TO PLEAD OUR OWN CAUSE

AMERICAN ABOLITIONISM AND ANTISLAVERY
JOHN DAVID SMITH, SERIES EDITOR

*The Imperfect Revolution: Anthony Burns and the Landscape
of Race in Antebellum America*
GORDON S. BARKER

A Self-Evident Lie: Southern Slavery and the Threat to American Freedom
JEREMY J. TEWELL

Denmark Vesey's Revolt: The Slave Plot That Lit a Fuse to Fort Sumter
JOHN LOFTON   NEW INTRODUCTION BY PETER C. HOFFER

*To Plead Our Own Cause: African Americans in Massachusetts
and the Making of the Antislavery Movement*
CHRISTOPHER CAMERON

To Plead Our Own Cause

African Americans in Massachusetts and

the Making of the Antislavery Movement

CHRISTOPHER CAMERON

THE KENT STATE UNIVERSITY PRESS

Kent, Ohio

© 2014 by The Kent State University Press, Kent, Ohio 44242
Library of Congress Catalog Card Number 2013042583
ISBN 978-1-60635-194-9
Manufactured in the United States of America

LIBRARY OF CONGRESS CATALOGING-IN-PUBLICATION DATA
Cameron, Christopher, 1983–
To plead our own cause : African Americans in Massachusetts and the making
of the antislavery movement / Christopher Cameron.
pages cm. — (American abolitionism and antislavery)
Includes bibliographical references and index.
ISBN 978-1-60635-194-9 (hardcover) ∞
1. African American abolitionists—Massachusetts—History. I. Title.
E445.M4C36 2014
326'.80922—dc23
2013042583

18 17 16 15 14   5 4 3 2 1

Contents

Acknowledgments

This book began nearly a decade ago as a ten-page paper on religion in the British and American abolitionist movements. My undergraduate adviser at Keene State College, Gregory Knouff, encouraged me to develop the paper into a larger project, and this study is the final result. I am indebted to Greg for his support and friendship over the years. Matthew Crocker's course on the Early Republic was instrumental in my deciding to pursue history, while Joseph Witkowski and Vincent Ferlini both chose me to serve as their undergraduate teaching assistants, which were important experiences when deciding to enter academia. Antonio Henley and Amanda Powell at the University of New Hampshire's Ronald E. McNair Program successfully convinced me to attend graduate school, and I will be forever grateful that they did so. Many thanks also to Funso Afolayan, my McNair mentor, for guiding this project along at its earliest stages.

I cannot say enough about the invaluable support, advice, and encouragement I received from my dissertation adviser, Heather Andrea Williams, as well as the insightful criticism and assistance of my dissertation committee members at the University of North Carolina—Kathleen DuVal, Lloyd Kramer, Laurie Maffly-Kipp, and Jerma Jackson. Other members of the faculty there who commented on portions of the work include John Wood Sweet, Jacquelyn Hall, and Rebecka Rutledge Fisher in the English department. My graduate colleagues in the history department at UNC were similarly invaluable to the completion of this study. Randy Browne carefully read each chapter of the manuscript and always offered excellent criticism. This project is what it is largely due to his assistance.

Ben Reed, Jennifer Donnally, Eliot Spencer, Catherine Conner, Brandon Winford, and David Palmer read parts of the project and helped make both my arguments and writing stronger. My colleagues at the University of North Carolina at Charlotte likewise read portions of the manuscript in our department's Brown Bag Seminars. I very much appreciate their excellent advice and support over the years. Special thanks to my colleague and series editor John David Smith, who was instrumental in this book's publication, as well as Manisha Sinha and the other anonymous reader at The Kent State University Press for their insightful comments and criticism.

I have received generous financial and research support from a number of different sources. These include the Department of Education's Ronald E. McNair Postbaccalaureate Achievement Program; the Royster Society of Fellows at the University of North Carolina; the UNC history department's Mowry Dissertation Fellowship; the Gilder Lehrman Institute of American History; and the Peabody Essex Museum. At UNC Charlotte, a Faculty Research Grant and a Small Grant were instrumental in helping me complete the manuscript. The staffs at the Massachusetts Historical Society, Boston Public Library, Congregational Library, Massachusetts Archives, Phillips Library at the Peabody Essex Museum, Rhode Island Historical Society, New-York Historical Society, and Schomburg Center for Research in Black Culture provided invaluable assistance.

Finally, I would like to thank my family. Alain and Lynn Cameron, as well as Rejean and France Cameron, opened up their homes during multiple research trips. Before she passed away, my grandmother Gisele and my grandfather, Real Cameron, did likewise. Many thanks also to my siblings, and to my wonderful wife, Shanice, for her love and encouragement. Most of all, I would like to thank my mother, Sylvie Cameron, for keeping me grounded and always being there for me. This book is dedicated to her memory.

Introduction

In one of the most significant antislavery tracts published in antebellum America, *Appeal to the Coloured Citizens of the World* (1829), David Walker, a black activist residing in Boston, articulated many of the most prominent themes in American abolitionism, including a rejection of the colonization plan, a call for black unity, and the idea that God would be on the side of the oppressed. "Though our cruel oppressors and murderers, may (if possible) treat us more cruel, as Pharoah did the children of Israel," Walker wrote, "yet the God of the Etheopeans, has been pleased to hear our moans in consequence of oppression; and the day of our redemption from abject wretchedness draweth near, when we shall be enabled, in the most extended sense of the word, to stretch forth our hands to the LORD our GOD."[1] Walker argued that even though whites treated blacks cruelly, God was on their side and would answer their cries for freedom. Central to Walker's vision of freedom for blacks was the assistance of the Almighty. At the same time, though, Walker argued that African Americans must take the initiative and work to free themselves. "There must be a willingness on our part, for GOD to do these things for us," he argued, "for we may be assured that he will not take us by the hairs of our head against our will and desire, and drag us from our very, mean, low and abject condition."[2]

While most studies of the antislavery movement begin their examination in the 1820s, Walker's blend of religious and political rhetoric in the cause of abolitionism was a tactic African Americans had employed in the fight against slavery since the eighteenth century. One such predecessor was a

1

free black man named Caesar Sarter of Newburyport, Massachusetts, who published an essay on slavery in 1774 asking supporters of slavery, "Why, in the name of Heaven, will you suffer such a gross violation of that rule by which your conduct must be tried, in that day, in which you must be accountable for all your actions, to, that impartial Judge, who hears the groans of the oppressed and who will sooner or later avenge them of their oppressors!"[3] As Walker would later do, Sarter argued that a righteous God would be on the side of slaves and would judge America for the sin of slavery.

It is a common understanding in the scholarship on abolitionism that the radical abolitionist movement did not begin until the 1830s. David Walker's *Appeal* and William Lloyd Garrison's publication of the *Liberator* beginning in 1831 are seen as the opening salvos in this new, radical phase of the antislavery movement. Sarter's rhetoric and calls for immediate emancipation, however, along with that of many of his contemporaries in Massachusetts, suggest that eighteenth-century abolitionism was just as radical as its nineteenth-century counterpart and that the origins of abolitionism in America can be found among blacks in Massachusetts. This is the first study to trace these origins to African Americans in the Bay State and explore the significance of Calvinism to their antislavery ideology.

The demographics of Massachusetts, rights given to slaves within the colony, and the injunction of ministers to Christianize slaves aided in the formation of a black community that began to challenge slavery in the public sphere during the revolutionary period. In Massachusetts, slavery itself was shaped heavily by Old Testament law, which said that slaves should have specified rights. Thus, early Puritans allowed slaves to petition the government and bring cases in court. Furthermore, religious leaders in the colony urged their parishioners to Christianize slaves, a practice that extant church records indicate was followed by a number of owners. The fact that slaves never made up more than 5 percent of the colony's population and the lack of overt rebellions (such as the 1739 Stono Rebellion in South Carolina) made the colony more conducive to allowing slaves liberties that they were summarily denied elsewhere.

The centrality of Massachusetts in Revolution-era politics also greatly contributed to black political activity, as blacks both drew from and critiqued whites' religious tenets and political arguments for freedom from British rule to argue for freedom from slavery. Blacks in Boston began making these arguments in the public sphere in 1773 by presenting petitions that employed religious rhetoric similar to what Sarter would use one year later, transforming Reformed theology into an argument for abolition. Petitioning was the most successful strategy black activists employed, as it pushed the Massachusetts General Court to consider laws abolishing slavery on more than one occasion and was partly responsible for the 1788 law prohibiting slave trading among state residents. Other tactics included publishing essays and books of poetry, suing for freedom, and creating institutions to serve as the basis for antislavery organizing.

Among these institutions was the first antislavery committee in America. While this honor is usually reserved for the Pennsylvania Abolition Society, first organized in 1775, a committee representing slaves in Massachusetts formed by 1773 and began its campaign to bring about abolition. They first petitioned the General Court in 1773, and records indicate that its efforts spurred the colonial legislature to pass an abolition bill the next year. After Prince Hall formed the African Masonic Lodge in 1775, that body took the lead in future petitions, again spurring the Massachusetts General Court to consider an abolition bill in 1777 and later calling for equal access to educational facilities in the state. The African Masonic Lodge would continue to play a vital role in Boston's black community and the larger abolitionist movement from the revolutionary era through the 1830s.

Along with more traditional forms of abolitionist organization, this book explores the black emigration movement of the late eighteenth and early nineteenth centuries and argues that emigration was an important component of antislavery activity during this period. African American leaders such as Paul Cuffe and Prince Saunders proposed emigration to Sierra Leone and Haiti as a means of both thwarting the international slave trade and inducing southern slaveholders to liberate their bondmen. Some masters argued that they could not free their slaves because it was unclear what their political and social status would be in America, so emigration emerged as a strategy that could alleviate this concern. While this movement never had the impact that Cuffe or Saunders envisioned, it served the practical purpose of connecting black leaders across the North and providing for cooperation between white and black abolitionists throughout the Atlantic world.

In the late 1820s, the national antislavery movement was centered in Boston, a phenomenon I trace to its origins through an examination of blacks' community-building efforts in Massachusetts in the years of the early republic. By doing this, I hope to shed new light on both the study of the "first emancipation," the period in which African Americans gained freedom in the North, and blacks' broader struggle for the freedom of all slaves in the early nineteenth century. Furthermore, while the subjects of this book are located in Massachusetts, I examine the broader contributions of African Americans to the political and religious ideology of America in its earliest years and the ways in which developments in England, Africa, and the Caribbean informed black abolitionism in Massachusetts. As such, this study is both a social and intellectual history of black abolitionists that places their actions within the context of global freedom struggles by whites and blacks from the era of the American Revolution to the antebellum period.

The field of abolitionist studies has certainly thrived over the years, and there have been a number of excellent works published in this area, yet few have examined the important relationship between Reformed theology and black abolitionism, and even fewer stretch their analyses back into the eighteenth century. In the first definitive study of the northern antislavery movement, Arthur Zilversmit claimed that "the history of the early abolitionist movement is essentially the record of Quaker antislavery activities," a claim that effectively excluded blacks, none of whom belonged to the Society of Friends or were allowed to participate in abolitionist organizations that Quakers ran in the eighteenth century.[4] While Zilversmit's study, along with Brycchan Carey's recent analysis of antislavery rhetoric, focuses primarily on Quaker abolitionists, David Brion Davis has examined the foundations of antislavery ideology throughout the Atlantic world in the Age of Revolution. Despite the sweep of Davis's seminal works, he slights the importance of blacks' antislavery thought and activities. More recently, historians such as Margot Minardi have explored the significance of eighteenth-century abolitionism, yet her important book *Making Slavery History* is concerned more with the memory of early abolitionists than the activists themselves.[5] Richard Newman's *Transformation of American Abolitionism* examines the movement in Pennsylvania during the eighteenth century, arguing for a shift from gradual to immediate emancipation by the 1830s.[6] In this book I challenge Newman's perspective by arguing that Massachusetts was at the center of the abolitionist movement from its inception and that calls for immediate emancipation were present in blacks' writings from the 1770s.

Those scholars who have focused on the political activity of black abolitionists have centered their attention primarily on the years after 1830. This is due to a misconception among historians such as Benjamin Quarles and Herbert Aptheker that early black abolitionists were too conservative in their approach and did not have a significant impact on the achievement of abolition. These scholars argue that most black abolitionists after 1830 were more radical because they called for an immediate end to slavery as opposed to its gradual abolition. This separation of radicalism versus conservatism into disparate time periods is no longer adequate. Black abolitionists articulated arguments that were best suited to their time period and local context. For some, this meant supporting gradual emancipation plans. But for most it meant arguing for an immediate end to slavery in no uncertain terms. I argue that the radical abolition movement did not begin during the antebellum period but, rather, in Revolution-era Massachusetts.[7]

Even as there has been an increasing amount of scholarship on nineteenth-century black abolitionists, there remains a dearth of literature on early black intellectual history. However, Mia Bay, Patrick Rael, and Laurie Maffly-Kipp, among others, have made important contributions to this field. Bay examines the racial ideology of African Americans toward whites in the period from 1830 to 1925, in part because she found a lack of sources for this topic in the earlier period. Rael's work has a shorter chronological focus, examining identity building in black communities between 1820 and 1860, while Maffly-Kipp explores the production of "race histories" from the late eighteenth century to the 1920s. I complement these important additions to the field by examining not only the political activity of black abolitionists in the eighteenth century but also the ideological origins of their political thought.[8]

In Massachusetts, these ideological origins lie primarily in late-seventeenth- and early-eighteenth-century Puritan thought, which shaped both the religious beliefs and political activity of black abolitionists in the late eighteenth century. John Saillant has made the connection between Puritanism and black politics in his biography of black abolitionist Lemuel Haynes, in which he argues that Haynes blended republican political philosophy with the New Divinity theology that dominated late-eighteenth-century

Calvinism in his critiques of the institution of slavery. I demonstrate that this was also the case among blacks in Massachusetts, such as Phillis Wheatley, Prince Hall, and Caesar Sarter.[9]

At one time or another, these three activists employed the rhetorical form of the Puritan jeremiad, yet few scholars have touched on the black jeremiad's origins during the eighteenth century. This sermonic form was a ritual that Puritan ministers had engaged in since the seventeenth century as a means to fight the perceived religious decline among their parishioners. Sacvan Bercovitch's *American Jeremiad* explores the significance of the jeremiad for American literature and politics into the nineteenth century but does not note its use by black thinkers. Those who do explore blacks' appropriation of the jeremiad, such as Wilson Jeremiah Moses and David Howard-Pitney, focus on nineteenth-century activists such as David Walker and Frederick Douglass. However, I argue that Caesar Sarter initiated the tradition of the black jeremiad with his 1774 essay on slavery, which claimed that blacks were God's new chosen people and that slavery's supporters would soon face God's wrath for their actions.[10]

Studies of Puritanism as a whole and biographies of early-eighteenth-century Puritan leaders such as Cotton Mather and Samuel Willard do not touch on the implications of Puritan thought and the system of slavery it set up for later black abolitionists. Harry Stout's work on preaching in New England, for instance, devotes one page to the relationship between white revolutionary ideology and abolition but does not examine the thought of African Americans. Richard Lovelace's *American Pietism of Cotton Mather* has a brief discussion of Mather's justification of social hierarchies but does not explore Mather's thoughts on slavery and their prevalence throughout colonial Massachusetts. Works on Samuel Willard, such as Ernest Benson Lowrie's *Shape of the Puritan Mind,* similarly neglect to examine Willard's ideas toward slaves. An exception is Richard Bailey's *Race and Redemption in Puritan New England,* though his study ends at the late colonial period, stopping short of an examination of Calvinism and black abolitionism.[11]

This book builds on these works by developing the important links between Reformed theology, the institution of slavery, and the rise of the antislavery movement. I argue that blacks in Massachusetts initiated organized abolitionism in America and that their antislavery ideology had its origins in Puritan thought and the particular system of slavery that this religious ideology shaped in Massachusetts. The political activity of black abolitionists was central in effecting the abolition of slavery and the slave trade within the Bay State, and it was likewise key in building a national antislavery movement in the years of the early republic. Even while abolitionist strategies were evolving, much of the rhetoric and tactics that well-known abolitionists such as William Lloyd Garrison and Frederick Douglass employed in the mid-nineteenth century had their origins among blacks in Massachusetts during the eighteenth century.

1

Puritans and Slavery

Masters, give unto your Servants, that which is Just & Equal, Knowing that ye also have a Master in Heaven.

—Colossians 4:1

Well then, poor Ethiopians, do you now stretch out your Hands unto the Lord; even those poor Black Hands of yours, the Lord calleth for them.

—Cotton Mather

The history of Puritanism and African American life are two fields of inquiry that are not often tied together. Doing so, however, greatly enriches our understanding of African American religion and politics, including the origins of black abolitionist thought as well as the transatlantic influence of the Puritan movement. To understand the ideology of Puritanism and its effect on African American life in Massachusetts, it is useful to briefly explore the background of the Puritan migration to the colony.

Under the rule of James I and Charles I in the early seventeenth century, English Puritans experienced increasing persecution for continuing the work of the Protestant Reformation to purify the Church of England of the remnants of Catholicism. King James and King Charles saw the Puritan movement as an assault on their authority, which they believed should be absolute in both civil and ecclesiastical matters. Both monarchs forbade preaching by ministers, instead insisting on preapproved readings from a common prayer book. Charles I also rejected the idea of a priesthood of all believers, seeking instead, as the head of the Church, to dictate religious belief and practices to the populace. By the 1610s and 1620s, authorities were imprisoning and executing Puritans at an alarming rate, prompting many to flee England.[1]

Many Puritans at first fled to the Netherlands. But finding that country's culture and manners strange, they decided to found the Plymouth colony in 1620. Their primary goal was to practice their religion freely in a place where they could raise their children in a language and culture familiar to them. The Puritans who left England aboard the *Arbella* and six other ships in the spring of 1630 to settle the Massachusetts Bay colony similarly wanted to practice their religion freely, but they did not want to separate themselves completely from their English brethren, as the earlier Puritans who landed at Plymouth wanted to do.[2] Instead, they aspired to establish a godly community that would serve as a shining light for their brethren back in England. In his famous sermon "A Model of Christian Charity," probably delivered before the voyage to Massachusetts, John Winthrop told his listeners: "We must consider that we shall be as a city upon a hill. The eyes of all people are upon us."[3] If they succeeded in establishing a godly community in New England, the Puritans believed they could bring old England back to the ways of God.

Among the key beliefs of these early Puritans was the absolute sovereignty of God. For them, this was his chief attribute, even above benevolence. They believed that all men deserved damnation but that God's benevolence had led him to choose some people as his Elect, those who would find themselves in heaven after death. While one could certainly look for signs of election, a good Puritan could never be sure if he had been chosen, a mind-set that often led to great anxiety over one's spiritual fate. Although the belief in predestination and its mysteries produced apprehension among many, it also made for a more egalitarian view toward conversion and evangelism, as ministers could argue that all people, including blacks and Native Americans, might be among God's Elect.[4]

For the Puritans, conversion to Christianity was both an experience and a process. The initial justification, or realization that one was among the Elect, represented the experiential aspect of conversion. The individual might hear a particularly relevant sermon and become convinced of their sinful nature. This was often followed by a period of spiritual anguish, in which people were sure they were going to hell, followed by a feeling of relief, perhaps coming after a vision or dream about Jesus. By the end of the first decade of settlement, it was common for churches to require an oral account of the justification process as an admission for membership. But conversion did not end there. Sanctification followed justification and was a process whereby individuals strove to live the rest of their lives according to God's precepts. If they thrived economically and appeared to be upright and Godly, this was evidence that they were among the Elect, but their adherence to Calvinism meant that they could never be sure.[5]

While salvation was uncertain for even the most Godly in Puritan society, damnation was almost assured for those who rejected God and followed Satan. This damnation affected the individual but could also have an impact on the larger society. In a follow-up to his passage arguing that Massachusetts residents must be "a city upon a hill," John Winthrop claimed that if they were not, "wee shall shame the faces of many of gods worthy servants, and cause theire prayers to be turned into Cursses upon us till we be consumed out of the good land whether wee are goeing."[6] Winthrop articulated his belief that New Englanders had a covenant with God to follow his biblical commands. If they broke the covenant, it would affect those around the world who the Puritans were trying to influence and bring back to the ways of God. But it would also mean that "the Lord will surely breake out in wrathe against us be revenged of such a periured people and make us know the price of the breache of such a Covenant."[7] This wrath could include natural disasters, famine, or attacks by Indians.

Ideas concerning God's sovereignty, man's covenant with him, and original sin gained strength from the cultural domination of a group of powerful ministerial intellectuals during the earliest years of settlement. This cultural domination had four major elements: authority conferred on these ministers, consensus among the intelligentsia, attention and deference of the laity in public, and the suppression of religious heresies. Thomas Hooker and John Cotton were two of the most prominent ministers. Both had immigrated to Massachusetts Bay in 1633, and it was Cotton who insisted on the test of saving grace that came to be practiced in most Congregational churches. One reason ministers wielded such great power in the colony was Puritan biblicism, the idea that they were the only figures capable of interpreting the Bible, which they did using ancient languages and hermeneutical techniques. Over time, divisions between the magistrates and ministers resulted in the loss of cultural domination by the ministerial class, yet they continued to wield an important influence over social and intellectual life in Massachusetts well into the eighteenth century.[8]

Puritans' religious thought played an important role in their approach toward the institution of slavery. Massachusetts' first law regarding slavery demonstrates a sort of ambivalence toward holding people in bondage. In 1641 the colony officially authorized slavery in its legal code the *Body of Liberties*. "There shall never be any bond slaverie, villinage or captivitie amongst us," it reads in part, unless it be lawfull captives taken in just warres, and such strangers as willingly selle themselves or are sold to us. And these shall have all the liberties and Christian usages which the law of God established in Israell concerning such persons doth morally require.[9] The statute expressly authorized slavery when the captives were the result of just wars, such as the 1637 Pequot War, or were outsiders sold to them, such as Africans in the Atlantic slave trade. By guaranteeing slaves "the liberties and Christian usages which the law of God established in Israell," Puritan magistrates demonstrated the influence of the Old Testament on their ideas about slavery and their recognition that the slaves among them were not merely property but human beings before the law. These liberties included freedom by slaves from arbitrary punishment, especially leading to death. In 1672 colonial leaders amended the law to make slavery a heritable condition by dropping the phrase "such strangers," making it possible for blacks born in Massachusetts to be slaves for life.[10]

From the early years of settlement in Massachusetts, masters used African slaves for a variety of purposes. Initially, slaves helped develop the economic infrastructure of the colony by clearing land, building barns, breaking up soil, building docks, and making roads. They generally worked twelve hours a day, yet the stamina of the owner determined the pace of work, because he usually labored alongside his servants and slaves. Until the Revolution, most residents of Massachusetts earned their living by farming, and masters used many slaves in agricultural work. Whites also used black slaves as domestic workers, and in the coastal regions a number of blacks worked in the shipping industry, either aboard ships or as ship joiners, carpenters, and rope makers. Other slaves worked as blacksmiths, caulkers, bakers, shoemakers, and tailors.[11] Extant records indicate the importance of slavery to the colonial economy. In a letter to his brother-in-law, Governor John Winthrop, Emmanuel Downing expressed his wish for another Indian war, writing, "If upon a Just warre the lord should deliver them into our hands, wee might easily have men woemen and Children enough to exchange for Moores." Downing wrote to Winthrop that he did not believe the new colony could thrive without a sufficient stock of slaves and claimed that slavery was a much more profitable system of labor than indentured servitude. "I suppose you know verie well how wee shall maynteyne 20 Moores cheaper then one English servant," he told Winthrop.[12]

While the number of African slaves throughout New England always remained relatively small compared to the southern colonies, the numbers do not begin to tell the story of how important slavery was to the region. Most enslaved Africans were clustered along the seacoast in major towns, which meant that slave populations were heaviest where those of the region's political and cultural leaders, the mercantile elite, lived and worked. Even though slavery was not absolutely central to the New England economy, it did help to diversify it, partly by freeing masters to work outside the home, and was an important factor in the transition to capitalism.[13]

In Massachusetts specifically, and New England more broadly, slaveholders often regarded themselves as benevolent patriarchs and better masters than those elsewhere in the Atlantic world. They prided themselves on giving slaves what they felt was adequate clothing and proper medical attention. Yet the image of the good master in colonial New England is largely a myth. The long hours demanded of slaves could be very taxing. And unlike their southern counterparts, female slaves in New England who reproduced were actually more of a liability to their master than a boon. In what would become an early harbinger for the tragedies associated with the internal slave trade, newspapers in colonial Massachusetts sometimes advertised masters' offers to give away the children of their female slaves.[14]

Despite what could be the harsh nature of slavery in Massachusetts, Puritan-influenced law granted slaves some of the liberties and rights of Christians in accordance with biblical precepts. A revision to the Massachusetts legal code and a case of magistrates returning enslaved Africans to their homeland further highlights the influence Puritan thought wielded on ideas about slavery in the colony. The 1646 *Body of Liberties* provided that "every man whether Inhabitant or foreigner, free or not free shall have libertie to come to any publique Court . . . and either by speech or writeing to move any lawfull, seasonable, and materiall question, or to present any necessary motion, complaint, petition."[15] By giving both free and unfree individuals the right to bring cases in court and petition for redress of grievances, Puritan authorities recognized in part the humanity and rights of slaves that colonies such as South Carolina summarily denied, a recognition based on the scriptural basis of their views on slavery.

Events regarding kidnapped slaves in 1645 similarly point to the religious influence on ideas about slavery. During that year, two merchants, Mr. Smith and Mr. Keser of Boston, traveled to the coast of Africa where they attacked a village, killed 100 people, and kidnapped two men to sell as slaves. Smith and Keser brought the Africans back to Boston, and Richard Saltonsall immediately petitioned the General Court to prosecute Smith and Keser because "it is apparent that Mr. Keser upon a sabboth day gave chace to certaine Negers; and upon the same day took divers of them; and at another time killed others." Saltonsall accused the two of murder, "manstealing," and breaking the Sabbath, all of which were "expressly capitall by the law of God."[16] In October 1645, the House of Deputies granted Saltonsall's petition and ordered "that Capt Smith and Mr Keisar be laid hold on and committed to give answer in convenient time thereabouts."[17] According to John Winthrop, colonial magistrates freed the slaves because Smith had kidnapped them, an unacceptable method of attaining slaves under the 1641 statute.[18]

Puritan ministers supported the magistrates' recognition of slave rights in the colony with their own injunctions for masters to treat their bondmen properly. Samuel Willard, minister at Boston's Old South Church from 1678 to 1707, wrote that no master "hath an Arbitrary Power over his servant, as to life and death." This drew from the book of Exodus, which mandates punishment for those who take the life of a slave. Slaves were to practice patience and submission at all times, but if a servant "be injuriously treated, he may make his Orderly application to the Civil Magistrate, whose Duty it is impartially to afford him a redress, upon a clear Proof of it."[19] Cotton Mather similarly enjoined slaves to obey their masters in all things, except when their masters told them to do something sinful.[20] Although both Willard and Mather supported the system of slavery, as did the magistrates who drew up the laws regarding bondage, their concessions to slaves' humanity paved the way for freedom suits and organized black abolitionism.

One of the most well-known freedom suits in Massachusetts history came from an enslaved man named Adam Saffin in 1701. In 1694 John

Saffin, a wealthy landowner and magistrate of the Massachusetts Bay colony, drew up a document placing his slave Adam under the service of his tenant, Thomas Shepard, for seven years. At the end of this period Saffin promised to "make free my said Negro man named Adam, to be fully at his own dispose and liberty as other Freemen are or ought to be . . . Always Provided that the said Adam my servant do in the mean time go on chearfully, quietly, and industriously in the lawful business that either my self or my Assigns shall from time to time reasonably set him about or imploy him in."[21] According to Saffin, he rented Adam to Shepard because "knowing the said Negro to be of a proud, insolent and domineering spirit . . . I thought to work upon his natural Reason; and for his own benefit to oblige him to obedience . . . I promised him his Freedom." After two years it was clear that Adam was not performing his duties as Saffin or Shepard hoped, so Shepard encouraged Adam by giving him a piece of land on which to plant tobacco, where Adam made £3 a year. Despite these allowances Adam grew "so tolerably insolent, quarrelsome and outragious," according to Saffin, "that the Earth could not bear his rudeness."[22] Shepard asked Saffin to take Adam back one year before his term was to expire, which Saffin did.

But in March 1700, while Saffin was on a trip, Adam left Saffin's house and proceeded to go about Boston at his leisure. On Saffin's return, Adam told him that he must go and see Samuel Sewall, who produced the court document Saffin had drawn up in 1694 and informed him that he should free Adam as promised. Saffin replied that Adam had not fulfilled his side of the bargain and did not deserve his freedom. Adam then sued Saffin, and the case eventually went before the Superior Court of Judicature, on which Sewall sat. The court awarded Adam his freedom in 1703 based on the earlier promise of manumission, despite Saffin's having brought forth at least five witnesses testifying that Adam was, among other things, "a very disobedient, turbulent, outragious and unruly Servant in all respects these many years."[23] After the case, Adam remained in Boston as a free man, showing up in the selectmen's records on a number of occasions as a "free negro or mulatto" required to perform service for the city in lieu of militia duty.[24]

Samuel Sewall, an influential merchant and member of the Massachusetts Superior Court of Judicature, the first independent court in the Western Hemisphere, had also been one of the judges on the witchcraft court of Oyer and Terminer in 1692. Five years later, Sewall appeared in front of his congregation at the Old South Church and repented for his role in the 1692 Salem witchcraft trials. According to one of his biographers, Sewell spent the rest of his life trying to atone for this role.[25] On 19 June 1700, while Adam's case was ongoing, Sewell noted that "having been long and much dissatisfied with the Trade of fetching Negros from Guinea; at last I had a strong Inclination to Write something about it . . . when I was thus thinking, in came Brother Belknap to shew me a Petition he intended to present to the General Court for the freeing a Negro and his wife."[26] Sewall further noted that "Mr. C. Mather resolves to publish a sheet to exhort Masters to labour their Conversion. Which makes me hope that I was call'd of God to Write this Apology for them; Let his Blessing accompany the same."[27]

Sewall published *The Selling of Joseph: A Memorial* five days later, on 24 June. It was the first antislavery tract printed in New England, and while it did not succeed in gaining widespread support for abolition among whites, it outlined a number of arguments against slavery that became important to later abolitionist writers. Sewall wrote, "It is most certain that all Men, as they are the Sons of Adam, are Co-heirs, and have equal Right unto Liberty."[28] He also countered arguments for slavery that claimed blacks were the children of Ham, pointing out that it was actually Ham's son Canaan who was cursed. Finally, Sewall refuted a common justification for slavery by arguing that conversion was not an excuse for enslaving Africans, because men were not to do evil to bring about positive results.[29]

Even as Sewall deplored the enslavement of Africans, he presented a problem for blacks because he upheld and helped popularize the racialized attitudes among whites that allowed slavery to flourish. In *The Selling of Joseph,* he posited that it would be impossible for whites to incorporate blacks into the body politic because "there is such a disparity in their Conditions, Colour, and Hair." He further felt that "as many Negro men as there are among us, so many empty Places are there in our Train Bands, and the places taken up of Men that might make Husbands for our daughters."[30] In his mind, the importation of black men to the colony prevented white male emigration, a situation that could contribute to military weakness with the empty spots in militia training units and create an imbalance of the sexes. To address the problem of too many black slaves in the colony, Sewall advocated bringing in more white indentured servants, partly because, he contended, blacks continually sought their freedom yet could "seldom use their Freedom well."[31]

Sewall circulated his pamphlet among colonial leaders of Massachusetts, and just one year after he published his tract, the Boston selectmen passed the following resolution for the representatives of the general Court: "The Representatives ar farther desired To Promote the Encourrageing the bringing of white servts and to put a Period to negros being Slaves."[32] While colonial leaders neither debated nor enacted a gradual abolition law, the resolution demonstrates the early formation of ideologies of black inferiority that would play a central role in Massachusetts and across the British North American colonies.

Shortly after Sewall declared blacks unfit for inclusion in the body politic, colonial leaders' ideas of European cultural superiority spurred concrete actions on their part to ensure that blacks would have an inferior political and social status. These actions included encouraging employers to import white indentured servants instead of black slaves, because they believed whites could make the colony more prosperous, and urging legislators to restrict blacks' participation in the colonial militia, as service in the militia was a badge of citizenship they did not want extended to blacks. Instead of bearing arms for the colony, the selectmen ordered "each Free negro & mollatto man of this Town, forthwith to attend and perform four days Labour, abt repaireing the streets or Highwayes wch is to be part of their Servi[c]e for this present year."[33] Free blacks and Indians had to perform at least four days of highway repair, but some, like Adam Saffin, had to perform eight days of service. In addition to general highway duty, in 1721 the selectmen ordered blacks to clean the streets and remove dirt to prevent smallpox from spreading. The evidence suggests that even as some blacks achieved freedom in the Massachusetts polity during the early eighteenth century, colonial leaders attempted to keep them in an inferior status by denying them traditional participation in the colonial militia, forcing them instead to perform manual labor.[34]

Despite the presence of these racial ideologies and government attempts to exclude blacks from the body politic, African Americans' joining and participating in Congregational churches ensured that whites did not completely disenfranchise them and that blacks gained access to the rhetoric and worldview of Puritanism. Some Puritan ministers began to emphasize evangelism toward the bondmen in their midst, a situation that would later aid in blacks' development of an antislavery movement during the revolutionary period. There were many reasons for this ministerial emphasis on conversion, not least of which was the belief that a large contingent of unconverted strangers among the Puritans might bring God's wrath on their holy experiment. Ministers such as Samuel Willard and Cotton Mather noted that masters had a Christian duty to tend to the souls of their bondmen, and Congregational churches baptized both slaves and free blacks and admitted them as members. Blacks attended and joined Puritan churches from the late seventeenth century to the era of the American Revolution and beyond, allowing them to acquire some of the rhetorical tools with which they successfully undermined slavery in the colony.

Samuel Willard insisted that slaves were part of Massachusetts' larger familial and religious institutions. During Willard's occasional sermons, those given during the midweek service and published after his death as the *Compleat Body of Divinity,* he noted that the word *servant* "applied to all such in a Family as are under the Command of a Master." Like many New Englanders of his time, Willard used the words *servant* and *slave* interchangeably. While there were differing degrees of servitude, Willard's sermons demonstrated that he believed servants were a part of the family in which they resided. Consequently, he argued that "there is a Duty of Love which Masters owe to their servants . . . and the poorest slave hath a right to it."[35] This duty of love, according to Willard, meant that masters should watch over both the bodies and souls of their slaves, seeing to their physical health and conversion to Christianity. Willard's views echoed the 1646 statute from the *Body of Liberties,* which stated that all inhabitants of the colony had the right to petition and bring suits in court. Willard's notion and the earlier law stating that slaves should have the same rights as other Christians were most likely conceived to prevent masters from abusing their slaves. Blacks could capitalize on these privileges, however, to gain recourse to the legal system when they believed they were treated unjustly. These injustices often involved promises of freedom that masters later disallowed for one reason or another, as in the case of Adam Saffin.

Cotton Mather echoed Willard's sentiments in his writings during the late seventeenth and early eighteenth centuries, specifically addressing the conversion of blacks and the reciprocal duties between masters and slaves. On 13 November 1698, Mather recorded in his diary: "This Day, I baptized four Negro's; and the Lord helped mee, to make this Action, a special Occasion of my glorifying Him: especially, with what I then spoke unto the rest of that Nation."[36] Eight years later, he noted receiving a slave as a gift from his congregation, a somewhat common occurrence in eighteenth-century Massachusetts. According to Mather, this gift was "a mighty Smile of Heaven" on his family. He named the slave Onesimus and determined that, with God's help, he "would use the best Endeavors to make him a Servant of Christ."[37]

In naming his slave Onesimus, Mather likened himself to the apostle Paul, who, in a letter to Philemon, indicated that he had befriended his slave Onesimus while imprisoned, and the two had grown so close that Paul considered the slave to be like a son to him. Paul advised Philemon to receive the slave "not now as a servant, but above a servant, a brother beloved."[38] Like Paul, Mather viewed all slaves as potential brothers in Christ, giving him a sense of obligation to his slaves as a master and to the free blacks in his congregation as a minister. Mather's diary also indicates that he viewed slavery as an institution that God sanctioned, because he accepted a slave from his parishioners and attributed their kindness to God smiling down on him. While many of his writings and sermons discussed his understanding of the slaveholders' obligations to his slaves, he never intended blacks to use his efforts at conversion to attack slavery.

As a minister, Mather felt obligated to convert slaves and free blacks as well as instruct them in the knowledge of God, both of which became important to the formation of a black community in Boston. He noted in May 1718: "I have a Number of black Sheep in my Flock, which it is time for me again, to send for; and pray with them, and preach to them, and enquire into their Conduct, and encourage them, in the ways of Piety."[39] Even prior to baptizing the four blacks in 1698, Mather had been ministering to the enslaved since at least 1693, when he wrote that "a company of poor *Negroes,* of their own Accord, addressed mee, for my Countenance, to a Design which they had, of erecting such a Meeting for the Welfare of their miserable Nation that were Servants among us."[40]

Mather agreed to the formation of the Society of Negroes and drew up rules for the organization. The blacks were to meet on Monday evenings, praying together and listening to a sermon that Mather prepared for them. They were also to "at all Times avoid *wicked Company*" and to admit none to their meetings without the consent of "the *Minister* of God in this place." Members were to abstain from the sins of drunkenness, lying, stealing, and disobedience. They also pledged that "Wee will, as wee have Opportunity, sett ourselves, to do all the good Wee can to the other *Negro-Servants* in the Town."[41] The language of these rules suggests that they were a synthesis of the views of the blacks and of Mather. On the one hand, it appears that Mather wanted to control who could participate in the society as a possible way of limiting slave resistance, while, on the other hand, the slaves' input is evident in their desire to do all they can to help other blacks, evincing a spirit of Christian brotherhood.

The formation of this society reveals the importance of evangelism to blacks among white leaders in Boston. But, more significantly, it demonstrates blacks' desire for fellowship with other blacks in colonial Massachusetts. It was the slaves themselves who wanted to form the Society of Negroes, according to Mather, indicating a clear interest in communion with other blacks. At a time when whites segregated blacks to "Negro pews" in their churches, and many slaves lived in households with few other slaves, this society would have been an important source of communal ties for blacks. Throughout the eighteenth century Atlantic world, churches and religious societies served a dual function of mentorship and kinship. Coming together in religious organizations helped new Africans in the Caribbean adapt to their lives as slaves and provided slaves with new kinship groups, since the slave traders had severed their old ones during the Middle Passage. For blacks in Massachusetts, the Society of Negroes also became a means of education. In 1721, Mather wrote, "I have at my own single Expense for many years, maintained a Charity-Schole for the Instruction of Negro's in Reading and Religion," indicating that the Society of Negroes helped blacks achieve literacy, a development that historians have argued was vital to both slave resistance and political activity among blacks.[42]

In addition to supporting the Society of Negroes, Mather published works aimed at convincing fellow Puritans to convert their slaves. In 1696 he published *A Good Master Well Served,* a tract of about fifty pages that he originally preached as a sermon in his Second Congregational Church. Here Mather articulated four main duties that masters owed their servants, including work, food, and discipline. The fourth, and most important, was that masters "care about the souls of your servants." Mather noted that "when any servant comes to live with you, the God of Heaven does betrust you with another precious and immortal soul; a soul to be instructed, a soul to be governed, a soul to be brought home unto the Lord." While recognizing that not all servants would be God-fearing ones, Mather posited that masters should not allow their servants to openly sin. Like Willard, he felt that "masters indeed should be fathers unto their servants," instructing them in piety and knowledge of the Christian religion.[43]

In *The Negro Christianized,* Mather expanded on these themes and addressed those who may have felt that converting African slaves would free them or make them less valuable. For masters with lingering doubts about whether conversion to Christianity would mean freedom, he assured them that "the State of your Negroes in this World must be low, and mean, and abject; a state of Servitude . . . Something then, let there be done, towards their welfare in the World to Come."[44] This "something," of course, was instructing them in the knowledge of God, and Mather furthered this process by recommending in the tract specific catechisms for slaves, as well as Bible verses they should learn and questions about the Ten Commandments they should be able to answer. For those masters who feared that Christianity would make their slaves less diligent, Mather told them to "be assured, Syrs; Your Servants will be the Better Servants, for being made Christian Servants."[45] He argued that religion could only make slaves more dutiful, patient, and faithful and would actually be a prop to the institution of slavery rather than a hindrance.

The attitude toward evangelizing slaves in Massachusetts had more in common with Iberian colonies than those in British North America. While white southerners were often opposed to Christianizing their slaves until the mid-eighteenth century, ministers in Massachusetts emphasized conversion of Africans beginning in the seventeenth century. This situation in Massachusetts was similar to Spanish and Portuguese slave colonies, where the Catholic Church secured for slaves the right to the sacraments. Indeed, the outlook of New England colonists drew heavily from that of their Iberian predecessors in the New World, especially in the belief that the devil had occupied it unmolested for centuries and it was now their job to introduce Christianity to the land. This shared cultural outlook drew from their medieval past and influenced both their evangelization efforts toward Native Americans and, later, Africans.[46]

One of the reasons that Puritans feared blacks' conversion to Christianity less than other British North American colonies was the smaller slave

population. Massachusetts contained virtually no blacks in 1641, the year
that the General Court first legalized the institution. As a result, colonial
leaders were not in constant fear of slave rebellions. The population of
Africans in Massachusetts would remain small over the next century,
with only 1,374 blacks in Boston and about 4,000 in the entire colony.
Unlike other British colonies in the New World, Massachusetts remained
a "society with slaves" for roughly 150 years and never transitioned into a
full-fledged slave society.⁴⁷ The proportion of blacks there never reached
more than 2.2 percent of the population, numbers that contrast sharply
with southern colonies such as Virginia and South Carolina and the British Caribbean islands of Jamaica and Barbados. While no more than 1,000
slaves lived in Massachusetts in 1700, by 1670 Barbados already had 35,000
slaves, compared to 25,000 whites, and Jamaica had 9,000 slaves to 8,000
whites. In the first decade of the eighteenth century, Virginia imported
7,700 slaves, bringing the total number close to 20,000, or 40 percent of
the entire population. South Carolina surpassed Virginia in terms of the
proportion of slaves in its population, achieving a black majority by the
year 1708. In 1740 there were 40,000 slaves compared to 20,000 whites
in South Carolina, prompting incessant fears among the slaveholding
class about rebellion and resistance. These fears were well-founded, as a
group of slaves in the colony carried out the Stono Rebellion in 1739 and
attempted to escape to Spanish Florida. Whites stamped out the rebellion,
and the legislature passed a harsh slave code that denied slaves the right
to hold property, congregate, or learn how to read.⁴⁸

Demographics was one important factor that influenced the development of slavery and the rights blacks could exercise while in bondage. But
the original intentions of colonial settlers in emigrating were even more
significant. In Virginia, most settlers were young, male, and in search
of wealth. They were looking for riches such as precious metals or the
opportunity to develop staple crops that they could sell on a large scale.
Slavery was not part of the settlers' original plans; yet, after the discovery
of tobacco, it quickly became the prominent labor type in the colony and
overtook indentured servitude as the primary form of labor by the end
of the seventeenth century. After the tobacco boom in Virginia, British
colonists settled Barbados with the hopes of replicating Virginia's success. But neither tobacco nor cotton flourished there, so they switched
to sugar in 1640-60, achieving great success with that crop. Most of the

early settlers to South Carolina came from Barbados, where land had grown scarce and resources were monopolized by the most prominent slaveholders. They brought their system of slavery with them from the West Indies, as well as their slaves, and immediately began searching for a staple crop that would thrive, which they found in rice in 1695.[49]

These situations contrast sharply with those of Massachusetts, where the residents emigrated primarily for religious, not economic, reasons, which meant that some masters began to heed the injunctions of Willard and Mather to treat their slaves as part of the family and see to their religious upbringing. Slaves' conversion to Christianity in Massachusetts began in 1641 with the baptism of Reverend Stoughton's enslaved woman and became more widespread in early eighteenth century when the Royal African Company lost its monopoly on slave trading and the direct importation of slaves to Boston increased. During the decade from 1690 to 1700, the black population in Massachusetts rose from 400 to 800 people, although their proportion of the total population remained at just 1 percent. These numbers would nearly quadruple over the next forty years, to nearly 3,100 blacks living in the colony by 1740.[50]

During this same period, ministers at Boston's First Congregational Church baptized thirty-two blacks, some slave and some free. These baptisms included both children and adults, as in the case of Luse Bush, who was "Received into full communion with the church and baptized and her child Peter" on 26 September 1702.[51] This record indicates that a minister baptized Luse and that the congregation accepted her as a member. Puritan churches did not confer membership easily. To achieve this status, Luse would have had to demonstrate godliness and knowledge of the scriptures. She would have also had to give an "account of saving grace" from God or a testimony aimed at convincing the congregation that she had been converted. It is possible that Luse gave this testimony to the congregation herself, but because she was a woman, it is more likely that a man spoke for her.[52]

Other Congregational churches in Boston saw African Americans undergoing baptism and becoming church members, although they were not full members because they did not have voting privileges (see table 1). At Brattle Street Church, home congregation of some of Boston's wealthiest residents, twenty-four blacks were baptized from 1709 to 1736. Over the same period, thirty-three blacks were baptized at the Old South Church,

Samuel Willard's former congregation. Cotton Mather was also successful in bringing slaves into the Christian fold, baptizing four blacks in 1698 and sixteen more from 1716 to 1736, among them his own slave, Ezor, and Ezor's son, Abraham. As at the First Congregational Church, Mather's church both baptized African Americans and admitted them into membership in the congregation. Being baptized and becoming members in these churches suggests that the ministers saw blacks as spiritually eligible for salvation and that masters were heeding the advice of men such as Mather and Willard to care for the souls of their enslaved people, allowing for the influence of Puritan religious ideas to spread among the black populace.[53]

This influence became apparent during the Great Awakening in Massachusetts, the period out of which come the first written accounts of African Americans' religious ideas. The revival period began in 1734 in the western part of the state, Northampton, under the stewardship of Jonathan Edwards. Edwards's grandfather, Solomon Stoddard, had initiated periodic revivals of religion during the early eighteenth century, but none approached the scope of the Northampton revival of 1734-35. In *A Faithful Narrative,* an account of the revivals written in 1737, Edwards described the conversion of more than 300 people in his community alone. According to Edwards, the revivals touched at least thirty-two other communities in the Connecticut River Valley. Edwards also mentioned that "several Negroes . . . appear to have been truly born again" during the revival and that nine blacks joined his church, including one of his own slaves.[54] His recognition of black conversions further underscores the importance of the Great Awakening to African Americans and indicates that Boston was not the only area of the state where whites introduced blacks to Puritan religious precepts.

Edwards's account of the earlier revivals played a key role in initiating even greater revival activity later in the decade. After reading Edwards's *Faithful Narrative,* George Whitefield of England came to preach in the American colonies in 1739 and helped precipitate a flood of black conversions. On the morning of 28 September 1740, Whitefield preached at the Old South Church "to a very crowded auditory" and, that evening, to the congregation at Brattle Street Church. He wrote in his journal that after giving these two sermons, "at their request, I then went and preached to a great number of Negroes on the conversion of the Ethiopian."[55] In this biblical story the angel of God commanded Philip to travel south from

Jerusalem to Gaza, where he encountered an Ethiopian eunuch. Philip and
the eunuch spoke about scripture and Jesus, and the eunuch asked Philip,
"See, here is water; what doth hinder me to be baptized?" Philip replied,
"If thou believest with all thine heart, thou mayest."[56] For the slaves and
free blacks to whom Whitefield preached, this story would have conveyed
the idea that all are equal in the sight of God and that they had just as much
right to salvation as white people, including their masters.

   The efforts of evangelists such as Jonathan Edwards and George
Whitefield seem to have paid off. During the five-year period from 1739 to
1744, both Brattle Street Church and Old South Church saw a rise in black
baptisms (and probably church attendance) with thirty-four receiving the
sacrament in the former congregation and twenty-six in the latter. While
there are not extant records from all congregational churches during
this period, the preceding sample from the four primary Congregational
churches in Boston shows that nearly 175 African Americans were either
baptized or admitted to church membership before and during the Great
Awakening. In the years after the revival period, 1745-75, at least seventy-
eight more blacks were baptized in both the Old South and Brattle Street
churches, individuals who came of age during the time of the American
Revolution and the antislavery movement in Massachusetts. These
numbers represent 3-4 percent of blacks in the colony being baptized or
admitted to church membership by 1745. However, this sample comes
from only Boston churches, so the proportion of black Christians in
Massachusetts was closer to 15 percent of the black population in what
would become an important area of abolitionist activity twenty years
after the Great Awakening.[57]

   African Americans also helped forward the Great Awakening in Massachusetts by participating in church splits and exercising spiritual leadership, both of which assisted them in further internalizing and articulating
the discourse of Reformed theology. One such split occurred in Ipswich,
where New Lights, the supporters of the revivals, formed the Congregational Church of Chebacco. Of the original twenty-two members, four
were slaves, including Flora, who left a brief account of this revival period.
Flora was the slave of Thomas Choate of Ipswich, a seacoast community
about twenty-five miles north of Boston, and she gave a testimony in 1746
concerning the state of her soul and her desire for communion with the
church. She had been a lay exhorter, demonstrating the opportunities

Table 1. Black Baptisms and Admissions to Membership in Congregational Churches, 1700-76

Old South Church	1709-38	1739-44	1745-75
Male	23	9	18
Female	10	17	21
Children	12	10	27
Total	33	26	39
Brattle Street Church	1709-36	1739-44	1745-76
Male	14	19	21
Female	10	15	18
Children	3	9	27
Total	24	34	39
Second Congregational Church	1702-36	1739-44	1745-76
Male	10	2	1
Female	8	1	2
Children	4	2	0
Total	18	3	3
First Congregational Church	1700-31	1741-49	1750-74
Male	15	5	0
Female	17	0	2
Children	22	5	2
Total	32	5	2

Sources: Richard D. Pierce, ed., "The Records of the First Church in Boston, 1630–1868," *Publications of the Colonial Society of Massachusetts*, vol. 39 (Boston: The Society, 1961), 101–13; Richard D. Pierce, ed. "The Records of the First Church in Boston, 1630–1868," *Publications of the Colonial Society of Massachusetts*, vol. 40 (Boston: The Society, 1961), 370–425; Second Church Record Book, Volume 4: *Baptisms and Admissions, 1689–1716*, and Volume 5: *Baptisms and Admissions, 1717–1741*, Massachusetts Historical Society, Boston; *The Manifesto Church: Records of the Church in Brattle Square Boston, with Lists of Communicants, Baptisms, Marriages, and Funerals: 1699–1872* (Boston: Benevolent Fraternity of Churches, 1902), 100–187; Old South Church Records, microfilm reel 4, Congregational Library, Boston.

blacks gained during the Great Awakening, yet she fell into sin and felt that her moral shortcomings hurt the revival cause.

According to Flora, her chief sins as an exhorter were "spirituall Pride, Ingratitude, Unwatchfulness and Levity or Lightness"—some of the same sins that Puritan ministers had decried in their seventeenth-century writings on the declining piety of New Englanders. Her confession was the means by which she would become a church member, and it revealed a realization that she was a sinner. She experienced a subsequent feeling of grace, which she felt God helped her achieve by "bringing home to [her] soul some Texts of holy Scripture." Flora further wrote that while in a state of sin "God gave me a Spirit of Prayer, out of the Deep I cry'd to him . . . and the Lord heard, to my Surprize & Astonishment, he ran to my Relief."[58] Her language reveals the importance of Calvinist thought to blacks in Massachusetts. She registered her surprise that God had reached out to her, evincing a feeling of depravity on her part and absolute sovereignty on the part of God, both staples of Calvinist rhetoric.

The presence of black exhorters such as Flora caused many individuals to oppose the revivals. Charles Brockwell, an Anglican missionary for the Society for the Propagation of the Gospel (SPG) in Salem, wrote derisively that "Men, Women, Children, Servants, & Nigros are now become (as they phrase it) Exhorters."[59] Charles Chauncy, minister of Boston's First Congregational Church, similarly wrote in his *Seasonable Thoughts on the State of Religion* that "another Thing that very much tends, as I apprehend, to do Hurt to the Interest of Religion, is the Rise of so many Exhorters . . . there are among these Exhorters, Babes in Age, as well as Understanding. They are chiefly indeed young Persons, sometimes Lads, or rather Boys: Nay, Women and Girls; yea, Negroes, have taken upon themselves the Business of Preachers."[60] Along with his opposition to black exhorters, Chauncy opposed religious affections in general, which explains why his congregation was not among those that gained a significant number of new converts during the Great Awakening. His and Brockwell's opposition to black exhorters such as Flora also suggests that this practice was becoming increasingly widespread in some locales, a testament to the influence these revivals had on both blacks' conversions and their gaining some measure of social standing in colonial Massachusetts.

The work of itinerant minister Daniel Rogers further confirms the growing presence of black exhorters in Massachusetts. Rogers was a Congregational minister who traveled the eastern seaboard preaching with both George Whitefield and Gilbert Tennent. While in Kittery, in eastern Massachusetts, during May 1742, Rogers noted that "a Negroe man servant of Colonel Pepperell's broke out and spoke in a wonderful manner of the sweet love of Jesus which he said he felt in his heart to great degree that he could die for Christ. He exhorted all to come and talke of the love of Christ. Another negroe man servant of Colonel Pepperell cryed out in distress."[61] Rogers was beginning to feel that the evangelical work of ministers such as Edwards, Whitefield, and himself was having the desired effect among the black population. While on another visit to the eastern part of the state, less than one year after his stay at Colonel Pepperell's, he spoke to a young woman who had "a view of ye coming of ye kingdom of God, and particularly of ye negroes being brought into It, and that the Scripture figures of It—viz. ye Stretching out ye hands to Christ 68 Psalm 31 vers. Which word has at this day been remarkably fulfilled in the conversion of many poor negroe slaves in New England."[62]

While many of Rogers's entries discuss his efforts at promoting Christianity among blacks, like Whitefield he makes it clear that it was often the blacks themselves who desired religious instruction. Shortly before the split that formed Flora's congregation in Ipswich, Rogers was in town and noted that "at the Desiree of Some Negroes who came from Rowley, a meeting was called and Mr. Jewel preached in the evening discoursing with poor negroes. The Spirit of God came Sweetly upon me in Faith and Love—we prayed and gave thanks."[63] After the split that formed the Congregational Church of Chebacco, Rogers preached there periodically, perhaps encouraging Flora's efforts at exhorting others to come to Christ.

Less than twenty years after Flora's testimony to the church, another series of revivals swept over the community of Ipswich, initiating conversions that further provided blacks with the religious language central to the abolitionist activity they would begin in the 1770s. Among these new black converts in the 1760s was Phillis Cogswell, a forty-year-old slave of Jonathan Cogswell. Phillis initially began attending church during the revivals of the 1740s, but she never became a full member and felt a decline in piety over the years. Her decision not to join a church changed with the onset of the Seacoast Revivals of the 1760s, however. Like Flora, Phillis had to give a testimony to the Congregational Church of Chebacco in order to become a member, and her wording similarly evinces the influence of Reformed theology on her worldview. In discussing her awareness of depravity, she wrote, "I was made sensible my heart was nothing but Sin, and that I had never done any Thing but sin against God and it would have been just with God to cast me into hell."[64] Her ideas echo that of Jonathan Edwards's famous "Sinners in the Hands of an Angry God" sermon, in which he told sinners that "the sword of divine justice is every moment brandished over their heads, and 'tis nothing but the hand of arbitrary mercy, and God's mere will, that holds it back."[65] After Phillis's recognition of her sinful state came the relation of God's mercy, when "Christ appeared lovely to my soul.—Sin appeared odious to me, and I tho't I should never sin any more."[66] Her testimony highlights the importance of Christianity to blacks in the colony and the growing influence of Calvinist thought on their own rhetoric.

Calvinist tropes of original sin, God's absolute sovereignty, and notions of the covenant became increasingly important among slaves and free blacks during the revival period in Massachusetts. Individuals such as Cotton Mather and Samuel Willard had tried for years to evangelize blacks, and ministers built on their efforts in the mid-eighteenth century. The growing importance of Reformed thought among African Americans would be a key component in their experience in Congregational churches, as the testimony of Flora and Phillis Cogswell suggests. The Reformed tradition and its theology would likewise provide the foundation for the black critique of the institution of slavery that developed less than ten years after Phillis Cogswell's conversion narrative in the Congregational Church of Chebacco.

2

Black Abolitionist Writers in the
Age of Revolution

Three years before the Seacoast Revivals swept through Massachusetts and led to the conversion of slaves such as Phillis Cogswell in 1764, another enslaved girl named Phillis landed in Boston after her forced migration from Africa. This latter Phillis was also given her master's surname, Wheatley, and, also like Phillis Cogswell, underwent conversion and displayed the influence of Reformed theology on her own religious beliefs. Unlike Cogswell, however, Wheatley became widely known on both sides of the Atlantic for her publication of a book of poems in 1773 and her correspondence with individuals such as Samuel Hopkins and the Earl of Dartmouth. She received her freedom shortly after publishing her book of poetry in 1773, and she later wrote against slavery in a published letter and other poems. Just months later, Caesar Sarter, another former slave, initiated the tradition of the black jeremiad with his "Address to Those Who are Advocates for Holding the Africans in Slavery." And in 1775, Lemuel Haynes, the first ordained black Congregational minister in New England, also began composing poems and later an antislavery essay attacking the institution on religious grounds.

The ideas contained in these individuals' poetry and antislavery essays represent the maturing of the religious ideology that blacks in Massachusetts had been inundated with since the early eighteenth century. Whereas Flora and Phillis Cogswell's conversion narratives evince the influence of Calvinism but do not discuss other societal matters, the writings of blacks such as Wheatley and Sarter apply the ideas of Calvinist ideology to a political critique against the institution of slavery and racial inequality. In mixing their religion and politics, these black writers continued a long-standing tradition among white Puritans of explaining the secular world in religious terms.

Religion was not the only way these black writers made their case against slavery, however. While it is difficult to separate the secular from the religious in Phillis Wheatley's work, there are a number of elements in her poetry that speak to both the natural rights and republican ideologies so popular during her day. So, too, with Lemuel Haynes, who used the very arguments white revolutionaries employed in the struggle for independence for the purposes of abolition. Haynes, Wheatley, and Sarter, while drawing from revolutionary ideas, also initiated a radical critique of republicanism and the Reformed tradition for their compromises with slavery, and they helped undermine justifications for slavery by their very acts of producing literature and entering the public sphere of rational, critical debate.[1]

Individual black writers of the revolutionary period were responding to the flowering of racialist literature that depicted blacks as subhuman because of their supposed inability to reason. In his posthumously published *Essays, Moral and Political,* Scottish philosopher David Hume wrote: "I am apt to suspect the negroes to be naturally inferior to the whites. There scarcely ever was a civilized nation of that complexion, nor even any individual eminent either in action or speculation. No ingenious manufactures amongst them, no arts, no sciences."[2] Writing just four years earlier, in 1773, Richard Nisbet, a West Indian living in Philadelphia, published a defense of slavery in which he similarly articulated an ideology of white superiority. Speaking of blacks, he surmised that "it is impossible to determine, with accuracy, whether their intellects or ours are superior, as individuals, no doubt, have not the same opportunities of improving as we have: However, on the whole, it seems probable, that they are a much inferior race of men to the whites, in every respect."[3] Like Hume, Nisbet argued that blacks were inferior because "they are, in their own country, said to be utterly unacquainted with arts, letters, manufactures, and everything which constitutes civilized life."[4] Nisbet expounded on Hume's reasoning, however, further postulating that blacks were inferior to whites because of a propensity for constant warfare and their lack of belief in a supreme being. Although Hume was opposed to the institution of slavery, between them these writers articulated the primary arguments that would be used to defend slavery and cast aspersions on Africans during the era of the Enlightenment, namely that black people were superstitious, had produced no literature or art, and had not made any significant contributions to scientific knowledge. It was in order to refute ideas like these and defend both their humanity and right to equality that writers such as Phillis Wheatley took up the pen.[5]

Phillis Wheatley was born in West Africa in 1753, probably in the area between the present-day countries of Ghana and Gambia. When she was about seven or eight years old, she was captured and brought to America aboard the slave ship *Phillis*. This ship made at least four trips to the coast of Africa between 1760 and 1764, docking three times in Massachusetts and once in South Carolina. Wheatley was among the seventy-five slaves on this ship when it landed in Boston in 1761, and it was there that John Wheatley, a prominent businessman, purchased her.[6] Wheatley's life was not the typical slave experience, even for an urban slave, as her owners recognized her precociousness and encouraged her education by giving her few household chores to perform. She turned out to be a prodigy, acquiring a mastery of the English language in a little over a year and, according to her master, learning to read "the most difficult Parts of the Sacred Writings."[7] Wheatley was baptized in the Old South Church in 1771. Her piety, together with her erudition, endeared her to some of the more important religious and literary figures of her day, including Mather Byles, Charles Chauncy, and Samuel Cooper, the minister who baptized her while visiting from his own congregation. These connections proved important in helping her get her writings published and in shaping her religious and political ideology.[8]

Phillis's mistress, Susannah Wheatley, was an intensely pious individual, and she helped introduce Phillis to an evangelical circle that spanned the Atlantic world, including such prominent individuals as George Whitefield and Selina Hastings, the Countess of Huntingdon. It was this latter connection that helped launch Phillis into international fame when she penned a poem honoring George Whitefield, which features two distinctly Calvinist ideas, predestination and uncertainty over salvation. In September 1770 the Wheatleys hosted Whitefield in their home, and Phillis was probably among the thousands to hear him preach in the Old South Church on 3 September.[9]

After Whitefield's death just weeks later at the end of September 1770, Wheatley penned "An Elegaic Poem, On the Death of that Celebrated Divine, and Eminent Servant of Jesus Christ, the late Reverend, and Pious George Whitefield." In one version of the poem, Wheatley has Whitefield speaking to Americans and Africans, saying, "Take HIM ye *Africans,* he longs for you; / Impartial SAVIOUR, is his title due."[10] By arguing that both blacks and whites were eligible for salvation, Wheatley spoke to the Calvinist idea of predestination. Just as ministers such as Cotton Mather and Samuel Willard had argued that blacks might be among the Elect, Wheatley, writing in the revolutionary era, claimed that God was no "respecter of persons." Her case for the impartiality of God's grace spoke to orthodox Reformed theology at a time when it was being undermined by the proliferation of both religious ideas and sects in the colony.[11]

Advertisements for this poem and reviews of Wheatley's work ran in many newspapers throughout New England, helping to introduce her work to a wide readership and to undermine proslavery arguments about black mental inferiority. The *Massachusetts Spy* advertised it as the production of "Phillis, a servant girl but seventeen years of age . . . She has been but nine years in this country from Africa."[12] The *New Hampshire Gazette* printed an extract of the poem and praised its quality, noting that "this excellent Piece ought to be preserved for two good Reasons, first in Remembrance of the great and good Man, Mr. Whitefield, and second on Account of its being wrote by a Native of Africa, and yet would have done Honor to a Pope or Shakespeare."[13] Both of these ads highlight the exotic quality of the author, having come from Africa and in the colonies only a few short years. Wheatley capitalized on this recognition, and her future publications contained numerous references to Africa and her identity as an African. The ads also demonstrate the favorable reception of her work, important to her fight against the institution of slavery.

Wheatley's poem honoring Whitefield, along with her mistress's evangelical connections, helped make her work known to an important patron, Selina Hastings, the Countess of Huntingdon. Hastings, who was herself a staunch Calvinist, supported the work of various black Atlantic figures, including James Albert Ukawsaw Gronniosaw and John Marrant. Gronniosaw published a slave narrative in 1772 that contains a scene that has been seminal to the interpretation of African American literature and helps illuminate the importance of Wheatley's work in challenging notions of

African inhumanity. Gronniosaw's narrative primarily covers his spiritual journey, from a young man in Africa with an idea of a supreme being to his enslavement and eventual conversion under the auspices of his master, who was himself an evangelical preacher. At one point in the narrative, however, Gronniosaw writes that his first master

> used to read prayers in public to the ship's crew every Sabbath day; and when I first saw him read, I was never so surprised in my life, as when I saw the book talk to my master; for I thought it did, as I observed him to look upon it, and move his lips.—I wished it would do so with me. As soon as my master had done reading I follow'd him to the place where he put the book, being mightily delighted with it, and when nobody saw me, I open'd it, and put my ear down close upon it, in great hope that it wou'd say something to me; but I was very sorry and greatly disappointed, when I found it would not speak, this thought immediately presented itself to me, that every body and every thing despis'd me because I was black.[14]

Gronniosaw recounts his alienation from Western culture, and thereby civilization, because of his inability to read, which is itself because of his blackness. He later overcomes this alienation by becoming literate, accepting Christianity, and producing works that authors such as David Hume and Richard Nisbet said blacks had never done, which, because of this, made them inferior to whites. Thus, for black Atlantic authors such as Gronniosaw and Wheatley, reading and writing became the means by which they could prove their ability to reason and their humanity, and undermining arguments for slavery in the process.[15]

Just one year after Gronniosaw published his narrative, Wheatley journeyed to England to regain her health and oversee the publication of her *Poems on Various Subjects, Religious and Moral,* a book that established her fame as a literary figure and contributed to the growing critique against slavery in the Atlantic world. In what is perhaps the most well-known poem from this book, Wheatley wrote,

> 'Twas mercy brought me from my *Pagan* land,
> Taught my benighted soul to understand
> That there's a God, that there's a *Saviour* too.
> Once I redemption neither sought nor knew

Some view our sable race with scornful eye,
'Their colour is a diabolic die.'
Remember, *Christians*, *Negros*, black as *Cain*,
May be refin'd, and join th'angelic train.[16]

In the first half of this poem, Wheatley employed a few Calvinist motifs, specifically the theological ideas that Samuel Hopkins articulated in his work *The Nature of True Holiness.* Hopkins was the leading proponent of the New Divinity, a school of ministers influenced by the ideas of Jonathan Edwards and which represented the major theological legacy of the First Great Awakening. Among the New Divinity ministers were Jonathan Edwards Jr., Joseph Bellamy, and Hopkins, who had studied under Edwards in the 1740s and preached in Wheatley's home congregation, the Old South Church, in 1768. In his doctrine of disinterested benevolence, Hopkins required from individuals complete self-denial, even to the point of being willing to go to hell for God's glory. This doctrine had important implications for individuals, but it also articulated an answer to the problem of evil, positing that God allows suffering to promote a greater good. It is this that Wheatley spoke to in the first half of her poem when she claimed that it was due to God's mercy that she was enslaved, as this eventually allowed her to become a Christian. Rather than apologizing for slavery, as her words suggest, Wheatley articulates her belief that under all circumstances, God has the ability to bring good out of evil. In the second half of the poem she switches gears and directly attacks ideas of racial inequality by arguing again that blacks are just as eligible for salvation as whites and thus should not be seen as inferior.[17]

Wheatley's poetry also evinces the influence of Puritan covenant theology, the school of thought that came into being during the seventeenth century when Puritan leaders such as John Winthrop sought to explain New England's relationship with God. In her poem "On the Death of General Wooster," she subtly employed covenant theology to argue against slavery, asking,

How, presumptuous shall we hope to find
Divine acceptance with th' Almighty mind—
While yet (O deed ungenerous!) they disgrace
And hold in bondage Afric's blameless race?

In these few lines, Wheatley argued that America would not be successful in the revolutionary war of the 1770s if it continued to enslave blacks, because this practice was immoral and a breach of New England's covenant with God. This would not be the case if Americans abolished slavery, she argued, telling the colonists to "Let virtue reign—And thou accord our prayers / Be victory our's, and generous freedom theirs." Once the colonists became virtuous enough to abolish slavery, according to Wheatley, they would achieve success in the war with Britain.[18]

In an earlier letter to Native American minister Samson Occom, she made the same argument, writing that "in every human Breast, God has implanted a Principle, which we call Love of Freedom; it is impatient of Oppression, and pants for Deliverance . . . God grant Deliverance in his own Way and Time, and get him honor upon all whose Avarice compels them to countenance and help forward the calamities of the Fellow Creatures.[19] She made a similar claim to that of many white revolutionaries, arguing that all men and women have a desire for freedom and a hatred of tyranny. She also subtly noted that like white revolutionaries, blacks were getting tired of being held in slavery and might soon take matters into their own hands. She was not looking for revenge, according to the letter, but merely to convince slaveholding colonists that it was a sin to hold Africans in bondage and that they should emancipate their slaves or face undesirable consequences.

Wheatley's application of covenant theology relates to the influence of republicanism on her work and, in turn, the contribution of her work to republican ideology. Whereas a number of ministers used the crisis with Great Britain to argue that the colonists must practice virtue, secular political thought also stressed the importance of virtue in building a republic. Indeed, for many Americans the very meaning of the Revolution was the new, republican world they would create for themselves. Republican political theory could easily be adapted to the ministerial focus on virtue, leading to the emergence of the Puritan ethic, a secularized version of Puritan morality. Tied in with ideas from classical Greece and Rome, the thinkers of the revolutionary era argued that virtue was found in the core values of industry, frugality, simplicity, temperance, and, above all, a willingness to sacrifice for the common good. Wheatley's work speaks to many of these core themes.[20]

Perhaps the most obvious way that Wheatley's poetry displayed the influence of republican ideology was her constant use of classical motifs. Wheatley's literary predecessors, including such figures as Alexander Pope and John Milton, certainly constituted one influence on her classical style, but it was also very much a product of her time. Many American political writers of the 1760s and 1770s took classical names and used classical quotes—as Wheatley did in much of her poetry—to demonstrate their erudition and to help shape their values and behavior. Looking back on the great republics of antiquity, and especially the causes of these republics' downfall, writers such as John Dickinson and Thomas Jefferson stressed the importance of virtue for success in building a contemporary republic.[21]

Wheatley's work spoke to the most important aspect of republican virtue for the American revolutionaries, namely the willingness to sacrifice individual interests to the common good. In the letter to Mary Wooster accompanying her poem on the general, she wrote that "it was with the most sensible regret that I heard of his fall in battle, but the pain of so afflicting a dispensation of Providence must be greatly alleviated to you and all his friends in the consideration that he fell a martyr in the Cause of Freedom."[22] According to Wheatley, Wooster should not be mourned but valorized because he gave up his individual interests in the pursuit of freedom for his country.

Wheatley's connection with George Washington further underscores the influence of republicanism on her worldview. Washington was one figure during the revolutionary era that fit the classical ideal perfectly, as he was restrained, temperate, dignified, and independent. By 1775, Washington was also known for his martial valor, one of the qualities that could make a nation great, according to republican political theory. In her 1775 poem to Washington, Wheatley praised him for displaying this valor, writing,

> Thee, first in place and honours,—we demand
> The grace and glory of thy martial band.
> Fam'd for thy valour, for thy virtues more,
> Hear every tongue thy guardian aid implore![23]

By connecting herself to Washington and everything he represented, she once again displayed the impact of republican ideology on her own political thought.

Phillis Wheatley soon became well-known, and enough people found her poetry impressive that even figures such as Thomas Jefferson contended with her work when writing about the character of black people. In Jefferson's *Notes on the State of Virginia,* published in 1782, he wrote of blacks: "It appears to me that in memory they are equal to whites; in reason, much inferior, as I think one could scarcely be found capable of tracing and comprehending the investigations of Euclid: and that in imagination they are dull, tasteless, and anomalous."[24] Jefferson went on to critique Wheatley's work, saying, "Among the blacks is misery enough, God knows, but no poetry . . . Religion indeed has produced a Phyllis Whately; but it could not produce a poet. The compositions published under her name are below the dignity of criticism."[25] Jefferson's harsh critiques of Wheatley here may have been motivated by his distaste for her religious perspective, yet his denunciations of blacks elsewhere reveal his belief that the two races could not live together in the same society.

These critiques, however, demonstrate that Jefferson was familiar with her work and felt it necessary to take the time to denigrate her. This points to the popularity of Wheatley in the colonies and throughout the world, as Jefferson originally wrote the *Notes* for circulation among intellectuals in France.[26] His essay indicates that there were people who believed Wheatley's poetry was evidence of black genius that could flourish under the right circumstances, and, as a slaveholder, this would have been threatening to Jefferson. Thus, he felt it necessary to imply that the "compositions published under her name" may not have been written by her at all.

This idea was shared by many at the time Wheatley first published her book, making it necessary for her to prove her ability to produce her own works before a self-styled committee of experts in Boston. The panel included her master, James Bowdoin, as well as John Hancock and Samuel Mather (Cotton Mather's son, and also a Congregational minister), and his cousin Mather Byles. Wheatley passed the test given her by these gentlemen, among others, and she included an attestation in her original book of poetry, which reads in part, "We whose Names are under-written, do assure the World, that the POEMS specified in the following pages, were (as we verily believe) written by PHILLIS, a young Negro Girl . . . She has been examined by some of the best Judges, and is thought qualified to write them."[27] Wheatley's book and her success passing this test convinced some of these Founding Fathers that blacks had the ability to produce literature of a high quality.

George Washington was similarly impressed by the power of Wheatley's intellect. In his reply to Wheatley's October 1775 poem addressed to him, Washington wrote that the poem's "style and manner exhibit a striking proof of your poetical talents; in honor of which, and as a tribute justly due to you, I would have published the poem." He then said that if Wheatley came to Cambridge, he would "be happy to see a person so favored by the Muses, and to whom nature has been so liberal and beneficent in her dispensation."[28] Washington's opinion is a far cry from Thomas Jefferson's argument that Wheatley was not even a poet and further demonstrates the power of her poetry to influence some people's minds concerning the mental capacity of an African American. While Washington was not driven to active support of the abolitionist movement during his lifetime, he did free all of his slaves on his death.[29]

In addition to her effect on some of the Founding Fathers, Wheatley exerted an important influence on white abolitionists on both sides of the Atlantic. In his 1773 pamphlet *An Address to the Inhabitants of the British Settlements in America Upon Slave-Keeping,* Philadelphia physician and future president of the Pennsylvania Abolition Society Benjamin Rush wrote, "There is now in the town of Boston a Free Negro Girl, about 18 years of age, who has been but nine years in the country, whose singular genius and accomplishments, are such as not only do honor to her sex, but to human nature. Several of her poems have been printed, and read with pleasure by the public."[30] Here Rush espoused a form of environmentalism, whereby all people, given the opportunity, could exercise rational faculties. In a similar vein, British abolitionist Thomas Clarkson, in his *Essay on the Slavery and Commerce of the Human Species,* reproduced some of Wheatley's work as evidence that blacks could write just as well as whites, observing that "if the authoress was designed for slavery, (as the argument must confess) the greater part of the inhabitants of Britain must lose their claim to freedom."[31] The argument he referred to was the same one Hume, Nisbet, Jefferson, and other writers employed concerning blacks' mental capacity rendering them fit only for slavery. Clarkson's reply to this argument moved beyond asserting blacks' mental equality to saying that Wheatley's work demonstrated evidence of some blacks' mental superiority.[32]

Wheatley's influence on white abolitionists not only proved that blacks were equal to whites, but her work may also have shaped the very arguments they employed to critique the institution of slavery. Among these individuals was Samuel Hopkins, whom she corresponded with and heard preach in Boston while visiting Newport, Rhode Island. She also had a close friend in Hopkins's church, a black woman named Obour Tanner, with whom she corresponded regularly. After returning from her trip to England, Wheatley wrote Hopkins, telling him she was sending seventeen of her books for him to sell and two more for her friend Obour. She also mentioned her happiness at the educational promise of two free black men about whom Hopkins had written her. He was training these two men, John Quamine and Bristol Yamma, for missionary work in Africa and regularly kept Wheatley updated on their progress. In a later letter, Wheatley told Hopkins she had printed 300 more books and would again like his assistance in selling them.[33]

In reading Wheatley's poems, Hopkins would have digested her arguments for the spiritual equality of blacks and the notion that although God brought blacks out of Africa and, through this method, Christianized them, whites were still hypocritical for holding their fellow men in chains. In his first antislavery publication, written in 1776, three years after Wheatley published her poems, he rejected the notion that slavery was a positive means of bringing blacks to Christianity, saying it was "a very great wonder and owing to an extraordinary divine interposition . . . that any of them should think favorably of Christianity and embrace it." Even if blacks did embrace Christianity, Hopkins argued that Christ commanded Christians "to go and preach the gospel to all nations, to carry the gospel to them, not to go and with violence bring them from their native country."[34]

Hopkins's antislavery argument, crafted three years after the publication of Wheatley's poems, employed some of the same themes she highlighted. Her poem "On Being Brought from Africa to America" argued that although slavery brought the gospel to her, racism and bondage were nonetheless sins because they made Christians treat their fellow men as less than human. When Hopkins published his first essay in 1776, he had probably also read Wheatley's published letter to Samson Occom in 1774, in which she argued that God would take revenge against Americans if they continued in their sinful ways. Hopkins employed this same argument in a 1776 antislavery sermon, noting that "tis impossible for God to save America this Day without a reformation. But as our hands are full of Blood his holiness and Justice oblige him to destroy us unless we wash ourselves by reformation."[35] In a second antislavery tract, published in

1793, he similarly asked, "Have we not all reason to fear that the vengeance of heaven will fall upon us, as a people, in ways perhaps which are not now thought of, unless we repent and reform?"[36] Calvinist ministers such as Hopkins had often spoken of God's covenant with New England and the consequences that would ensue were this covenant broken. African American writers such as Wheatley pushed some of these ministers to broaden their theological perspective to include the abolition of slavery as an essential component of this covenant.

Black writers throughout the colonies who were concerned with the fate of slaves and the question of abolition likewise read Wheatley's work. Among these individuals was Jupiter Hammon. In 1760, Hammon, then a forty-nine-year-old slave residing in Long Island, inaugurated the tradition of African American literature by publishing his poem "An Evening Thought: Salvation by Christ, with Penitential Cries." The poem's primary theme is prayer, with Hammon arguing that by calling to Christ, all people, white or black, could achieve salvation. His biographer, Sondra O'Neale, notes that, like Wheatley, most of his work is infused with Calvinist principles; however, in this poem he espoused a form of Arminianism—the belief that individuals can have an effect on their own salvation.[37] Also like Wheatley, Hammon's messages to slaves and his attacks on the institution were coded in biblical language. For instance, the first stanza in the above poem reads,

> Salvation comes by Jesus Christ alone,
> The only Son of God;
> Redemption now to every one,
> That loves his holy word.[38]

While he did not directly say anything about slavery in this excerpt, the word *redemption* alludes to being freed from sin and also to possibly being freed from slavery, as the ancient Israelites of the Bible had often referred to God as their redeemer.[39]

Hammon's next poem was written specifically for Phillis Wheatley in 1778, showing his familiarity with her work and his belief in the importance of her endeavors. He began the piece by noting, like Wheatley herself did, that she should "adore / The wisdom of thy God, / In bringing thee from distant shore, / To learn his holy word."[40] In the Calvinist, predestinarian perspective that Hammon shared with Wheatley, her forced migration and separation from her family was a means for God to introduce her to the gospel and let her be an example of what other Africans could achieve:

> That thou a pattern still might be
> To youth of Boston town,
> The blessed Jesus set thee free,
> From every sinful wound.[41]

Wheatley's application of Reformed theology to the problem of slavery was shared by black writers closer to home, one of whom has received little scholarly treatment in studies of the early antislavery movement. This individual is Caesar Sarter. Just six months after Wheatley's letter to Occom appeared in colonial newspapers, Sarter published an antislavery essay in the *Essex Journal and Merrimack Packet,* based in Newburyport, Massachusetts. Newburyport was a relatively new town of 3,600 people located about forty miles north of Boston. Ten years before its split from Newbury in 1764, there were fifty slaves in the town; however, census records do not indicate how many blacks were in Newburyport when Sarter first published this essay. Given that Newburyport is located on the coast, Sarter may have been a maritime worker, perhaps working as a sailor, carpenter, or rope maker, or he could have been a skilled worker in any number of trades in which black people worked, such as blacksmithing or barbering. Like Wheatley, Sarter had been captured in Africa and forcefully migrated to Massachusetts, where he spent twenty years as a slave and where he still had eleven relatives in bondage.[42]

This 1774 essay is Sarter's only known publication and has not received any scholarly treatment in the history of abolitionism in Massachusetts, even though it demonstrates both the influence of Calvinism and the political context of the American Revolution on black antislavery thought. His essay is also one of the most forceful early black critiques of the revolutionary tradition.

Sarter began by referencing the context of the Revolution, noting that "as this is a time of great anxiety and distress among you, on the account of the infringement, not only of your Charter rights; but of the natural rights and privileges of freeborn men," the colonists should know well that liberty is the greatest gift a person can enjoy.[43] Just as political writers in revolutionary Massachusetts, such as John Adams, often referenced the settling of the colony and the fact that early Puritans came to Massachusetts to enjoy liberty, Sarter connected blacks' struggles for liberty with the early Puritans, arguing—incorrectly, it turned out—that these settlers had "an utmost abhorrence of that Curse of Curses, Slavery."[44] He then asked his readers to imagine that they were enslaved, a rhetorical move that allowed him to highlight the horrors of slavery and appeal to the benevolence of his readers, one of the chief sources of antislavery thought in the Atlantic world.[45] "Suppose you were trepanned away," he wrote, "the husband from the dear wife of his bosom—the wife from her affectionate husband—children from their fond parents—or parents from their tender and beloved offspring."[46] Sarter recounted the indignities that accompanied the working of the slave trade, with Africans being "exposed to sale, with as little respect to decency as though you were a brute." If you chose to shed a tear over the loss of your loved ones, he told his reader, "you must be plied with that conclusive argument, that cat-o' nine tails, to reduce you to what your inhuman masters would call Reason."[47] This argument had the dual effect of allowing his reader to imagine themselves in a slave's place while also critiquing the slaveowners who misused the Enlightenment's emphasis on reason.

In addition to his appeal to the heritage of New Englanders and their benevolent nature, Sarter spoke to covenant theology. If his readers could imagine what these slaves went through, he wondered how supporters of slavery or slaveholders would hope to escape divine judgment: "Why, in the name of Heaven, will you suffer such a gross violation of that rule by which your conduct must be tried, in that day, in which you must be held accountable for all your actions, to, that impartial Judge, who hears the groans of the oppressed and who will sooner or later, avenge them of their oppressors!"[48] While Wheatley's letter to Occom earlier in the same year subtly said that God would "get him honor" on the colonists for slavery, Sarter had no compunction about saying outright that God would avenge blacks for the wrongs perpetrated on them. He then built his argument for the irrationality of slavery among people who sought freedom for themselves: "Would you desire the preservation of your own liberty?" he asked the colonists. "As the first step let the oppressed Africans be liberated; then, and not till then, may you with confidence and consistency of conduct, look to Heaven for a blessing on your endeavors."[49] Sarter contended that God would not assist the colonists in their struggle against Britain unless they stopped enslaving blacks and participating in the transatlantic slave trade, broadening covenant theology to speak to the problem of slavery.

Along with his particularly Calvinist critique of the institution of slavery, Sarter employed more general Christian themes in his work. "I need not tell you, who are acquainted with the scriptures, that this kind of oppression, is discountenanced by them," he wrote. This includes Exodus 20:16, which mandates death for those who steal human beings. And if colonists were really interested in spreading the gospel, the slave trade was not the way to go about it, because, according to Sarter, in America Africans were likely "to become ten fold more the children of satan, then we should probably, have been in our native country."[50] Finally, he noted, "If you are still determined to harden your hearts, and turn a deaf ear to our complaints, and the calls of God, in your present Calamities; only be pleased to recollect the miserable end of Pharoah, in Consequences of his refusal to set those at Liberty, whom he had unjustly reduced to cruel servitude."[51] In this statement, Sarter once again critiques American republicanism by comparing those who supported slavery to the biblical tyrant Pharaoh.

Closely related to Sarter's argument about Christianizing Africa was his direct rebuttal of arguments advanced by proslavery thinkers such as Nisbet. In reply to those who argued that Africans would be happier in America, he wrote that "though many think we are happier here than there, and will not allow us the privilege of judging for ourselves, they are certainly in error."[52] He contended that blacks' greater happiness in Africa stemmed from their being brought "from a land of innocence—from a land that flows, as it were, with Milk and Honey."[53] The idea that Africa was a land replete with natural resources characterized the writings of numerous abolitionists throughout the Atlantic world, including figures such as Olaudah Equiano and Anthony Benezet.[54] And to counter Nisbet's claims that Africans were uncivilized because they were constantly at warfare, Sarter responded, "Though 'tis true, that some of our wars proceed from petty discords among ourselves, it is as true, that the greater part of them and those the most bloody, are occasioned, in consequence of the Slave trade."[55]

Sarter's essay is significant to the history of abolitionism because he articulated some of the main streams of thought that would characterize black abolitionist discourse until the Civil War. He connected the struggle of black people to America's European settlers and the long-standing spirit of liberty in the colonies while appealing to the emotions of his readers by expounding on the horrors of slavery. Sarter also worked to tie slavery to the ethical and religious values Americans held dear, a connection that abolitionists were just beginning to make during the revolutionary period. And he also articulated the belief that African Americans were akin to the ancient Israelites in the trials they were undergoing in the New World, an argument that seventeenth-century Puritans had made before him about white New Englanders.

By tying in African American history with that of ancient Israel and speaking to the covenant that white New Englanders believed they had with God, Sarter's essay also initiated the tradition of the black jeremiad. For early Puritans, the jeremiad had been a means of joining social critique to spiritual renewal, and it was a ritual whose roots stretched back to John Winthrop's 1630 *Arbella* sermon, where he warned his listeners that success in their holy experiment rested on following God's strictures. For white ministers and magistrates alike, the jeremiad articulated a worldview whereby God was intimately involved in earthly affairs, an outlook that would have accorded well with traditional African cosmologies, as scholars have noted a similar lack of distinction between sacred and secular realms in African thought. Although Sarter has gone unnoticed by scholars of the black jeremiad, his claim that God, the "impartial judge," hears the groans of the oppressed slaves and will "sooner or later avenge them of their oppressors" places him squarely within the Puritan tradition of calling for spiritual renewal and a return to America's original promise of being a city on a hill.[56]

Lemuel Haynes was another writer who drew from Calvinist thought and the revolutionary tradition in critiquing the institution of slavery. Haynes, born in 1753, was the illegitimate child of a white mother and a black father. He was an indentured servant on a farm in Granville, Massachusetts, until 1774, when, like many other young men of his generation, he joined the militia and marched to Lexington, later serving with the Continental Army in Roxbury and Ticonderoga. Haynes was self-educated, often reading whatever he could get his hands on after working on the farm, and his education led him to dabble first in poetry and then to compose an antislavery essay and later to write and give sermons.[57]

Haynes's initial foray into the world of letters came in January 1774 when, still in the army, he wrote "A Poem, Occasioned by the Sudden and Surprising Death of Mr. Asa Burt." Like many of Wheatley's poems, this piece by Haynes was meant to console the family of a man who died too soon, at just thirty-seven. Also like Wheatley, Haynes began this work with a classical reference: "Awake my drousy Muse within, attend with awe profound."[58] This usage connected his work to the literary conventions of the day, much of which employed classical tropes, especially references to the muses. From there, Haynes, the narrator, went on to offer consolation to the family, assuring them that their father was resting safely in heaven. Evident was the influence of Calvinism, as he told the family that

> At first Affliction may seem hard,
> And penetrate severe,
> Yet they will profit afterward,
> To them that faithful are.
> Justice is God's own Attribute,
> With Wisdom 'tis subjoin'd;
> Why should a mortal Worm dispute
> And call a God unkind?[59]

While Haynes did not publish this essay, he did send it to the family of Asa Burt, and others probably saw it as well, providing them with an example of a learned and pious black man, an individual whose life and intellect countered those proslavery theorists who argued that Africans were inferior in every respect to whites.

Lemuel Haynes's second poem dealt not with the tragedy of an untimely death but with the tragedy "perpetrated on the 19th of April 1775 by a Number of the British Troops under the Command of Thomas Gage." Haynes titled this piece "The Battle of Lexington" and similarly began with a classical reference to the Muses, asking that "some Seraph now my Breast inspire." Haynes referred to the British in this poem as "Tyrants fill'd with horrid Rage" who came to Lexington to "slay the innocent." After recounting the British march on both Lexington and Concord and the initial attempts to peacefully resist, Haynes noted that the colonists had to retaliate as their freedom was under attack. Demonstrating the powerful rhetorical hold that the ideology of the American Revolution had on him, he wrote:

> For Liberty, each Freeman Strives
> As it's a Gift of God
> And for it willing yield their Lives
> And Seal it with their Blood.[60]

This idea that liberty was a gift from God infused the writings of other black abolitionists, who used it to promote their cause and to critique the declarations of those white revolutionaries who claimed they loved liberty and yet also held slaves.

Using the same covenant theology prevalent in the work of Wheatley and Sarter, Haynes asks his reader to

> Stop and see the Pow'r of God
> Who lifts his Banner high
> Jehovah now extends his Rod
> And makes our Foes to fly.

The reason that Britain is on the wrong side of God's will in this endeavor was that the country has become "Infamous in our Eye / Nearly allied to antient Rome / That Seat of Popery."[61] He then calls for the British to withdraw their troops from America and notes that the colonists would still be loyal to the king if he followed the law and did not tax them without representation. The poem ends in speculation on the cause of the colonists' troubles.

> Sin is the Cause of all our Woe
> That sweet deluding ill
> And till we let this darling go
> There's greater Trouble still.[62]

While in this poem Haynes did not explicitly refer to slavery as one of the sins causing the colonists' problems with England, his later writings do refer to slavery as a sin.[63]

After writing these two essays and finishing his service in the Continental Army, Haynes returned home to Granville, Massachusetts. He
received theological training after his military duty ended in 1776, and he
went on to become the first ordained black minister in America and the
first to preside over a primarily white congregation, taking up the pastor-
ship of a Congregational church in Rutland, Vermont, in 1788, where he
worked until 1818. Before this, however, while residing in Granville, Haynes
penned the antislavery sermon "Liberty Further Extended," which was
among the first abolitionist works to use the rhetoric of the Declaration
of Independence. He prefaced his essay by quoting the first sentence of
the second paragraph of the Declaration, which posits that all men have
natural, unalienable rights, and gave his reason for writing the piece: "As
Tyrony had its Origin from the infernal regions, so it is the Deuty, and
honner of Every son of freedom to repel her first motions. But while we
are Engaged in the important struggle, it cannot be tho't impertinent for us
to turn one Eye into our own Breast, for a little moment, and See, whether
thro' some inadvertency, or a self-contracted Spirit, we Do not find the
monster Lurking in our own Bosom."[64] The monster, of course, was the
institution of slavery, but Haynes was somewhat reserved in his attack on
colonists for the presence of the institution, arguing that the sinful nature
prevalent in all men is what likely influenced them to buy and sell slaves.

The sermon moved on to discuss the nature of liberty, drawing both
from the political context of Massachusetts and the Bible. Liberty is an
innate principle, Haynes said; thus, if a man infringes on another man's
liberty, he must expect to meet resistance, as the laws of nature call for all
men to defend their liberty. Haynes argued in no uncertain terms that, like
the white revolutionaries, it is in the very nature of black people to fight for
their liberty, and they would do so if whites continued to deprive them of
that most precious gift. He also argued that "liberty is a Jewel which was
handed Down to man from the cabinet of heaven . . . as it proceed from
the Supreme Legislature of the univers [*sic*], so it is he which hath a sole
right to take away."[65] He once again drew from his Calvinist background
to make his antislavery critique, arguing for the absolute sovereignty of
God in this matter of liberty and noting that any man's attempt to take it
away is acting "out of his own domain."[66]

"Liberty Further Extended" spoke to the notion of the equality of all
men before God. Haynes quoted the famous verse Acts 17:26 and posited

that "as all are of one Species, so there are the same Laws, and aspiring principles placed in all nations."[67] Since this is the case, if liberty is precious to the white man, he wrote, it must be so to the black man, and there is nothing in the Bible that can possibly justify the slavery of Africans. While God may have distinguished some human beings in point of ability, God has not distinguished between human beings in terms of natural rights, thus making slavery unjust and unlawful.

In an attempt to appeal to the emotions of his readers and warn them of the consequences of their actions, Haynes addressed the slave trade itself. He noted that those who engaged in this form of commerce instigated wars among the Africans in order to procure captives. On the ships themselves, he wrote, "there are generally many hundred slaves put on board a vessel, and they are Shackkled together, two by two, wors that Criminals going to the place of Execution . . . and their sufferings are so great, as I have Been Credibly informed, that it often Carries off one third of them on their passage."[68] In addition to this high death rate, many slaves chose to end their own lives due to the anguish they suffered. Turning to some of the same themes discussed in Sarter's essay, he then asked, "What must be the plaintive noats that the tend[er] parents must assume for the Loss of their Exiled Child? Or the husband for his Departed wife? And how Do the crys of their Departed friends echo from the watry Deep!"[69] For these crimes, Haynes argued that a just God must have vengeance on the colonists and slave traders. He did not mention the revolutionary context, as Wheatley and Sarter did, but asked, "What will you Do in that Day when God shall make inquisision for Blood . . . Believe it, Sirs, there shall not a Drop of Blood, which you have Spilt unjustly, Be Lost in forgetfullness."[70] By expounding on the horrors of the slave trade for the African people, for both those forcefully migrated to the colonies and those left behind, Haynes helped cement this rhetorical strategy as an effective one that abolitionists would use for years to come. He also placed himself within the ideological position staked out by writers such as Wheatley and Sarter, namely that slavery was a sin for which God would have His vengeance, either in this life or the next.

Haynes ended the essay by consciously refuting some of the most prevalent proslavery arguments of the period. To the argument that blacks were descended from Canaan, the biblical character whom Noah cursed because his father Ham saw Noah naked, Haynes responded that the curse did not outlast Christ's atonement on the cross. And to the ubiquitous claim that Africans were better off in slavery because they were brought out of a heathenish land, he replied, as Samuel Hopkins would that same year, that men are not to do evil so that good may come about. He further posited that "those Slavemerchants that trade upon the coasts of Africa do not aim at the Spiritual good of their Slaves."[71] Instead, they were merely concerned with profiting off their fellow men and living lives of luxury, both of which could be dangerous for a people trying to cultivate republican virtue. As his final admonition to the colonists, Haynes tied in the practice of slaveholding with America's efforts against Great Britain, telling them, "If you have any Love to yourselves, or any Love to this Land, if you have any Love to your fellow-men, Break these intollerable yoaks . . . for god will not hold you guiltless."[72]

While these early poems and essay were not published during Haynes's lifetime, they are important for the study of black abolitionism in Massachusetts because they demonstrate the degree to which Calvinism in particular, and Christianity in general, informed African American political thought in the colony. It's not likely that Haynes kept the ideas contained in these works to himself during the revolutionary era, and we know that he later published works and spoke about the institution of slavery from the pulpit on many occasions. From his pulpit in Rutland, Haynes used the ideas and rhetoric shaped by his experience in Massachusetts to continue to critique the institution of slavery, arguing that both Christianity and republicanism were inconsistent with holding human beings in bondage.[73]

In making this argument, Haynes and his contemporaries Phillis Wheatley and Caesar Sarter became key figures in the history of the early abolitionist movement. They helped broaden the scope of Reformed theology and give legitimacy to their moral critiques of the institution of slavery. While drawing from revolutionary ideas of liberalism and republicanism, they also critiqued the revolutionary tradition for its failure to adequately address the problem of slavery, warning the colonists of God's impending judgment on the nation. Together, they articulated some of the most significant arguments that abolitionists in their own and in the next century employed in the fight against both slavery and racial inequality.

3

Black Petitioning and Organized Abolitionism in Revolutionary Massachusetts

Around the same time that black writers in Massachusetts such as Phillis Wheatley, Caesar Sarter, and Lemuel Haynes were publicly critiquing the institution of slavery, groups of slaves began petitioning the colonial authorities for their freedom. Most students and scholars of early American history are familiar with Lord Dunmore's November 1775 proclamation, the significance of which cannot be overstated, as it led to the exodus of thousands of slaves to British lines and steeled the resolve of southerners who had been on the fence about whether to take up arms against England. Less familiar is an offer Massachusetts slaves made to Royal Governor Thomas Gage to fight for the British in exchange for freedom. According to Abigail Adams, in September 1774 there had "been in Town a conspiracy of the Negroes. At present it is kept pretty private and was discovered by one who endeavourd to diswaid them from it—he being threatend with his life." She wrote that the group of slaves carried out their conspiracy by getting an "Irishman to draw up a petition to the Govener telling him they would fight for him provided he would arm them and engage to liberate them if he conquerd." Gage decided not to act on the blacks' petition to fight for him, yet the whole affair made Abigail Adams "wish there was not a Slave in the province."[1]

This petition and four others that Massachusetts slaves submitted to the legislature and royal governor during the 1770s were part of a concerted effort by America's first antislavery committee to abolish the institution of slavery. While many historians claim that the Pennsylvania Abolition Society, organized in 1775, was the nation's first antislavery organization, a committee of slaves in Massachusetts began its efforts on behalf of the cause in January 1773. Not much is known about the functioning of this committee; however, it is clear that it was an organized group dedicated to achieving the abolition of slavery and the slave trade. Members established contacts with white political and religious figures that supported their cause, and they were able to disseminate their ideology through the expanding medium of print, with the petitions showing up in both newspapers and other abolitionist tracts. An examination of the records of governmental bodies such as the Massachusetts House of Representatives as well as the ideology expressed in other black petitions throughout New England demonstrates that blacks in Massachusetts were able to motivate people in power to support their cause and influence the ideas of other antislavery activists.

Organized black abolitionism during the revolutionary period was preceded by both individual acts of resistance from slaves and attacks on slavery and the slave trade by whites during the 1760s. Among the first white abolitionists to publicly voice his opposition to slavery was James Otis, the scion of an old Massachusetts family. James Otis Sr. was the Speaker of the Massachusetts House of Representatives in the early 1760s, and Otis Jr. was also a member of that body. Both father and son led the popular resistance in Boston to the Stamp Act and other Parliamentary taxes in the mid-1760s. In his 1764 tract *Rights of the British Colonies,* Otis deplored the practice of holding slaves because he viewed liberty as a gift from God that no man can take away. He further argued that slavery was a throwback to the days of barbarism and ignorance prevalent in the Dark Ages. While many of his contemporaries claimed that blacks were inferior to whites and deserved to be enslaved, Otis asked rhetorically, "Does it follow that 'tis right to enslave a man because he is black? Will short curled hair like wool instead of Christian hair, as 'tis called by those whose hearts are as hard as the nether millstone, help the argument?"[2] He believed that the colonists were being hypocritical in calling for their own natural rights while denying them to slaves and that the institution of slavery was harmful to white colonists on multiple fronts, among them because it stymied pace of Enlightenment and kept them from being able to value their own liberty.

Another white abolitionist to publicly voice his opposition to slavery during the 1760s was Nathaniel Appleton. Appleton's 1767 pamphlet *Considerations on Slavery* is significant both for the information it provides about the institution in Massachusetts and the arguments it sets forth, arguments that would serve as the crux for both white and black abolitionist thought for years to come. Among the first arguments that Appleton, the son of a Congregational minister, made against the slave trade was that it was "contrary to humanity, Christianity, the interest of the province, and of private families."[3] He further claimed that Massachusetts would be stronger economically and militarily by importing white servants instead of slaves, who, once freed, would help settle the province and defend it from enemies in a way that blacks could not because whites barred them from military service.

White servants would also be less likely to engage in rebellion as black slaves had throughout the Atlantic World, according to Appleton: "It must be constantly expected that a slave will improve every opportunity to throw off his burthen, and imposition. New-York, & most of the Southern colonies, and West-Indies, have experienced something of that, which is enough to make all those that set a just value upon domestic security, to tremble."[4] Appleton was likely referring to the New York slave conspiracy of 1741 when, authorities believed, slaves and some white allies tried to take over the city. Also, the large uprising in Jamaica in 1760–61, known as Tacky's Revolt, is something that Appleton and other whites would have read about in colonial newspapers. This uprising resulted in the deaths of sixty whites and an estimated 300–400 slaves and took over a year for authorities to quash. Although there were no more than 5,000 slaves in Massachusetts at the time, less than 2 percent of the population, there was a higher concentration in Boston (about 6 percent), leading Appleton to think that slaves in the colony would grow weary of their treatment and follow the example of enslaved blacks throughout the British Empire.[5]

Along with these practical considerations, Appleton stressed the moral question of slavery and its effects on both black and white people in Africa and Massachusetts. He maintained that the slave trade was destroying African life by promoting warfare and was harmful to African Americans in Massachusetts because it denied them the right to marry without fear of being sold and promoted the sale of older slaves who could no longer perform hard physical labor. Foreshadowing arguments Thomas Jefferson would famously make in the 1780s, Appleton also wrote that slavery was harmful to whites because it introduced haughtiness and cruelty into children in their treatment of slaves, character traits that then could carry over into other relationships. Speaking to the rising opposition of white colonists to the policies of Parliament, Appleton ended his appeal by noting, "It has always appeared very strange to me, how people can be so sensibly affected with what has but a remote tendency to deprive them of their smallest right or privilege, and yet remain so insensible of the deplorable state of so many of our species that live among us."[6]

Like Otis's remarks three years earlier, Nathaniel Appleton's pamphlet drew strength from the increasing emphasis on natural rights being voiced by white colonists throughout British North America and helped forward abolitionist sentiment in Massachusetts. On 4 March 1767, a bill for pre-venting the importation of slaves was read a first time in the House of Representatives.[7] Nine days later the bill was amended to "A Bill to prevent the unwarrantable and unusual Practice or Custom of inslaving Mankind in this Province, and the importation of Slaves into the same." This change is significant because previous action by colonial leaders had targeted only the slave trade and not slavery itself. The move reflects a growing discontent with the institution of slavery among the people of Massachusetts and some of their leaders. The amended bill was read a third time but did not pass, perhaps because legislators felt the governor would not approve of any restriction on slavery. Instead, the House brought a new bill that attacked only the slave trade, laying a prohibitive duty on all slave imports, but the Council passed a different version, and the two houses could not agree, thus killing the legislation. These efforts reveal the changing attitudes in the colony toward slavery and helped spur continued efforts by blacks, individual and groups, to seek their freedom.[8]

One way that white leaders feared blacks might try to undermine slavery was through clandestine church meetings. On 7 June 1771, white members of the Old South Church in Boston convened to discuss such meetings. The committee reported: "Whereas Danger is apprehended from the Slaves that are frequently left in the meeting house after the public worship is over— Voted that the sexton make diligent search on the Lord's day Evening . . . to see if any slaves are left in the house."[9] The slaves found lingering in the church were to be taken back to the sexton's house, where their owners could pay a fine to retrieve them.

From the church records, it is not clear what danger the committee feared would come out of slaves meeting in the church, but they certainly recognized that they themselves used meetinghouses for political purposes. Some may have felt meeting in churches was an opportunity for blacks to plan a revolt or rebellion of some kind. Just three years earlier, in October 1768, Massachusetts leaders dealt with a potential rebellion instigated by a British soldier. According to Boston selectman Joshua Henshaw, British army captain John Wilson got drunk one night and, as he was walking the streets of Boston, encountered a number of black men, whom he presumed to be slaves. He asked them if their masters were Liberty Boys, those en- gaged in resistance to the taxation policies of the British Parliament. The men gave the captain different answers, and he said that if their masters were Liberty Boys, they should go home, cut their masters' throats, and come back to him for protection. He also told them he would make them soldiers, which may be where some of the blacks who petitioned Gen- eral Gage six years later got the idea in the first place. It was this sort of threat, slave rebellions in the colonies and the larger Atlantic world, which convinced Nathaniel Appleton that the slave trade was detrimental to the security of white colonists.[10]

The selectmen took immediate action against Captain Wilson and any black people roaming the streets at night. In their meeting shortly after the incident, private citizens noted that they entered "their Complaint with the Selectmen against John Wilson Esqr. Of the 59th Regiment of Foot, for practicing on their Negro Servants to induce them immediately to enter into a dangerous conspiracy against their masters promising them their freedom as a reward." The selectmen secured affidavits against Wilson. This was a crime that could not be taken lightly, and to ensure that something like this did not occur in the future, "the Several Constables of the Watch [were] directed by the Selectmen, to be watchful of the Negros & to take up those of them that may be in gangs at unseasonable hours."[11] By restricting blacks' freedom of movement at night, authorities hoped to deflect what they saw as the dangers posed by their gathering in groups.

Whites may have also feared meetings by slaves in churches because of the potential for slaves to turn the message of Christianity into a lib- eration theology. During the Great Awakening, slaves such as Flora of Ipswich had capitalized on religious enthusiasm to become exhorters and lay claim to equality in religious affairs. Thereafter, slaves and free blacks continued to join and participate in churches where they would have further opportunity to internalize both the discourse of Calvinism as well as ideas about individual liberty and the duty of resistance to tyranny. From 1744 to 1770, at least twenty-seven blacks were baptized in the Old South Church, individuals who came of age during the time of the American Revolution and the antislavery movement in Massachusetts. In Boston's First Congregational Church only seven blacks were baptized from 1741 to 1774; however, over a similar period at Trinity Church forty-six blacks were baptized, and thirty-five received the sacrament at Brattle Street Church between 1745 and 1770.[12]

The increasing presence of blacks within white churches in Boston represented a threat to slavery, because as opposition to Britain from white colonists mounted, messages of resistance to British tyranny and opposition to slavery resounded from pulpits across the province. In an oration delivered at the Second Baptist Church of Boston, for example, John Allen declared that "if there be any vein, any nerve, any soul, any life, or spirit of Liberty in the Sons of America, shew your love for it; guard your freedom, prevent your chains; stand up as one man for your Liberty; for none but those, who set a just value upon this blessing are worthy to enjoy it."[13] It is likely that any slaves present in the church that day, or those who later read the printed edition of the pamphlet, would have applied Allen's principles to their own situation. Allen also displayed his friendship to the cause of abolition in the sermon, saying that "for mankind to be distressed and kept in Slavery by Christians, by those who love the Gospel of Christ; for such to buy their Brethren (for of one blood he has made all nations) and bind them to be Slaves to them and their heirs for life. Be astonished, ye Christians, at this!"[14] Nathaniel Niles, Calvinist minster of the North Church in Newburyport, similarly asked from his pulpit "God gave us liberty, and we have enslaved our fellow-men. May we not fear that the law of retaliation is about to be executed on us?"[15] During the revolutionary period, churches increasingly became politicized spaces where blacks could imbibe messages of freedom and the equality of man under God.

The religious basis of organized black abolitionism is clear from the very beginning of the first petition Massachusetts blacks submitted to Governor Thomas Hutchinson and the state legislature on 6 January 1773 asking for the freeing of slaves. The sole signer of the petition was a slave

named Felix, probably the same Felix Holbrook who signed a later petition. Although he was the sole signer, the wording of the petition makes
it clear that Felix was not writing for himself alone but for all slaves in
the province, and this petition is an important window into the ideology
and worldview of these enslaved blacks in revolutionary Massachusetts.
The petition began by telling the magistrates, "We desire to bless God,
who loves Mankind, who sent his Son to die for their Salvation, and who
is no respecter of persons."[16] These words put forth the biblical basis of
black protest against the institution of slavery and was a shrewd use of
the same language white colonists and ministers employed in their arguments for colonial freedom from British tyranny. The petitioners were
also making the case for racial equality by saying that God does not judge
people based on outward appearances but what is in their hearts. This
tactic is one that blacks such as Flora had employed during the Great
Awakening, one that black writers such as Phillis Wheatley would use in
her book of poems, and one that the black petitioners were employing
to undermine the power of slaveholders.

Religious ideas played a prominent role in the petitioners' arguments,
especially the question of how slavery affects virtue. They noted that
many slaves in the province are "virtuous and religious, although their
condition is in itself so unfriendly to Religion, and every moral Virtue
except Patience."[17] By stating that slavery is destructive to the virtue of
those in bondage, the petitioners used an idea common in the political discourse of the time. While white colonists were not themselves enslaved,
many political tracts discussed parliamentary taxation as a form of slavery,
and ministers throughout the colony remarked on the destructiveness of
any form of slavery to the virtue of a people. This idea was one Jonathan
Edwards articulated in his work, when he defined liberty as the freedom
to act morally without any constraints. The Calvinist ministry during
the revolutionary era used Edwards's idea to argue that men must have
natural liberty if they were to be able to do the will of God, just as the
petitioners' rhetoric indicates that they, too, felt liberty was necessary for
virtue. By pointing this out, they could gain allies among the ministerial
class that were making similar claims.[18]

Felix and the other petitioners further displayed the influence of Edwardsianism on their own religious and political thought by saying that
they would attempt to practice virtue to the best of their ability: "We have

no Property! We have no Wives! No Children! We have no City! No Country. But we have a Father in Heaven, and we are determined, as far as his Grace shall enable us, and as far as our degraded contemptuous Life will admit, to keep all his Commandments."[19] With this they showed the colonists the true extent of slavery and how it robbed them of a normal family life and squelched their sense of patriotism. But by saying they would keep God's commandments if his grace allowed them to, they employed a distinctly Calvinist approach, one that attributed any change of heart in a sinner to God's irresistible grace and not the efforts of people. Further, in the double entendre referencing their "degraded contemptuous Life," the petitioners again pointed out their poor temporal situation but also alluded to the Christian belief in original sin, an allusion that may similarly have appealed to ministers and the religiously inclined whites who were starting to question and speak against the institution of slavery.

Despite their claim that they had no city or country, the slaves put forth patriotic arguments to support their cause against slavery among those to whom religious appeals would have little effect. They wrote that while some blacks were "vicious," they were under the same laws as all other British subjects, and "there are many others of a quite different Character, and who, if made free, would soon be able as well as willing to bear a Part in the Public Charges."[20] Here the petitioners appealed to both the sentiment and pocketbooks of colonial leaders. They argued that freeing the slaves would produce many individuals loyal to the colonies, individuals who were virtuous and would contribute to God looking favorably on their country. At the same time, by saying those freed would bear their part in the public charges, they argued that abolition would result in higher tax revenue once freedmen became property owners and productive citizens.

Another appeal that the petitioners employed reveals their awareness of transatlantic antislavery politics, an important tool as activists on both sides of the Atlantic were stepping up their efforts to achieve abolition in the early 1770s. After their claim that "God is no respecter of persons," they noted that God "hath lately put it into the Hearts of Multitudes on both sides of the Water, to bear our Burthens, some of whom are Men of great Note and Influence; who have pleaded our Cause with Arguments which we hope will have their weight with this Honorable Court."[21] They referred to the general antislavery sentiment arising in the Atlantic world but probably also had in mind the specific case of James Somerset, a slave who had lived in Boston from 1765 to 1769 and who some of the petitioners may have known. Motivated by a desire for freedom and probably emboldened by the many acts of resistance and the growing emphasis on natural rights in Boston, Somerset ran away from Charles Steuart, his master, shortly after arriving in England. Steuart caught Somerset and detained him with the intention of shipping him to the West Indies. Granville Sharpe took on his case and secured legal assistance for Somerset. In the ensuing decision that Lord Chief Justice Mansfield delivered on 22 June 1772, Somerset was freed because, Mansfield argued, slavery was of such an odious nature that it could only be supported by positive law, of which there was none within England. While the decision did not actually free all slaves in England, the petitioners may have perceived the decision as such and used that information to bolster their own argument against slavery.[22]

The petitioners distributed their entreaty and its arguments against slavery in a few different media in order to reach as wide an audience as possible. The anonymous author of *The Appendix,* an antislavery tract, inserted the entire text of their petition into his publication, thereby assisting the slaves by circulating their work while also building off their arguments in his own essay. Where the slaves said they hoped the arguments that other abolitionists were advancing would have an effect on the provincial leaders, *The Appendix* author argued that slavery is contrary to the charter of Massachusetts, in effect saying that there was no positive law for slavery and the practice should end. His argument again spoke to the ambiguity of the *Body of Liberties* toward the institution of slavery, which stated that there should be no slaves in the colony but then proceeded to list exceptions to the rule. The "lover of constitutional liberty," as the author called himself, said of the slaves' efforts: "Great Success is expected from this Petition, since Those, who are the Guardians of our Rights, are led and influenced by the true Principles of Liberty."[23] But if it was not successful, he counseled, the blacks should seek other methods of redress, especially suing their masters.

In addition to placing their work in *The Appendix,* the petitioners managed to get it noticed in an essay published in the *Massachusetts Spy.* The anonymous author of the essay addressed the Massachusetts General Court: "Having seen a petition that is intended to be laid before you in the name of many slaves living in Boston and other towns of this province, praying that you would be pleased to take their unhappy state and condition under consideration."[24] This essayist also argued against slavery on the grounds that it violated the charter, which guaranteed liberty to all subjects of the British Empire. Although the petition did not appear verbatim in the essay, the slaves' activism was recognized and helped convince abolitionists to support their cause and to do so publicly.

While Felix and his fellow slaves were successful in airing their cause in multiple venues, the January 1773 petition did not lead to any legislative action. Thus, in April they submitted another petition arguing for the abolition of slavery and urging the legislature to do so as soon as possible. Instead of presenting this entreaty as a blessing to God, as they did the first, the petitioners mentioned the many efforts made "by the legislative of this province in their last sessions to free themselves from slavery."[25] Pointing out the seeming hypocrisy of American republicanism, they wrote, "We expect great things from men who have made such a noble stand against the designs of their fellow-men to enslave them. We cannot but wish and hope Sir, that you will have the same grand object, we mean civil and religious liberty, in view in your next session."[26]

The slaves' recognition of the legislature's fight for civil and religious liberty highlights another source of black antislavery thought, namely the battle for religious freedom waged by sects such as the Presbyterians, Baptists, and Methodists throughout Massachusetts. In his tract *Freedom from Civil and Ecclesiastical Tyranny,* Presbyterian minister Jonathan Parsons of Newburyport noted another inconsistency in the political rhetoric of Massachusetts' leaders who argued for civil freedom while clinging to a religious establishment. One of the leaders, Isaac Backus, a Baptist minister, was similarly active during this period in publishing calls for religious freedom. While in this instance the slaves used the struggle for religious freedom as a way to bolster their claim, they did not abandon the religious basis of their call for equal treatment, pointing out that, as with the colonists, "the divine spirit of freedom, seems to fire every humane breast." They left it up to the imagination of the petition's recipients to discern what would happen if this divine spirit were ignored.[27]

Like the previous petition, the slaves tried to appeal to ideas of patriotism to aid their cause. They said that while they could demand reparations for services rendered, they would not do so, but they would like to receive the same considerations that other countries gave their slaves. "Even the Spaniards," they wrote, "who have not those sublime ideas of freedom that English men have, are conscious that they have no right to all [to] the services of their fellow-men, we mean the Africans . . . therefore they allow them one day in a week to work for themselves."[28] Referring to the Spanish practice of *coartación,* whereby slaves who earned enough money could purchase their freedom, the petitioners wisely made the enemies of the English seem more humane, thereby appealing to their sense of cultural superiority, prevalent especially among Congregationalists opposed to Roman Catholicism.

Along with their appeals to religion and patriotism, the petitioners tried to allay whites' fears about living in a multiracial society where blacks were not controlled by slavery. They claimed that they were "willing to submit to such regulations and laws, as may be made relative to us, until we leave the province."[29] This argument was necessary because of the ubiquitous claims by proslavery advocates that blacks could only be contained under slavery, and, if freed, they would disregard the law. In addition to obeying the law while in the province, the slaves assured the magistrates that they had no intention of staying, writing that they wanted to leave "as soon as we can, from our joint labours procure money to transport ourselves to some part of the Coast of Africa, where we propose a settlement."[30] Anticipating the calls for colonization that would arise during the late eighteenth century, the petitioners tried to appeal to the racial sensibilities of those who deemed Africans inferior as well as to the purse strings of those who opposed abolition because of how it would affect the poor rolls and town budgets.

The petitioners again publicized their ideas in multiple venues, helping to influence those in power and the larger public. In the second edition of his tract *On the Beauties of Liberty,* John Allen wrote that because the slaves could not get their April 1773 petition published in the newspaper, he "shall comply with the request of an advocate for a multitude of these distressed People, who are unjustly held in Bondage by those who profess to act on principles of Liberty and Religion, by inserting the following piece."[31] The piece he inserted was the full text of the April petition, an inclusion that was significant because Allen's pamphlet was one of the most popular during the revolutionary era and assisted greatly in spreading the petitioners' antislavery message to a wider readership.

The Massachusetts House of Representatives also heard the grievances of the slaves and came closer than they ever had to abolishing the trade.

While the petitioners' tone remained deferential throughout the piece, they did say to the legislature, "We cannot but expect your house will again take our deplorable case into consideration, and give us that ample relief which, as men, we have a natural right to."[32] The members formed a committee to consider the matter.[33] Three days later the committee recommended that the petition be tabled until the next session, which it was. At the start of the next session, in January 1774, the slaves' second petition was read again, along with another memorial from them, and both the House and Council passed a bill in March 1774 to prevent the importation of slaves. The bill would have become law had Governor Thomas Hutchinson signed it, but instead he dissolved the General Court on 9 March 1774, the day after receiving the bill from the legislature, due to recent armed hostilities between the English and the colonists.[34]

When a number of Bostonians destroyed tea belonging to the East India Company, resulting in the Coercive Acts and a change in executive leadership, the petitioning slaves believed this might be more conducive to their needs. After the Crown replaced Governor Hutchinson with General Gage, the committee immediately petitioned him and the legislature once more, hoping that where they had failed to convince Hutchinson they might be able to convince Gage. From the original April 1773 petition and that of May 1774, the tone changed markedly, switching from a humble entreaty to more forceful assertions of their rights, stating that "your Petitioners apprehend we have in common with all other men a naturel right to our freedoms without being depriv'd of them by our fellow men." Boldly asserting their equality with whites and a claim to freedom, the committee argued that they were "a freeborn Pepel and have never forfeited this Blessing by aney compact or agreement whatever."[35] Here they displayed knowledge of Locke's natural rights theory, which posited that individuals in society give up some of those rights by compact to secure protection. These ideas were common in both the pulpit and political arena, and articulating them would have surely caught the attention of those who used the same discourse to argue against British taxation.

The petitioners also continued to employ the religious rhetoric common in the previous petitions, although they now did so more frequently. They twice referenced the hypocrisy of Christians owning slaves, noting early that they had been "held in a state of Slavery within the bowels of a free and christian Country" and remarking later that they were "brought hither to be made slaves for Life in a Christian land."[36] Whereas earlier they had noted that many blacks were virtuous, in this petition they said that many of them are sincere members of the Church of Christ and, because of this membership, felt a duty to bear the burdens of other Christians, including their own masters. But they could not do so while in a state of slavery, nor can their masters do the same for them: "How can the master be said to Beare my borden when he Beares me down with the Have chanes of slavery and operson against my will"?[37] Their rhetoric was infused with biblical metaphors and aimed to make the slaves seem more virtuous and Christian than their own masters. Along with these entreaties, the slaves argued that, in general, bondage rendered them "incapable of shewing our obedience to Almighty God."[38] Being a part of white's churches throughout Massachusetts, the slaves recognized that appealing to religion and virtue would be surefire ways of getting their arguments heard and possibly acted on.

Closely tied to religious ideas in revolutionary Massachusetts were ideologies of gender, and the petitioners similarly spoke to those to achieve their goal. They asked how, if they continue to be enslaved, "the wife [can] submit themselves to there husbands in all things How can the child obey thear parents in all things?"[39] They voiced a desire for norma-tive patriarchal relationships, which they claimed were impossible under slavery, since masters have the power to sell children at will and separate wives and husbands whenever they choose. By appealing to the norma-tive gender ideologies of white colonists, the slaves employed a tactic that other marginalized groups of the period used to gain respectability. When the Baptists started becoming more prominent in Massachusetts during the Great Awakening, their worship services were seen by many as distinctly feminine because of their emotionalism and sensuality. Baptists also allowed women to participate in services to a far greater degree than was acceptable in Congregational churches. These practices changed in the late eighteenth century, however, when, to gain respectability, the Baptists started participating more in politics, seen as a strictly masculine domain, and then discouraged the type of worship and female participation that had been prevalent in their churches during the 1740s and 1750s. The Baptists' were successful in gaining respect and toleration, and by claiming that they, too, wanted to live by those same patriarchal ideals, the slaves hoped to gain respect and freedom.[40]

This petition also showcases the slaves' demands for immediate emancipation, as opposed to the gradual abolition most scholars have seen as a staple of early abolitionism. They asked Gage and the legislature to "cause an act of the legislative to be passed that we may obtain our Natural right our freedoms and our children be set at lebety at the years of twenty one."[41] From this line it is clear that they wanted freedom for themselves without qualification, having already suffered under slavery for many years. They did propose freedom for their children at twenty-one years of age, which may seem like a gradual emancipation plan but was in fact very different from the *post nati* emancipation statutes that Connecticut and Rhode Island passed in 1784. Given the economic context in which they wrote, it appears that the petitioners were angling to get apprenticeships for their children.[42] Probably aware that they could not educate their children as well as they would have liked, their call seems calculated to give their children training in a useful trade while also securing their own, immediate freedom. Furthermore, most gradual abolition plans passed during the revolutionary and early national periods actually freed no slaves, thus the petitioners plans differed markedly from those that scholars have seen as the staple of eighteenth-century abolitionism.[43] While a number of scholars have commented on the acquiescence in gradual abolition as an argument for the nonradicalism of early black and white abolitionists—with some even saying that the early antislavery movement was a failure—a close examination of the wording of this appeal reveals a desire among this antislavery committee for immediate release from bondage.[44]

When Thomas Gage did not act on the slaves' initial petition for freedom, other slaves in the province continued to try to effect abolition through the legal system. On 14 June 1775, the Worcester Committee of Correspondence passed a resolution against slavery after blacks protested being held in bondage. The resolution, which was printed in the *Massachusetts Spy* one week later, said that "the Negroes in the counties of Bristol and Worcester, the 24th of March last, petitioned the Committees of Correspondence . . . to assist them in obtaining their freedom."[45] It is unclear whether this petition was delivered orally or in writing, but it did prompt the Committee of Correspondence to make it known publicly that they "abhor the enslaving of any of the human race, particularly the Negroes of this country."[46] The committee promised, in addition, to make any endeavors they could in bringing about the freedom of slaves in

Massachusetts. Like their Boston counterparts, the slaves and free blacks in Bristol and Worcester organized to help achieve their goals and were successful in getting whites to support their cause publicly.

At this same time, a former slave in Boston named Prince Hall began his thirty-year tenure as Massachusetts' most eminent African American abolitionist. Hall, who was born in Barbados on 12 September 1748, was relocated to Boston by his master. He educated himself and became a lay minister to an informal worship group in Cambridge, a position that made him influential in Boston's black community. He also worked as a leather dresser and caterer and was widely known among whites and blacks as an honest, hard-working leader. Hall purchased his freedom in 1770. Among his most significant accomplishments, and a move that made him the recognized leader of Boston's black community, was his organization of the African Masonic Lodge in 1775, the first formal all-black institution in America.[47]

In January 1777, Hall led a petition drive to the state legislature and argued against slavery on many of the same grounds as previous petitions but employed a more radical tone. Seamlessly interweaving Christian rhetoric with secular ideologies of natural rights, Hall wrote, "Your Petitioners apprehend that they have in Common with all other men a Natural and Unaliable Right to that freedom which the Grat Parent of the Unavers hath bestowed on all menkind."[48] He repeated the earlier claims of both individual black abolitionist writers and the black antislavery committee to an equality that stemmed from both nature and God. The petition further stated that "a Life of Slavery Like that of your petitioners Deprived of Every social privilege of Every thing Requiset to Render Life Tolerable is far worse then Nonexistence."[49] Echoing Patrick Henry's famous line, "Give me liberty or give me death," the petition's rhetoric can certainly be read as a veiled threat of rebellion. It suggested that, if forced to suffer under the harsh yoke of slavery much longer, slaves in Massachusetts might be willing to risk forfeiting their lives to gain their freedom, as thousands of slaves in the southern states were doing at that time and as groups of slaves in Boston had offered to do three years earlier.[50]

Hall and the other 1777 petitioners displayed a familiarity with the political rhetoric of both white colonists and black abolitionists. "[In imitat]ion of the Lawdable Example of the Good People of these States," they wrote, "your petitioners have Long and Patiently waited the Evnt of petition after petition By them presented to the Legislative Body of this state."[51] Again their rhetoric marked a radical departure from the tone of earlier slave petitions by propounding another veiled threat to the colonists, implying that their response to repeated injustice and tyranny might be the same as the revolutionaries'. They ended by asking for a restoration "to the Enjoyments of that which is the Naturel Right of all men," demanding immediate emancipation for themselves and for their children to receive their freedom at twenty-one years of age.[52]

As in the April 1773 petition, Hall and his fellow petitioners' latest entreaty pushed the legislature into action. On 18 March 1777, the Massachusetts legislature received "a petition of Lancaster Hill, and a number of other negroes, praying the Court to take into consideration their state of bondage, and pass an act whereby they may be restored to the enjoyment of that freedom which is the natural right of all men. Read and committed to Judge Sergeant, Mr. Dalton, Mr. Appleton, Col. Brooks, and Mr. Story." In a little more than three months, the House of Representatives responded by drawing up "A bill intitled an Act for preventing the Practice of holding Persons in Slavery."[53] While many white abolitionists of the time were calling solely for an end to the slave trade, the petitioners were able to convince legislators to attack the institution of slavery itself. The House read the bill twice but tabled it until it consulted with the Continental Congress. This action effectively killed the legislation, since the Continental Congress was comprised of a number of supporters of slavery.

This appeal was also unsuccessful in effecting legislative change, yet it appears that the actions of Boston's slave and free black communities were influencing the debate on slavery within the colony, and their ideas and tactics may have subsequently impacted those of black abolitionists outside Massachusetts. Just two years after Massachusetts' blacks' last petition, slaves in Connecticut and New Hampshire petitioned their respective legislatures for freedom, often employing the same arguments that the slaves in Boston had used. In 1777, Hall had wrote that Massachusetts slaves were "Unjustly Dragged by the hand of cruel Power from their Derest friends and sum of them Even torn from the Embraces of their tender Parents"; just two years later, Connecticut slaves similarly appealed to the sentiment of legislators by noting that "many of your Petitioners, were (as they verily believe) most unjustly torn, from the Bosom of their dear Parents, and Friends."[54] And just as Massachusetts blacks had woven

Enlightenment ideas of natural rights with Christian notions of equality under God, Connecticut blacks wrote, "We are Convinced of our Right (by the Laws of Nature and by the whole Tenor of the Christian Religion, so far as we have been taught) to be free."[55]

The petition of New Hampshire slaves to their legislature in 1779 employed similar themes and arguments. They claimed that "the God of nature gave them life and freedom, upon the terms of the most perfect equality with other men" and noted that freedom was a gift from God and one that all men have a duty to fight for.[56] They also tried to appeal to the sentiments of their readers, writing that "often is the parent's cheek wet for the loss of a child, torn by the cruel hand of violence from her arching bosom; Thus, often and in vain is the infant's sigh for the nurturing care of its bereaved parent."[57]

Blacks in Connecticut and New Hampshire likely learned about the earlier petitions in Boston in a variety of ways. The appearance of the petitions in newspapers and abolitionist tracts no doubt drew the attention of slaves in other locales. The *Essex Journal,* where Caesar Sarter published his antislavery piece, was located in Newburyport, a town just twenty miles from Portsmouth, New Hampshire, where the slaves who submitted their 1779 petition resided. Popular pamphlets discussing the principles of freedom, such as John Allen's widely circulated *Oration on the Beauties of Liberty,* similarly provided slaves in other areas a chance to imbibe the ideas, tactics, and boldness to air their own grievances. Other slaves were probably influenced by personal contacts. Prince Whipple, for instance, a soldier and one of the signers of the 1779 New Hampshire petition, spent time in Massachusetts during the war and may have met black abolitionists such as Prince Hall, who was also a soldier.[58] Similarly, Peter Lewis of Stratford, Connecticut, the town where the 1779 petition originated, served time in the military outside of Boston in 1775, and Nero Hawley and Cesar Edwards, two other slaves from Stratford, also saw action in Massachusetts. These men all gained their freedom by serving in the military and may have either established contacts with black abolitionists in the Boston area, or heard of their efforts from local blacks.[59]

As blacks in Massachusetts and throughout New England began gaining their freedom, they extended the debate over slavery to the arena of racial equality. The proposed 1778 Massachusetts constitution would have excluded blacks, Indians, and mulattoes from voting, and some towns in the province rejected it for this reason. While the later 1780 constitution did not exclude blacks from voting, local custom did in many places, including Dartmouth. Two brothers, Paul and John Cuffe, had refused to pay taxes there from 1777 to 1780 because of this exclusion from the political process, and they, along with five others, petitioned the General Court for relief.[60]

The Cuffes were the freeborn children of Ruth and Cuffe Slocum. Ruth was a freeborn woman of Indian descent, and Cuffe Slocum was a native born African sold into Massachusetts slavery in 1728. Slocum bought his freedom in 1745 and was able to purchase a 120 acre farm in Westport, Massachusetts, in 1766. Paul and John inherited the family farm on the death of their father in 1772 and shouldered the responsibility of caring for their mother and three younger sisters. In 1775, at the age of sixteen, Paul Cuffe went to sea and traveled on whaling ships to the Gulf of Mexico and the West Indies. While on his third voyage in 1776, his ship was captured by the British and he was briefly imprisoned in New York before returning to Westport. He sailed to the Caribbean again in 1778 and the following year decided to go into business with his brother, building a small boat for conducting trade with the islands just off the Massachusetts and Rhode Island coasts. These many experiences proved formative to Paul's growing political consciousness, allowing him to witness the treatment of blacks throughout the Western Hemisphere and to become conversant with the discourses of natural rights and the duty of resisting tyranny. His familiarity with these discourses is evident in the petition he and six others submitted in February 1780.[61]

The petitioners—John Cuffe, Adventum Child, Samuell May, Pero Howland, Pero Russell, and Pero Coggeshall—started by noting their Africanness and the legacy of slavery: "That we being chiefly of the African extract and by reason of long bondage and hard slavery we have been deprived of enjoying the profit of our labour or the advantage of inheriting estates from our parents as our neighbours the white people do having some of us not long enjoyed our own freedom."[62] Although the Cuffe brothers did not suffer these disadvantages, having been born free and inherited a farm, they still felt the pinch of taxation and resented being taxed "contrary to the invariable custom and practice of the country"—that is, without the benefits of representation. They argued that the taxes were actually harmful to the common good because they would reduce blacks in that locale to paupery, making the town responsible for their welfare. From the petition it is difficult to tell whether they objected solely to the tax or to being taxed without representation, but chances are they disliked both.[63]

The petition also pointed out the many services that blacks had rendered to whites in the state, both while enslaved and after being freed. After noting again that they could not vote in town meetings and had no voice in choosing representatives, the petitioners wrote, "We take it as a heard ship that poor old negroes should be rated which have been in bondage some thirty, some forty and some fifty years and now just got their liberty some by going into the service and some by going to sea." Employing some of the same religious discourse common to earlier petitions in Massachusetts—such as praying for God to influence those in power to be merciful to the poor and give unto those who ask of them—they asked the General Court to "grant [them] relief from taxation while under our present cirsumstances."[64]

While this petition was not an abolitionist one per se, in that it did not ask for the end of slavery, it was a part of the burgeoning antislavery movement among blacks in Massachusetts. While the movement's primary focus was on getting both slavery and the slave trade abolished, equally important to many black activists was the struggle for racial equality and economic opportunity. John and Paul Cuffe continued to wage their struggle for both after the General Court did not act on their petition. In early 1781, the brothers challenged the Dartmouth town meeting to explicitly deny them the franchise, and while they did not win this battle, they did have their taxes reduced from £154 to £8.12 and had tax evasion charges against them dropped. This struggle is significant, since it came at a time when the Cuffes were just starting their business and needed the extra capital. It is also important in the history of abolitionism because it shows how, for blacks in Massachusetts, other freedom struggles, such as ones for racial equality and economic opportunity, could not be divorced from the fight against slavery.[65]

The efforts of African Americans in Massachusetts to abolish slavery during the revolutionary period represent nothing less than the beginning of organized abolitionist activity in America. Two years before white Philadelphians formed the Pennsylvania Abolition Society and twelve years before the formation of the New York Manumission Society, Massachusetts blacks had established an antislavery committee that worked to influence public policy through petitioning the legislature and encouraging the production of antislavery literature by white abolitionists. While a gradual abolitionist sentiment did dominate the abolitionist activity of members of these more formal antislavery organizations, the members of the black antislavery committee in Massachusetts called only for an immediate end to slavery, placing their tactics squarely within the "radical" antislavery tradition that scholars have attributed primarily to abolitionists working in the 1830s and beyond.

4

Abolition of Slavery and the Slave Trade

In the same year that Paul Cuffe and his fellow activists presented their petition for relief from taxes to the Massachusetts General Court, the people of the Bay State ratified what is today the oldest functioning constitution in American history. Drafted by John Adams, Samuel Adams, and James Bowdoin (the latter two of whom actively assisted the 1773 black petitioners in getting their voices heard in the legislature), the Massachusetts constitution went into effect on 25 October 1780. This document, with its three equal branches of government, bicameral legislature, and strong executive, is widely known for having influenced the general frame of the U.S. Constitution. To some contemporaries, it was also widely known for having led to the downfall of slavery in the state. Lawyers, jurists, slaveholders, and African Americans alike interpreted the first article—"All men are born free and equal, and have certain natural, essential, and unalienable rights; among which may be reckoned the right of enjoying and defending their lives and liberties; that of acquiring, possessing, and protecting property; in fine, that of seeking and obtaining their safety and happiness"—as having effectively abolished the institution of slavery.[1]

The constitution was not the only factor that led to the downfall of slavery in the Bay State, however; abolition came about due to a convergence of forces. In his response to a query from historian Jeremy Belknap in 1795, Vice President John Adams argued that slavery ended because white workers did not want to compete with slave labor. This was especially true in the tough economic times that Massachusetts saw in the wake of the American Revolution. "The common white people," Adams wrote, "or rather the labouring people, were the cause of rendering negroes unprofitable servants. Their scoffs and insults, their continual insinuations, filled the negroes with discontent, made them lazy, idle, proud, vicious, and at length wholly useless to their masters, to such a degree that the abolition of slavery became a measure of oeconomy."[2]

Other correspondents gave different answers to Belknap's query respecting abolition in Massachusetts. Samuel Dexter, a successful Boston merchant and representative to the General Court, responded that few had spoken against slavery or the slave trade until the Stamp Act crisis. Before that, most had agreed that Christianizing Africans was a positive result of the trade, but afterward publications in newspaper and pamphlet form became more common. With the 1780 Massachusetts Constitution, blacks started taking their freedom into their own hands. Dexter noted that "soon after the establishment of the constitution of Massachusetts one negro after another deserted from the service of those who had been their owners, till a considerable number had revolted. Some of them were seized, and remanded to their former servitude. Certain individuals of these brought actions against those who had been their masters, and the success of the negroes in these suits operated to the liberation of all, who did not voluntarily remain with their former owners."[3]

Belknap himself credited popular opinion with bringing down the institution. Writing to St. George Tucker of Virginia, who was contemplating a gradual abolition plan for that state, Belknap posited that antislavery publications from men such as James Otis and Nathaniel Appleton and the many black petitions of the 1770s had helped weaken public support for slavery. Blacks were well aware of the 1772 Somerset decision and began suing their masters in earnest during the 1770s, with few, if any, losing their cases, according to Belknap. What finished the job in his mind was a series of court cases that culminated in 1783 with a decision that many contemporaries and later historians have interpreted as having abolished slavery in the state, one similar to the views expressed in the Somerset decision. For Belknap, this decision was "a mortal wound to slavery in Massachusetts."[4]

Massachusetts' route toward abolishing slavery varied from those of other northern states, which took action against the institution during and immediately after the Revolution. Slavery ended in Vermont under the state's 1777 constitution, passed the same year that the Massachusetts legislature debated abolition but took no action. Then, in 1780, Pennsylvania enacted its gradual abolition law, a statute that freed no slaves immediately but liberated the children of slaves when they turned twenty-eight. In 1784 Connecticut and Rhode Island followed suit, with Connecticut's gradual abolition law freeing the children of slaves at age twenty-five. By 1804, both New York and New Jersey had also passed laws gradually abolishing slavery. Massachusetts never did so, but, according to contemporaries such as New Haven pastor Jonathan Edwards Jr., the Commonwealth did not need to because all their slaves were freed via court decision.[5]

Although this decision didn't come until the famous Quok Walker case initiated in 1781, slavery had been under attack in the Massachusetts court system from the early revolutionary period. From 1760 to 1779, African Americans initiated twenty freedom suits. The earliest cases did not generally attack the institution of slavery itself, but instead focused on a broken contract or specific point of law. This was true of Jenny Slew's lawsuit, which became the first such challenge to slavery in the court system in more than half a century. On 5 March 1762 Jenny Slew of Ipswich, Massachusetts, sued her master, John Whipple, for her freedom, claiming that because her mother was white, Whipple had illegally held her in slavery and that she should be immediately freed. After repeated continuations, in September 1765 Slew's case was on the docket of the Inferior Court of Common Pleas in Newburyport. This court rejected Slew's claim to freedom, but she immediately appealed and won her case before the Superior Court of Judicature at Salem in 1766 on the grounds that her mother was white. Slew won £4 in damages and court costs and gained her freedom. According to John Adams, who was present when the judges decided in favor of Slew, Justice Oliver declared that "this is a contest between liberty and property—both of great consequence, but liberty the most important of the two."[6] In the midst of an increasing emphasis on property rights among American colonists, and Bostonians in particular, Slew's case convinced the judges that the right to liberty for a slave was more important than the master's right to property.

Slew probably drew attention from her contemporaries because freedom suits had not occurred in Massachusetts since the time of Adam Saffin's in 1700. The case also would have interested those who were used to seeing men, not black women, participate in court. In the docket books of the Essex County Court of Common Pleas, the overwhelming majority of lawsuits were initiated by white men against other white men. Slew's suit was one example of how slave resistance could help erode public support for the institution of slavery in Massachusetts by showing masters that owning slaves could be even more unprofitable than it had already become after the Seven Years' War. In the wake of an economic depression following this conflict, many masters in Massachusetts had little work for slaves to perform, leading to increased sales of blacks out of the colony. With the possibility of losing money invested in a slave by court action, many masters would have thought twice about purchasing one in an already inhospitable clime for owning slaves.[7]

Other slaves in the province used Slew's approach and took to the judicial system to gain their freedom. In May 1768, an enslaved woman named Margaret petitioned the Middlesex County Inferior Court of Common Pleas for a writ of replevin, or the recovery of personal chattel, arguing that William Muzzy of Lexington had unjustly detained her in slavery. Margaret won her freedom in 1770. One year later an enslaved man named Caesar successfully sued his master in the Essex County Inferior Court of Common Pleas, arguing both a specific point of law (his master promised to free him in a contract) and that slavery was contrary to reason and the laws of God. Both of these cases came in the wake of early antislavery publications and popular protests against the Stamp Act and Townshend duties. As such, they illustrate the effect to which revolutionary political ideology and challenges to slavery by whites helped spur African Americans' responses to slavery in the colony. They are also significant because each successful lawsuit moved the state closer to abolishing slavery. By showing whites that their investment in slave property would likely not pay off, freedom suits during the 1760s and early 1770s reflected and contributed to the growing distaste with slavery among Massachusetts' white residents.[8]

These cases were too specialized to secure a general emancipation in the state because they often involved a specific promise of freedom to a slave. It was not until the suits of Quok Walker and Elizabeth Freeman that the constitutionality of slavery entered the debate, because prior to this point there had been no constitution to which lawyers could refer. Once the 1780 Massachusetts Constitution had been ratified, the courts became venues where slavery was seemingly most vulnerable. Earlier John Adams remarked that he never knew a jury to keep a man or woman enslaved on appeal.[9] The state's blacks faced better odds of gaining their freedom through the court system because they had to convince fewer people that they deserved freedom than they did in the legislature. Also, courts were comprised of local juries, and, as was the case with juries throughout the state and in institutions such as the Worcester Committee of Correspondence, local whites could be more receptive to the arguments of slaves than those in the state government, especially in areas where slavery did not figure prominently in the economy, such as western Massachusetts.

Elizabeth Freeman's case started in western Massachusetts, going before the Berkshire Court of Common Pleas at Great Barrington in August 1781. Freeman was about thirty-six years old and the slave of John Ashley, a judge who was the largest land- and slaveholder in Berkshire County. Ashley had been an important proponent of resistance to Parliament in the 1760s and a leading patriot during the 1770s when he played a prominent role in drafting the Sheffield Resolves of 1773, a document that articulated the rights of man and the aim of government. Much of Ashley's political activism took place in his own home, where Elizabeth would have been imbued with the rhetoric of the American Revolution. While this may have excited a desire for freedom in Elizabeth Freeman, it was not until February 1781 that she decided to pursue it in earnest. That month Hannah Ashley, John's wife and Elizabeth's mistress, grabbed a kitchen shovel in a rage and attempted to hit Elizabeth's sister with it. Freeman intercepted the blow and received a nasty scar on her arm. Shortly thereafter she decided to seek legal counsel from a neighbor and pursue her freedom.[10]

The neighbor was Theodore Sedgwick, who had graduated from Yale College in 1765 and later studied law under Mark Hopkins, the younger brother of Calvinist minister Samuel Hopkins. Sedgwick had settled in Great Barrington, Massachusetts, and become a friend and mentee of John Ashley, whom he helped draft the 1773 Sheffield Resolves. Along with Sedgwick, Tapping Reeve joined Freeman's legal team. Reeve was an early women's rights advocate, according to Freeman's biographer, and "he would later become famous for his Law of Baron and Femme, which became a critical contribution to helping women achieve legal status before the law."[11] Perhaps because of Reeve's experience in dealing with issues of gender and the law, he and Sedgwick decided to add a man to the suit as a co-plaintiff, which Freeman did by filing suit with another of Ashley's slaves, a man named Brom.[12]

The first step that Sedgwick and Reeve took in the case was to ask for a writ of replevin, "a form of action which lies to regain the possession of personal chattels which have been taken from the plaintiff unlawfully."[13] Unlike most legal actions of this kind, the personal chattels which the plaintiffs hoped to regain were their own bodies. Freeman and Brom argued that they were illegally held in slavery and requested the court to give them control over their own lives and labor, employing a similar argument as the 1774 petitioners, who had written that they "are a freeborn Pepel and have never forfeited this Blessing by aney compact or agreement whatever."[14] Along with requesting the writ of replevin, Sedgwick argued that it was illegal for slaves to be held in Massachusetts for three primary reasons. First, he claimed that Massachusetts had never specifically sanctioned the institution. This argument was seemingly influenced by the 1772 Somerset case, which was decided on the question of whether or not there was any positive law for slavery in England. Second, Sedgwick claimed that the laws that protected slavery were based on a legislative error, namely a misinterpretation of the 1641 *Body of Liberties*. And, last, he argued that even if slavery had legally existed in Massachusetts, the first article of the 1780 constitution had outlawed the institution.[15] It is not clear whether Freeman's case was decided on these constitutional arguments or on a more specific point of law. It is likely that it was the constitutional arguments that prevailed, however, because unlike earlier slaves who sued their masters, Freeman had no legal claim to freedom, such as a promise of manumission. The court decided to issue the writ of replevin and, when Ashley refused to honor it, declared that "the said Brom and Bett are not and were not at the time of the purchase of the original Writ the legal Negro Servants of him the said John Ashley."[16] Both Freeman and Brom received their freedom, and the court fined John Ashley 30 shillings.

After winning her freedom, Elizabeth Freeman went to work for the Sedgwicks, who moved to Stockbridge, Massachusetts, in 1786. That year she helped protect the Sedgwick home from mobs that were part of Shays's Rebellion, and by 1803 she was able to purchase five acres of land for herself in Stockbridge. She stopped working for the Sedgwicks in 1808, and, by the time of her death in 1829, she had accumulated nineteen acres of land, a considerable amount for a former slave at the time. Her character, work ethic, and demeanor impressed most of those who knew her and became in themselves a practical refutation against ideas of racial inequality. Just four years after helping Freeman secure her freedom, Theodore Sedgwick joined the Pennsylvania Abolition Society. In 1831 Sedgwick, who by this time had served Massachusetts as a U.S. representative and senator, as well as a state Supreme Judicial Court justice, wrote of Freeman, "If there could be a practical refutation of the imagined natural superiority of our race to hers, the life and character of this woman would afford that refutation . . . she had nothing of the submissive or the subdued character, which succumbs to superior force, and is the usual result of the state of slavery."[17]

Unlike Elizabeth Freeman's case, Quok Walker's 1781 freedom suit did involve a promise of manumission, but it instead was decided on the question of slavery's constitutionality in Massachusetts. Quok Walker was the son of Mingo and his wife, Dinah, all three of whom James Caldwell purchased in 1754, when Quok was just nine months old. In 1763 James Caldwell died, passing along ownership of Quok to his wife, Isabell, who later married Nathaniel Jennison. On Isabell's death in 1773, Quok became the property of Nathaniel Jennison. According to Quok, however, both James Caldwell and Isabell Jennison had promised to free him, promises that Nathaniel Jennison refused to honor. So in April 1781, Quok ran away to work for John and Seth Caldwell, the younger brothers of his original owner.[18]

Jennison soon found Walker in his new situation, beat him, and took him back to his home. Walker then sued Jennison for assault, in effect claiming the right to be secure in his own person. In turn, Jennison sued John and Seth Caldwell for £1,000, claiming that the brothers enticed his slave away. Walker won his case against Jennison and Jennison won his case against Caldwell—both in the same court. These decisions were clearly contradictory, but they came about because of their timing. In the latter case, Jennison produced a bill of sale for Quok, leading to his victory against the Caldwells. In the former case, Quok's attorneys argued for his freedom on both moral grounds and the earlier manumission promise, and, as juries throughout the state had done for close to twenty years, they came down on the side of liberty and declared Walker a free man in June 1781.[19]

After these two decisions, both Jennison and the Caldwells appealed their losses. However, Jennison's appeal of the fine for assault and the decision to free Walker was dismissed because his lawyer did not file the correct paperwork. In September 1781, in the case *Caldwell v. Jennison,* the court overturned the earlier decision, which held John and Seth Caldwell liable for damages to Jennison. So, after all of the legal wrangling, Quok Walker won his freedom by successfully suing Nathaniel Jennison for assault. The court had initially made a contradictory ruling when it said that John and Seth Caldwell were liable to Jennison for the loss of Walker's employment; but in overturning this decision, the court supported the decision that granted Walker his freedom.[20]

Historians have debated whether the 1781 cases were the ones that truly ended slavery in the state or whether it was the case that finished in 1783, the year Nathaniel Jennison was tried for assaulting Walker. Had Jennison won the case, slavery's legality would presumably have been upheld. The case appeared before the Supreme Judicial Court at Worcester in April 1783, with Robert Treat Paine serving as the prosecutor and William Cushing as the chief justice. Paine had served on committees in the General Court that considered the January and April 1773 black petitions and had expressed antislavery sentiments in writing. He did not argue the case on constitutional grounds but on the grounds that Walker had been promised his freedom and should not have been subject to assault. William Cushing, however, in his charge to the jury, stated that

> our Constitution of Government, by which the people of this Common-wealth have solemnly bound themselves, sets out with declaring that all men are born free and equal-and that every subject is entitled to liberty and property—and in short is totally repugnant to the idea of being born slaves. This being the case, I think the idea of slavery is inconsistent with our own conduct and the Constitution; and there can be no such thing as perpetual servitude of a rational creature.[21]

Cushing interpreted the first article of the 1780 Massachusetts Constitution as having abolished slavery in the state. He also significantly broadened the scope of the case by addressing the institution of slavery as a whole rather than just the enslavement of Quok Walker, an approach that Lord Chief Justice Mansfield had refused to do in the 1772 Somerset decision. Many blacks had appealed to the legislature for relief from bondage, and their efforts finally pushed the judicial branch to take an activist stance and assert itself as an interpreter of the law. Cushing's charge to the jury was not a legal decision per se, and thus cannot be seen as having abolished slavery in Massachusetts. But, like the earlier Somerset decision, it showed that slavery had no support in positive law. It also went even further by specifically arguing that slavery was repugnant to the 1780 constitution. After this, masters were loath to hold blacks in slavery because they could challenge their bondage with impunity. By the time of the 1790 census, there were officially no slaves in the Bay State.[22]

Just a few years after the Quok Walker case, abolitionists throughout the Atlantic world stepped up their efforts to end the international slave trade. In 1787, Granville Sharp and Thomas Clarkson helped found the English Society for Effecting the Abolition of the Slave Trade, while the following year French abolitionists founded the Societe des Amis des Noirs (Society of Friends of the Blacks). To be sure, British abolitionists had been active well before the late 1780s. Granville Sharp, for instance, had been working to free blacks through the judicial system since 1767, the year he helped secure the freedom of Jonathan Strong, and five years later he brought the Somerset case before Mansfield. And Thomas Clarkson's famous essay on the legality of the slave trade was published in 1785. But it would not be until two years later that the British movement became organized, as Massachusetts blacks had done in 1773.[23]

American activists replicated the efforts of their European counterparts and were successful in getting the slave trade abolished in New England. During the summer of 1787, the New England Yearly Meeting petitioned the Rhode Island legislature to end slave trading among its residents, and within months lawmakers had passed a bill doing just that. The brevity of the debate actually surprised activists such as Samuel Hopkins, who had prepared for a protracted and bitter struggle. Rhode Island Quakers soon turned their attention to abolishing the slave trade in Connecticut, which they helped do in 1788. They felt this was necessary because merchants and slavers could easily transfer their enterprises outside of Rhode Island and conduct business as usual. With the slave trade abolished in most New England states, Rhode Island activists soon formed the Providence Society for Abolishing the Slave Trade to enforce the new statutes. Abolitionists formed the group in January 1789, and their goals were threefold. First, they wanted to suppress the African slave trade. Second, members felt that blacks should be able to exercise constitutional rights. And third, the group wanted to draw attention to the plight of those whites who, like Africans, "may be carried into slavery at Algiers or elsewhere."[24]

The slave trade was also a heated topic of debate at the Constitutional Convention. On 21 August 1787, Luther Martin, a delegate from Maryland, proposed a ban on the slave trade that sparked one of the most heated discussions of the convention. Martin argued that "it was inconsistent with the principles of the revolution and dishonorable to the American character" to allow the importation of slaves in the Constitution.[25] Roger Sherman of Connecticut was also opposed to slavery, but he did not think the convention should take up the question for fear it would hinder chances of creating a union, what delegates from the Deep South threatened would happen if abolition was a part of the Constitution. John Rutledge and Charles Cotesworth Pinckney, both of South Carolina, stated in no uncertain terms that their state would not join the union if a ban on slave trading went into effect. Rutledge noted that he would exempt northerners from having to participate in the defense of the South were a slave rebellion to occur, countering one of the main northern arguments for abolition. And Pinckney stated that even if he were to agree on an abolitionist measure, his constituents would soundly reject such a frame of government. Eventually these issues were resolved when the New England states agreed to allow slave importations for at least twenty more years in exchange for the South dropping its insistence on a two-thirds majority vote for all navigation laws. The heated nature of the debate shows what an important issue slave trading had become.[26]

It was in this context that Prince Hall resumed his public antislavery activities, petitioning the General Court once more, this time to protest the kidnapping of three black Masons and ask the legislature to outlaw slave trading in Massachusetts. After the Revolution, merchants in Massachusetts resumed the international slave trade. Even with slavery effectively abolished in the state, vessels continued to sail to Africa, sell slaves in the West Indies, and bring back goods such as sugar and molasses in the triangle trade. Some captains, however, did not bother to go to Africa and instead kidnapped blacks in America to sell in the West Indies. This is exactly what occurred in Boston in January 1788, when a Captain Hammond enticed three members of the African Masonic Lodge aboard his ship to sell them as slaves in Martinique.[27] As a response to this act, Prince Hall and twenty members of the African Masonic Lodge presented a petition to the General Court on 27 February 1788: "Your Petitioners are justly allarmed at the enhuman and cruel Treetment that Three of our Brethren free citizens of the Town of Boston lately Receved."²⁸

Hall and his fellow Masons revealed their awareness of kidnapping as an ongoing problem in the commonwealth and appealed to their audience's pocketbooks to stymie the practice: "We can aseuer your Honners that maney of our free blacks that have Entred on bord of vessels as seaman and have been sold for Slaves & sum of them we have heard from but no not who carred them away."²⁹ The result of these kidnappings, according to Hall, was that "many of us who are good seamen are obliged to stay at home thru fear and the one help of our time lorter about the streets for want of employ."³⁰ The petitioners asserted the importance of seafaring as an occupation for black Bostonians and appealed to the legislature to keep this avenue of employ open, lest the town be forced to support blacks on the poor rolls because they can find no other work.

Although the primary purpose of this petition was to protest and put an end to kidnappings on the American side of the Atlantic, Hall also argued for the abolition of the African slave trade in general: "One thing more we would bege leve to Hint, that is that your Petetioners have for sumtime past Beheald whith greef ships cleared out from this Herber for Africa and there they ether steal or case others to steal our Brothers & sisters." Recounting some of the horrors that Africans were subjected to in the Middle Passage, the petitioners appealed to the Christian sensibilities of their audience, remarking that "after haven sported with the Lives and Lebeties fello man and at the same time call themselves Christians: Blush o Hevens at this."³¹ While this petition was a very short one, its powerful language and the fact that members of the African Masonic Lodge initiated it demonstrate the way that this fraternity acted as an antislavery society and as an organization that could connect the interests of blacks in Boston with those of Africans throughout the Atlantic world.

Even before Hall submitted this petition, he was working to publicize the kidnapping to sympathetic whites in Boston and elsewhere in the country. Historian and minister Jeremy Belknap noted how he "had some conferences with Prince on the subject" of the petition and that the kidnapping story appeared in newspapers as far as New York.³² Months after Hall submitted the petition, Ebenzer Hazard of New York wrote to Belknap and told him, "I now return to you Prince Hall's petition. It will appear in one of our newspapers on Monday, when a trial will come on between one of our masters of vessels and a member of the society for promoting the manumission of slaves, who accused the former of kidnapping negroes."[33] The full text of Hall's petition, signed by him, also appeared in the 24 April 1788 edition of the *Massachusetts Spy* in Worcester.[34] Hall's work helped connect both him and his organization to whites who agreed that the slave trade should be abolished and show abolitionists as far as New York that the kidnapping of free blacks was a national problem that they needed to address.

Hall's February 1788 petition and two others submitted to the Massachusetts legislature that same month by Quakers and a group of Boston ministers spurred the General Court into action. On 26 March 1788, the legislature passed "An Act to prevent the Slave-Trade, and for granting Relief to the Families of such unhappy Persons as may be kidnapped or decoyed away from this Commonwealth." The law recognized Hall's complaint that blacks were continually subject to kidnapping, noting that, "by the African trade for slaves, the lives and liberties of many innocent persons have been from time to time sacrificed to the lust of gain."[35] They went on to mandate stiff fines for all those involved in trading slaves to any state in America or any nation, including a £50 fine for every African sold as a slave and a £200 fine for every vessel outfitted for the slave trade. And although the legislature's action came as the result of three petitions, and not just Hall's, the petition of the Masons was important in spreading awareness of black kidnappings.

Hall's petition succeeded in both securing the abolition of the slave trade in Massachusetts and the return of the three members of his lodge, Wendham, Cato, and Luck. When these three were shipped to Martinique they refused to work as slaves, despite serious floggings, and the media attention prompted Governor John Hancock to write the governor of Martinique to have the three men shipped back to Boston. The governor obliged and returned the Masons to Boston in late July 1788. According to Jeremy Belknap, their return "caused a jubilee among the blacks," although the captain of the ship was never apprehended. Prince Hall took them to see Belknap, who had been instrumental in getting them returned and the trade abolished, and for Belknap their appreciation was "much more than a balance for all the curses of the African dealers, distillers, &c., which have been liberally bestowed upon the clergy of this town for promoting the late law against their detestable traffick."[36] Belknap's words indicate the true importance of Hall's efforts, which, combined with those of others, were able to bring about the abolition of the slave trade.

After helping push the General Court to prohibit slave trading in Massachusetts, Jeremy Belknap joined with other New England activists in opposing slavery throughout the Northeast. Of the hundreds of members to join the Providence Abolition Society after its formation in January 1789, sixty-eight hailed from Massachusetts, including Congregational ministers such as Belknap and Quaker businessmen like William Rotch of New Bedford. Only three members of the society in its early years were from Connecticut, including Levi Hart and Jonathan Edwards Jr. David Howell served as its first president and Moses Brown as treasurer for a number of years. Similar to Boston's black antislavery committee, the Providence Abolition Society vowed to enforce anti-slave trading laws throughout New England by prosecuting those who skirted the laws. It had its ideological foundation in Christianity: "It having pleased the Creator of mankind to make of one blood all Nations of men, and having by the diffusion of his Light manifested that however diversified by Colour, Situation, religion, or different states of Society, it becomes them to consult and promote each Other's happiness, as Members of One great family."[37]

The Providence Abolition Society had counterparts in other northern states and attempted to coordinate efforts in order to develop a widespread antislavery movement. The Pennsylvania Abolition Society reorganized for a third time in 1787, and Providence abolitionists modeled their 1790 incorporation charter on that of their predecessor. The two groups began a formal correspondence in August 1789 and shared literature and strategies, jointly petitioning Congress in December 1790. While the Providence Abolition Society consisted of a number of members from around New England, they decided not to enlarge their scope because they did not want to discourage the formation of similar groups. At its February 1790 meeting, the group resolved to write corresponding members from Boston urging them to form their own antislavery organization. But while there were informal African American abolitionist organizations, such as the African Masonic Lodge, no formal abolitionist society was formed in Boston until the Massachusetts General Colored Association came together in 1826.[38]

African Americans were wholly excluded from participating in groups such as the Providence and Pennsylvania abolition societies. Ideologically, they may have eschewed the groups had they been given the opportunity to participate, because many white abolitionists denied that the general abolition of slavery was their primary goal. For instance, the 1794 meeting of the Convention of Delegates from the Abolition Societies of the United States noted that "the petitioners who have met your committee, on this occasion, have, for themselves, in very explicit terms, disclaimed any request or desire of legislative interference for the purpose of a general emancipation of the slaves already in the United States; and they have declared to your committee, that they believe this to be the general sense of their societies."[39] Instead, the committee pushed for a ban on American citizens participating in the foreign slave trade. African American activists continued to work through groups such as the African Masonic Lodge, however, while also developing new strategies and institutions for achieving racial equality in the early republic.

5

Massachusetts Blacks and the Growth of the Northern Antislavery Movement

Even as they secured the abolition of the slave trade, African Americans in Boston still had to wage a struggle against racial discrimination. Indeed, the very law that abolished the slave trade in the state singled out blacks for "warning out." The measure stated that

> no person being an African or Negroe . . . or a citizen of some one of the United States; to be evidenced by a certificate from the Secretary of the State of which he shall be a citizen, shall tarry within this Commonwealth, for a longer time than two months, & upon complaint made to any Justice of the Peace within this Commonwealth, that any such person has been within the same longer than two months, the said Justice shall order the said person to depart out of this Commonwealth.[1]

If any such blacks did stay in Massachusetts for longer than two months, they had to leave the state, and any who refused to do so faced jail time with hard labor. Laws such as these reflected the fears of Massachusetts residents, and northerners in general, that with the end of slavery blacks would become a burden on both the public rolls and the jail system. Indeed, even before the General Court passed this law, authorities in Boston tried to get rid of blacks they deemed "strangers." At the Boston Board of Selectmen's meeting of 10 October 1781, "the Clerk [was] directed to write the Selectmen of Ipswich acquainting them a Negro Boy named Jettero, born at Ipswich but had lived some time with Mr. Dodge of Wenham, is now sick in our Alms house & that a considerable expense will accrue to the Town of Ipswich if he belongs there, unless soon removed to Ipswich."[2] A little over a year later, "the Selectmen upon application by several of the Inhabitants, have determined to make choice of a suitable Person, to warn Negros & others to depart the Town."[3] City and state leaders demonstrated during the 1780s that with the end of slavery and the slave trade in Massachusetts, they wanted the Bay State to be as free of blacks as possible.

For their part, many African Americans were determined to stay and carve out lives for themselves in Massachusetts. Despite efforts to get rid of blacks who they felt did not belong there, the selectmen were sometimes receptive to black petitions for certain municipal services. In February 1789, they noted that "application having been made the Selectmen by a number of Blacks, that they might have use of Faneuil Hall for once, to accommodate them in hearing an African preacher, lately arrived with a good recommendation—Liberty was granted that they might have use of the Hall for an Afternoon."[4] This African preacher was likely John Marrant, who arrived in Boston that same month. The only restrictions the selectmen set were that services must be held during a weekday and around 3:00 P.M. to protect the blacks from hostile whites.

Persistence paid off for black petitioners to the selectmen. In September 1789, African Americans asked for permission to have one of their own color bury their dead, likely because whites did not follow what they saw to be the correct burial practices. The board denied this petition, as well as one that came before them two years later, because "it was the opinion of the Selectmen that the request could not be granted, as it would interfere with the present regulations & the duty of those Sextons, to whom are committed the care of the several burial Places."[5] One year later Boston's blacks went before the selectmen once again. But the third time was apparently a charm, as the selectmen noted that "on the petition of the Blacks that Henry Richard Stevenson, may have the care of burying the Blacks—Voted that the said Stephenson have a License to take care of the Funerals of the Blacks, in all respects except breaking Ground."[6] This would allow Stevenson to prepare the bodies of the black deceased in accordance with African, West Indian, and Christian customs.

As in the earlier efforts to attack slavery and the slave trade, the African Masonic Lodge took the lead in articulating the race consciousness and moral code that would assist blacks in their endeavor to gain equality, which for them meant the equal application of the law and freedom from racist violence. Black Freemasonry in the 1780s was formed in the context of the migration north from southern states and the West Indies, which was central to the "creation of institutional conceptions of free black identity and community."[7] The lodge's formation in the context of increased migration from others parts of the United States, Africa, and the West Indies meant that Masonic leaders such as Prince Hall had to find some way to create a sense of common purpose among blacks if he wanted to unite them to work toward becoming respected citizens.

Hall aimed to do this by publishing his lodge's annual St. John's Festival speeches, with John Marrant's 1789 sermon being the first installment in a series of three speeches that articulated the goal of black Freemasonry and Hall's vision of uplift for blacks in the United States. Marrant's life and travels provide an excellent example of how religious and political ideas circulated among blacks in the Atlantic world. Born free on 15 June 1755 in New York, he soon moved to Charleston, South Carolina, with his family. In his teens he was a well-known musician. In 1769 he went to a revival meeting, where he heard George Whitefield preach, and, after an emotional period during which he felt God would cast him into hell, he converted to Christianity. Marrant soon left his home and ended up among the Cherokee Indians, were he eventually began preaching. He continued his ministry work among the Cherokees, Creeks, and Catawbas of South Carolina and then served in the British Navy during the American Revolution, which involved traveling around the Atlantic, including a stint in the West Indies. After the war, he went to England, where he was ordained in the chapel of Phillis Wheatley's patron, the Countess of Huntingdon, in 1785.

Like early black abolitionist writers, Marrant was a Calvinist who believed that God had an active hand in earthly affairs. (On his way to the black Loyalist colony of Nova Scotia, Marrant noticed many passengers swearing and playing cards and remarked, "I spoke to them about their wicked ways; that God's frowns are upon us by reason of their wickedness on board the ship, but it was fruitless."[8]) In many ways, he considered himself a prophet who would help rescue fellow blacks from their sins and build a new nation. In December 1785, he preached from Acts 3:22-23, which reads: "For Moses truly said unto the fathers, A prophet shall the Lord your God raise up unto you of your brethren, like unto me; him shall ye hear in all things whatsoever he shall say unto you. And it shall come to pass, that every soul, which will not hear the prophet, shall be destroyed from among the people."[9] Marrant labored among the black Nova Scotians for three years, but a lack of funding from England forced him to leave. From there he sailed to Boston, arriving in February 1789. Samuel Stillman, a white minister in Boston, soon introduced him to Prince Hall, and Marrant resided with Hall and joined the African Masonic Lodge, becoming its pastor and giving the St. John's Festival speech that year.[10]

The twin goals of Marrant's speech were to help build communal ties among blacks and demonstrate "the anciency of Masonry." Marrant prefaced this speech, which he styled as a sermon, with Romans 12:10, which tells Christians to show each other brotherly love. He then told his audience that "being all members of the body of Christ with the Church, we ought to apply the gifts we have received to the advantage of our brethren."[11] Marrant's brand of Christianity called for active benevolence to those less fortunate, as did the New Divinity theology of white abolitionist Samuel Hopkins. Along with calling for his audience to be "kindly affectioned" toward each other, Marrant blasted white racism, asking, "What can these God-provoking wretches think, who despise their fellow men, as tho' they were not of the same species as themselves?"[12] To counter the racist ideology so prevalent in his day, Marrant linked Masonry with Christianity and Africa, arguing that God made paradise "border upon Egypt, which is the principal part of the African Ethiopia." He asked, "What nation or people dare, without highly displeasing and provoking that God to pour down his judgments upon them.—I say, dare to despize or tyrannize over their lives and liberties, or incroach on their lands, or to inslave their bodies?"[13] Here he displayed the Calvinist rhetoric common among earlier black abolitionists such as Caesar Sarter and Phillis Wheatley, rhetoric that would have continued to appeal to Congregational ministers. He also demonstrated his sensitivity to those still enslaved, despite the fact that it did not exist where he lived, a result of his time spent in Charleston and in the West Indies.

After this critique of slavery, Marrant directly linked Masonry with Africa. He wrote that Masons were responsible for the construction of Babylon and the ancient Egyptian city of Heliopolis. And he also posited Masonry as a cosmopolitan order, as the Masons who worked on Solomon's Temple "were of different nations and different colours, yet they were in perfect harmony among themselves, and strongly cemented in brotherly love and friendship." At a time when white Masons were prejudiced against their black brethren, Marrant called for them, and the larger white society, to put aside their prejudices and treat blacks as equals. He ended his sermon by noting that "ancient history will produce some of the Africans who were truly good, wise, and learned men, and as eloquent as any nation whatever, though at present many of them in slavery, which is not a just cause of our being despised."[14] Africa had produced men capable attaining the same heights as whites, according to Marrant, and any deficiencies that contemporary critics may point to were a result of their state of bondage, not any innate differences between the races.[15]

John Marrant's sermon was built on the rhetoric of earlier black activists in Massachusetts. According to literary scholar Joanna Brooks, Marrant "restored the abandoned Calvinist concept of the covenant community as a site of regeneration, and he redeveloped this covenant theology for the black Atlantic."[16] While this concept had not been entirely abandoned, given blacks' articulation of covenant theology during the 1770s, her assessment of Marrant's contribution demonstrates the importance of his ideas in the development of African American intellectual history. With Marrant's arguments for benevolence and the "anciency of Masonry" established, it was now up to Prince Hall to further articulate his aims for the black community in his two published speeches.

Hall delivered his 1792 *Charge* during the festival of St. John the Baptist and endeavored to show his audience the duties of a Mason. The first of these was belief in "one supreme Being, that he is the great architect of the visible world, and that he governs all things here below by his almighty power."[17] Like Marrant's earlier sermon, Hall assumed that his listeners would blend Christianity with the principles of Masonry to guide their lives. After belief in a supreme being, Masons, according to Hall, must adhere to the laws of the land in which they dwell, listen to the magistrates, and take no part in any violent conspiracies or rebellions. Indeed, during Shays's Rebellion, Prince Hall had volunteered to raise black troops to help quash it, perhaps as a way to publicly demonstrate the patriotism of African Americans. "The next thing is love and benevolence to all the whole family of mankind, as God's make and creation."[18] According to Hall, Masons must love and assist without regard to color, even if they felt others wrongfully abused them.

Hall also appealed to African heritage and pride in order to build a communal consciousness among the Masons in his audience and those blacks who would later read the published tract. He hoped that his audience would follow the example of African church fathers such as Tertullian and Augustine, "so far as your abilities will permit in your present situation and the disadvantages you labour under on account of your being deprived of the means of education in your younger days." Hall demonstrated his awareness of the effects of slavery and racism in depriving blacks of an education but said that he looked "forward to a better day; Hear what the great Architect of the universal world saith, Aethiopia shall stretch forth her hands unto me."[19] Education was an important topic to Hall. In October 1787 he and "a great number of blacks" petitioned the Massachusetts General Court to secure equal access to educational facilities for blacks. Noting that they paid their taxes like other citizens, the petitioners remarked, "We are of the humble opinion that we have the right to enjoy the privileges of free men. But that we do not will appear in many instances, and we beg leave to mention one out of many, and that is of the education of our children which now receive no benefit from the free schools in the town of Boston."[20] Hall and his fellow petitioners recognized the importance of education in the new republic and the potential it had for raising themselves to a level equal with whites.

In his second charge, delivered in 1797, Prince Hall once again referenced the accomplishments of Ethiopians in Christian history. He first noted that the Ethiopian Jethro instructed Moses, "the great law giver," on how to properly run the courts and choose candidates for office. In addition to Jethro's role in establishing the Mosaic legal system, the apostle Philip rode with an Ethiopian eunuch, and Solomon conversed with the Queen of Sheba, also an Ethiopian, on points of Masonry. For Hall, these facts demonstrated that color should not be a factor for Christian fellowship, a point that applied to whites as much as blacks. By recounting for his audience the great achievements of Africans and referencing the biblical verse that would become a staple of black political rhetoric during the nineteenth century and beyond, Psalm 68:31, Hall aimed at building a group identity that could facilitate the transition of "Africans" from regions throughout the Atlantic into "African Americans."[21]

Hall believed that the creation of a group identity was necessary because of the racism that blacks in Boston continued to face and the state of millions of Africans still in bondage. And he contended that patience for blacks was necessary because "were we not possess'd of a great measure of it you could not bear up under the daily insults you meet with in the streets of Boston; much more on public days of recreation, how are you shamefully abus'd . . . helpless old women have the clothes torn off their backs, even to the exposing of their nakedness."[22] For those who had been enslaved in the West Indies, such as Hall, this treatment of blacks in Boston must have been eerily reminiscent of such bondage, and it led him to call first for benevolence to all mankind, but particularly those in distress. "Among these numerous sons and daughters of distress," Hall wrote, "I shall begin with our friends and brethren; and first, let us see them dragg'd from their native country, by the iron hand of tyranny and oppression . . . to a strange land and a strange people, whose tender mercies are cruel."[23] Here Hall recounted some of the horrors of bondage to elicit feelings of benevolence for his readers. He also articulated a vision of blacks as a covenanted community by alluding to Psalm 137:4: "How shall we sing the Lord's song in a strange land." Prior to this, the psalmist noted that "by the rivers of Babylon, there we sat down, yea, we wept, when we remembered Zion."[24] Clearly thinking of the nation of Israel in this text, Hall likened black people to God's former chosen nation and argued that African Americans were his new chosen ones.

Despite the struggles that blacks had endured in this "strange land," Hall believed that a change for the better was coming soon and that blacks must prepare themselves for that day. "My brethren, let us remember what a dark day it was with our African brethren six years ago in the French West-Indies. Nothing but the snap of the whip was heard from morning to evening; hanging, broken on the wheel, burning . . . but blessed be God, the scene is changed; they now confess that God hath no respect of persons, and therefore receive them as their friends, and treat them as brothers. Thus doth Ethiopia begin to stretch forth her hand, from a sink of slavery to freedom and equality."[25] In mentioning the Haitian Revolution, Hall aimed to inspire hope in his readers by providing an example of what blacks there had achieved.

This revolution began on the northern plains of the French colony of Saint Domingue in August 1791 and lasted until 1804, when Haiti declared itself an independent republic. Even before gaining independence, however, the rebellious slaves had pushed the French National Convention to abolish slavery in all its territories and spurred a massive emigration of both whites and blacks to the United States. Many of these people brought stories of the successful revolt, something American masters did not want their slaves to learn about. Authorities in Charleston blamed a 1793 plot to overthrow slavery on blacks from Saint Domingue. One white resident there believed that "the negroes and mulattoes intended to serve us as the inhabitants of Cape-Francois were served."[26] Newspapers in the North also expressed the fear of slave revolt in the South. An article in the *Boston Gazette* said that "emissaries were expected from St. Domingo, to assist and even to take the lead in this infernal business."[27] So in referencing this revolution, Hall spoke to whites' fear of the revolution in Saint Domingue spreading to the United States while at the same time assuring blacks that the time of freedom from racism and slavery was soon coming. And to make sure that it did come, blacks must exercise their rational faculties regardless of their level of education and get rid of the fear of man. He was speaking to African Americans and, rhetorically at least, to Africans, noting that an essential part of discarding the fear of man was halting the slave trade, as many African people carried it on because they feared Europeans or other African nations.[28]

By using African history and Masonry to express the moral code that blacks should follow—namely belief in God, conformity to his will and the laws of the land, and benevolence to their fellow man—Prince Hall became one of the first articulators of pan-Africanism and Ethiopianism. According to historian Chernoh Sesay Jr., "Ethiopianism represents one metaphor, among others, for those literary, political, and spiritual traditions begun by Africans and New world blacks who described Africans and their diasporic antecedents not as separate peoples . . . but as an imagined collective, as a 'people.'"[29] While many scholars have looked to the 1820s work of Alexander Young and David Walker for Ethiopianist ideas, they were present in the writings of both Hall and Marrant thirty years earlier and presaged the development of black nationalist ideologies in the early nineteenth century. And along with articulating Ethiopianism, these texts became central to the creation of a black public sphere, as they were printed for distribution in Boston, Providence, and Philadelphia, thus helping connect black leaders in these disparate locales.[30]

The growth of black Freemasonry also served to connect African American leaders on the Atlantic seaboard in the late eighteenth and early nineteenth centuries. After visiting Boston for Prince Hall's 1792 *Charge*, black Masons from Providence wanted to establish a lodge in their own city. Some of these Masons had been initiated in foreign lodges and some in Prince Hall's, and in 1797 Hall gave nine of them a charter to begin Hiram Lodge No. 3 in Providence.[31] That same year Peter Mantore, who was initiated into the Masons in Europe, requested that Prince Hall charter a lodge in Philadelphia. "In the name of the most holy Trinity, Father, Son and Holy Ghost," he wrote, "we most respectfully solicit you, Right Worshipful Sir, for a Dispensation for an African Lodge." He further indicated that "the white Masons have refused to grant us a Dispensation, fearing that black men living in Virginia would get to be Masons, too. We would rather be under you, and associated with our brethren in Boston, than to be under those of the Pennsylvania Lodge."[32]

Prince Hall was happy to comply with Mantore's request. Writing back just three weeks later, he said that he was aware that "there are a number of blacks in your city who have received the light of masonry, and I hope they got it in a just and lawful manner. If so, dear brother, we are willing to set you at work under our charter and Lodge No. 459."[34] Hall revealed his desire to have black Masonry throughout the country legitimized by being established through the proper Masonic channels. And like in his two charges, Hall's language indicated that for many blacks Masonry served a similar function as religion. Receiving the "light of masonry" could be compared to receiving the light of Christ; both allowed black men to build their lives on the strong ethical foundations of belief in God and practicing benevolence to their fellow man. Indeed, some of the most prominent black clerical and lay religious leaders of Boston and Philadelphia were Masons—Prince Hall, Richard Allen, Absalom Jones (pastor of St. Thomas African Episcopal Church), James Forten (Philadelphia's most prominent black layman), and Thomas Paul (pastor of the African Baptist Church in Boston).

In some ways, African lodges could act as churches for their members, yet they were open only to men and thus could not serve the spiritual and political needs of entire communities. This situation led to the establishment of the African Baptist Church in Boston. Since the seventeenth century, blacks in Massachusetts had attended, been baptized in, and become members of white churches. They attended the same services as whites but often wanted to learn about Christianity and worship with other blacks. Rising white racism and a desire for self-determination in the early nineteenth century thus facilitated a split from the First and Second Baptist churches in Boston, with Thomas Paul becoming the pastor of the new black church in 1805.

Paul was born in Exeter, New Hampshire, in 1773 and baptized there in 1789. From a young age, he wanted to enter the ministry and was ordained in New Hampshire in 1805. Prior to his ordination, Paul had joined the First Baptist Church in Boston, and although there were a number of black members in this congregation, they had been holding separate services since 1800. The year that Paul was ordained, he joined Scipio Dalton, a member of the African Masonic Lodge and the First Baptist Church, in raising funds for a black congregation. Dalton secured the assistance of Samuel Stillman, pastor of his church, and members of the Second Baptist Church in building their new meetinghouse, which opened its doors on 8 August 1805 with twenty-four members.[35]

The African Baptist Church was important to the antislavery movement and the growth of Boston's black community. Indeed, most black communities' growth was intertwined with abolitionism, as an important part of this movement was improving the condition of free blacks to show whites that there was nothing to fear from freed slaves. Among these whites to whom they would have wanted to display their respectability was Theodore Foster, president of the convention of the disparate abolition societies in America. In his address to "the Free Africans and other free People of color in the United States," Foster recommended a politics of respectability for black people, who should "at all times and upon all occasions . . . behave yourselves to all persons in a civil and respectful manner . . . We beseech you to reflect it is by your good conduct alone, that you can refute the objections which have been made against you as rational and moral creatures, and remove many of the difficulties, which have occurred in the general emancipation of such of your brethren as are yet in bondage."[36] Foster published this address in 1796 and also recommended that blacks attend church, refrain from hard alcohol, teach their children useful trades, be diligent in their callings, avoid idle amusements, and pay careful attention to the education of their youth.

Along with serving the spiritual needs of Boston's black residents, the African Baptist Church assisted in enacting this latter recommendation by housing the African School. Primus Hall, son of Prince Hall and also a black Mason, first obtained a license from Boston's Board of Selectmen to operate a school for blacks in 1798. The school was originally located in his home and was supported through subscriptions. In May 1799 the selectmen stated that "upon application of Prince Hall & others that Mr. Nester Pendleton a black man be licensed as a Schoolmaster to Instruct their black Children—Voted that the said Pendleton be licensed agreeable to the request of the Petitioners."[37] The assistance of white ministers such as William Ellery Channing and Jedidiah Morse kept the school going after 1801, but there was no permanent building for it until the African Baptist Church was built in 1805. With this new space, Primus Hall helped raise funds to turn the basement into a suitable schoolroom and completed the project in 1808. Although the school was technically a separate institution that had come under the control of the Boston School Committee, the church played an important role in its management. In March 1819, the Boston School Committee asked Thomas Paul "to report quarterly to this board the general state of the African school," demonstrating the interconnection of these two black organizations.[38]

The African School in Boston instructed its youth in grammar, writing, the sciences, and foreign languages and no doubt also inculcated abolitionist sentiments in its students. This was the case at the New York Free African School, where a young girl named Matilda Williams "spoke a piece on the slave trade" during an examination of the school in November 1817. African schools had the potential to challenge gender norms by providing women the opportunity to voice their ideas in public, and they also raised awareness about the institution of slavery among the black youth who would someday become the leaders of their communities. Thus, by housing the school for blacks in Boston, the African Baptist Church, like the African Masonic Lodge, prepared the generation of antislavery leaders that would come of age in the 1820s.[39]

The creation of the African Baptist Church was partly an outgrowth of a general revival of religion in Boston and helped spread the Second Great Awakening throughout the United States, which in turn became vital to the growth of antislavery sentiment in the North. In early 1803, the First and Second Baptist churches saw a rapid increase in baptisms and "a very considerable number of young people, who were deeply impressed with a sense of their condition, frequently visited their ministers and others with this inquiry, 'Sirs, what must we do to be saved?'"[40] These two congregations invited numerous itinerant ministers to their pulpits, and people from surrounding towns flocked to Boston to take part in the revivals. Overcrowding in these churches could easily have led to increased hostility to black members, but it was probably also the case that blacks themselves were among the new converts and that they desired their own congregation. After the African Baptist Church of Boston opened its doors, Thomas Paul continued the work of the revival by traveling to New York to help organize the Abyssinian Baptist Church, where he preached until the congregation found its own pastor. He also took an active role in the Boston Baptist Association, an organization that Baptists from New Hampshire and Massachusetts instituted in 1812 to encourage foreign and domestic missionary work. Paul's church contributed funds for the support of missions and the Baptist Education Society, and on at least three different occasions he served on committees to correspond with New Hampshire and Vermont Baptist associations.[41]

Paul's missionary work helped him build a network of support among the Baptist clergy, forward his goal of converting blacks throughout the diaspora to Christianity, and played an important role in the antislavery movement during the early nineteenth century. In 1823, he traveled to Haiti under the auspices of the Boston Baptist Association to do missionary work, and on his return he encouraged the migration of American blacks to the young republic. This effort and his work with the association helped fan the flames of revival throughout the hemisphere.

These revivals had their origin in the late-eighteenth-century revivals in Kentucky and soon spread to the East Coast. An important result of the Second Great Awakening was the spread of the doctrine of perfectionism, whereby individuals came to believe that if they could accept God and perfect themselves, they could also perfect society. Perfectionism led to the rapid proliferation of reformers involved in temperance and sabbatarianism, among other movements, but chief among these was abolitionism. By helping to build his own church, which grew from twenty-four members in 1805 to 103 by 1819, and contributing to the growth of churches elsewhere, Thomas Paul and the African Baptist Church became an important part of keeping the antislavery movement alive during a period in which most scholars argue there was a significant lull in abolitionist activity in America.[42]

Along with the African Baptist Church, the African Society of Boston

became an important venue for the spread of the antislavery movement
in the early nineteenth century. Organized in Boston in 1796, the African
Society aimed primarily to help indigent blacks support themselves in times
of sickness, although a widow could receive benefits from the society, provided that she "behaves herself decently, and remains a widow." Members
had to pay dues of a quarter each month and could receive benefits after one
year. The society promised that those who were sick would be supported
and those who died would be buried, "but it must be remembered, that
any Member bringing on himself any sickness or disorder by intemper-
ance, shall not be considered as entitled to any benefits or assistance from
the Society."[43] These strictures were similar to those of African societies
elsewhere in the North, as the New York African Society for Mutual Relief
also stipulated that its membership "shall consist of free persons of moral
character" and that any members caught gambling or drinking to excess
would be expelled. They likewise compared with the goals of mutual aid
societies around the Atlantic world, including organizations such as the
black *cofradias* in the Iberian colonies.[44]

The African Society of Boston and similar black institutions aimed to promote the same values of respectability that Theodore Foster recommended
that blacks throughout the United States adhere to if they wanted to help
those Africans still enslaved. Along with denying benefits to intemperate
persons, the society actively tried to police each others' morals, acting as a
progenitor to the African Baptist Church. The laws noted that "the Members
will watch over each other in spiritual concerns; and by advice, exhorta-
tion, and prayer excite each other to grow in grace, and in the knowledge
of our Lord and Saviour Jesus Christ."[45] In this respect, the African Society of Boston was similar to the Free African Society of Philadelphia that
Richard Allen and Absalom Jones formed in 1787, as this latter institution
held religious services, policed the morals of its members, and influenced
the creation of two separate black churches in 1794. By upholding these
emerging bourgeois values, the African Society of Boston appealed to
whites concerned with the fate of blacks in America and also became an
important component of the growing black community in Boston.[46]

The society also served as a venue for antislavery publications. In 1808
one of its members published an essay entitled *The Sons of the Africans*,
which recounted the history of slavery and blasted those who continued
to hold their fellow men in bondage. "Freedom, a thing so desirable to

most men," the author wrote, "and so hard to be obtained by many at the present time, will be the theme of our contemplation."[47] He argued that it was sin that introduced slavery into the world and caused the biblical Joseph's brothers to sell him into Egyptian slavery, but that God often rose up men in unlikely ways to accomplish his ends, as was the case with Moses. Moses' miraculous delivery of the Israelites from bondage "seems to demonstrate a truth like this: that it was displeasing to God to have any of the children of men exercise such a spirit of tyranny as Pharaoh there exhibited." He noted further that his contemporaries should mark Pharaoh's fate because "as that oppressor was destroyed, so will all others be, and meet with their reward either in this or in the world to come."[48]

Continuing the tradition of the black jeremiad that Caesar Sarter initiated in the 1770s, this member of the African Society of Boston argued that God would be on the side of the oppressed in America. By doing so, he also likened blacks to the Israelites of old, a rhetorical move that was gaining increasing currency among black authors of the early nineteenth century. For example, Absalom Jones, in *Thanksgiving Sermon,* preached that same year to commemorate the abolition of the slave trade, recounted the miseries that the Israelites suffered in Egypt and noted that since God redeemed that nation from slavery, he would do so for American blacks as well. By likening black people to the ancient Israelites, these authors invoked the spirit of a covenanted people and used Exodus as a metaphor for a black nation built on the shared heritage of slavery and exposure to racial discrimination.[49]

The African Society of Boston also contributed to the antislavery movement through public commemorations of the abolition of the slave trade. Beginning in 1808, blacks in Boston, Philadelphia, and New York City gathered together to commemorate abolition in the United States and Great Britain. Those in Boston also commemorated abolition within Massachusetts. (These celebrations took place on 1 January in some locales but were usually held on 14 July in Boston.) They consisted of a large meal and a parade through the city streets, which generally ended at the African Baptist Church, where on at least four occasions a white preacher gave a sermon or discourse to the assembled blacks. These commemorations contributed to the antislavery movement in three primary ways. First, they helped keep the memory of slavery and the slave trade alive for those who no longer suffered under bondage. Second, they forged kinship ties and a communal consciousness as participants exchanged food and toasts. And last, they helped forge alliances with white abolitionist ministers and other leaders by presenting images of organized, respectable black citizens. Among these white ministers were Jedidiah Morse, one of the founders of the Andover Newton Theological Seminary, and Paul Dean, who would later join a subcommittee on the African School, which was part of the Boston School Committee. These men gave addresses at the abolition commemorations in 1808 and 1819, respectively, that argued for the sinfulness of slavery and enjoined blacks to work hard and practice temperance in order to "shew to those around you, that you are worthy to be free."[50]

By inviting these ministers to take part in their commemorations, African Americans in early-nineteenth-century Massachusetts helped keep alive the interracial abolitionism that they initiated in the 1770s and contributed to the growing spirit of radicalism that characterized black politics throughout the eastern seaboard in the early republic. An important part of this radicalism involved laying claim to public spaces from which whites attempted to restrict them. In the mid-eighteenth century, blacks initiated Negro Election Days and enjoyed use of public spaces for up to a week beginning on the last Wednesday in May. While these celebrations did continue through the nineteenth century, abolition commemorations began to take their places after 1808 as the primary black holiday. Also, in Boston, whites began to resent and fight back against blacks' use of public space.

In 1797, Prince Hall indicated that blacks were "shamefully abus'd" in the public streets of Boston, and during the 14 July celebrations some whites began to publicly ridicule blacks' efforts to keep alive the memory of slavery and abolition. For some whites, these celebrations represented blacks overstepping their proper places. In a scornful broadside published in 1816, the author noted that "DE Afrikum Shocietee having done demself de high honour of pointing you one of dere Marshal to fishiate in grand porseshium on Monday next, being de fourtient day of de weak, respectfully beg leave to present you de aaccompanying uniform as de badge which will be worn on dis splendored rocasion."[51] The tract went on to mock the toasts of blacks and attempted to make the whole celebration appear ridiculous. The broadside's language also subtly recognized the accomplishments of educated, well-traveled blacks such as African School master Prince Saunders, of whom the author wrote, "De great Misser Prince Sarndurs. Wid one foot he wash his hand in de Atlantic, wid de oder he touch he calf a leg in de frog pond . . . de resplendum of his oloquence shine upon de nation like de full moon in eclipse, onny just he be as much shuperior to dem as two and two make six."[52] While the broadside was meant to ridicule the members of Boston's African Society and discourage future abolition commemorations, it demonstrates the extent to which African Americans were able to educate themselves, lay claim to public spaces, and contribute to the growth of the antislavery movement.

Like the African Masonic Lodge and the African Baptist Church, the African Society of Boston was instrumental to the growth of the black community and the antislavery movement in the early nineteenth century. This organization assisted needy blacks and helped them secure jobs and apprenticeships. It also helped build connections between the city's black and white activists in that would be central to the abolition-ist movement until the Civil War. Most important of all, however, were the ways in which the African Society kept alive the memory of slavery and the slave trade for Boston's black residents and encouraged them to remain active in the cause of those still enslaved.

6

Black Emigration and Abolition
in the Early Republic

In June 1812, Paul Cuffe wrote a letter to British abolitionist William Allen stating that he "thinks well of Establishing mercantile intercourse on the Cours of Africa to Replace to the Africans a trade in Lawfull and Leagull terms in lue of the Slave trade for it seems hard to them to be deprived of all opportunity of gitin goods as usuall."[1] Cuffe was referring to his plans for black Americans' emigration to Africa, plans that had been in the works for at least four years. Emigrationism, commerce, and abolitionism were intimately linked, he believed, because helping African nations develop legitimate trading alternatives would hasten the demise of the slave trade.[2]

The black emigration movement during the early nineteenth century served a number of different functions. On the one hand, for activists such as Paul Cuffe and Prince Saunders, it became a way to attack the Atlantic slave trade and provide asylum for those blacks freed from American slavery. African Americans would take specialized commercial and agricultural knowledge to help develop African economies and introduce Christianity to help convert the native inhabitants. They also believed that slaveholders would be more likely to free their slaves if there were a place outside of the United States to send them. On the other hand, black leaders like James Forten pursued emigration schemes in part to deal with the rising level of racism aimed at the free black population during the early republic. This racism manifested itself in the form of riots, efforts to disenfranchise blacks, and laws barring free black emigration to northern states such as Ohio and Pennsylvania.[3]

Emigrationism represented both a continuation of tactics and strategies that early black activists employed as well as some significant departures that influenced the future course of the antislavery movement in America. Interracial cooperation, institution building, and fostering connections throughout the Atlantic world were central to the work of black emigrationists. In viewing Africa, Haiti, and other regions as asylums for slaves who would eventually be freed, however, Cuffe, Saunders, and other leaders seemingly acquiesced to the gradualist sentiment that often dominated the antislavery ideology of white activists. In this sense, even as these leaders fostered important political connections, emigrationism represented something of a retreat from the radicalism of earlier generations of activists.

Schemes for emigration to Africa, in one form or another, had been present in America since the Revolutionary War. In their April 1773 petition to the Massachusetts General Court, black activists wrote that they desired "as soon as we can, from our joint labours procure money to transport ourselves to some part of the Coast of Africa, where we propose a settlement."[4] That same year Congregational ministers Samuel Hopkins and Ezra Stiles raised money to send two black men, John Quamine and Bristol Yamma, to evangelize in Africa. Yamma and Quamine, members of Hopkins' First Congregational Church in Newport, Rhode Island, "were hopefully converted some years ago; and have from that time sustained a good character as Christians."[5] These facts, combined with their being natives of Africa, made them perfect candidates for this evangelical mission, one that Hopkins hoped would be the vanguard of more widespread efforts. Hopkins and Stiles saw this effort as an opportunity to spread the Christian religion to what they saw as a heathen people. And they sought support for this plan because "it is humbly proposed to those who are convinced of the iniquity of the slave trade; and are sensible of the great inhumanity and cruelty of enslaving so many thousands of our fellow men every year . . . and are ready to bear testimony against it in all proper ways, and do their utmost to put a stop to it: Whether they have not a good opportunity of doing this, by chearfully contributing, according to their ability, to promote the mission proposed."[6] This endeavor also had the ability to undermine justifications for slavery. Many supporters of slavery during the eighteenth century argued that the slave trade was an effective means of bringing Christianity to Africans, but Hopkins retorted that Christ commanded Christians "to go and preach the gospel to all nations, to carry the gospel to them, not to go and with violence bring them from their native country."[7] In his mind, it was not acceptable for people to do evil that good may come of it, and sending missionaries to Africa could counter one of the most prevalent justifications for the slave trade.

Hopkins attempted to enlist Phillis Wheatley in his plan, with the aid of John Thornton, a London merchant and their mutual correspondent. While Wheatley ardently hoped the plan would succeed, she had no intentions of removing to Africa herself. "You propose my returning to Africa with Bristol Yamma and John Quamine," she wrote Thornton, "but why do you hon'd Sir, wish those poor men so much trouble as to carry me So long a voyage? Upon my arrival, how like a Barbarian Should I look to the Natives; I can promise that my toungue shall be quiet for a strong reason indeed being an utter stranger to the Language."[8] By this time, Wheatley was a free woman and did not want to leave her life in Boston for an unknown life in Africa. With the death of Quamine during the revolutionary war and a general lack of financial support, Hopkins's plan fell apart.

In November 1780, Newport Gardner and other blacks formed the Free African Union Society, a moral and benevolent organization that by the end of the decade began promoting black emigration to Africa. In January 1787 they wrote William Thornton, saying, "[it is] our earnest desire of returning to Africa and settling there."[9] Thornton was a Quaker from Antigua who had recently inherited slaves and wanted to free them and send them to Africa. By 1787, he had moved to Philadelphia and become an American citizen, and he told the members that he had "conveyed your sentiments to the committee on African Affairs in London," helping connect their efforts to those of activists throughout the Atlantic world. For Thornton, plans for emigration to Africa "combined philanthropy and profit"; he would show free blacks "how to achieve independence and wealth along Africa's commercially rich Ivory Coast and, at the same time, show masters a practical means of emancipation."[10]

Blacks in Massachusetts also began articulating their own plans for emigration in 1787. Black Bostonian Samuel Stevens wrote the Free African Union Society in June and told members that he and other blacks had met with Thornton and were interested in emigrating and getting blacks in other northern states to consider moving as well. In January 1787, Stevens was one of twelve black Masons (including Prince Hall) and seventy-three African Americans who signed a petition to the General Court requesting

the legislature's assistance for blacks' return to Africa. "We, or our ancestors have been taken from all our dear connections, and brought from
Africa and put into a state of slavery in this country," they wrote, "from
which unhappy situation we have been lately in some measure delivered
by the new constitution . . . But we yet find ourselves, in many respects,
in very disagreeable and disadvantageous circumstances; most of which
must attend us so long as we and our children live in America."[11]

This petition expressed some of the main goals that would come to
characterize black emigration plans on both sides of the Atlantic. First,
there was the notion that blacks could not and would not enjoy equality
while living among whites. Second was their claim that Africa was their
"native country which warm climate is much more natural and agreable
to us; and for which the God of nature has formed us." They also said
that "the soil of our native country is good and produces the necessaries
of life in great abundance." They believed there were large, uncultivated
tracts of land that needed only people to work it and make it productive.
And as would be the case with almost all emigration plans, the petitioners
argued that "the execution of this plan will, we hope, be the means of
enlightening and civilizing those nations who are now sunk in ignorance
and barbarity: and may give opportunity to those who shall be disposed,
and engaged to promote the salvation of their heathen brethren, to spread
the knowledge of Christianity among them and perswade them to embrace it."[12] Escaping white racism, opening up economic opportunity,
and spreading the gospel—these were the foundations on which African
Americans built their first plans for emigration.

From the outset, blacks were wary of this process being controlled by
others, especially whites. Samuel Stevens said, "We do not approve of Mr.
Thornton's going to settle a place for us; we think it would be better if we
could charter a vessel, and send some of our own Blacks." The members
of the Newport society could not have agreed more. While they thought
Thornton's idea of emigration was a good one, they did not fully trust
him and wanted to control the process themselves. Before they made
any definite moves, they were also "waiting and longing to hear what
has been the issue and success of the attempt made in England to make a
settlement of Blacks in Africa."[13] This "attempt" was the settling of Sierra
Leone, an endeavor initiated in part by a correspondent of Hopkins',
Granville Sharp.

In early 1786, Granville Sharp and other Londoners organized a committee to supply winter relief to the city's black poor, and in short order the endeavor flowered into a full-fledged emigration scheme. Just as the committee began its work, Henry Smeathman, a physician who had lived in Sierra Leone for nearly four years in the 1770s, offered up a plan for an African colony. He argued that staple crops such as rice and tobacco could be grown with ease in Sierra Leone, that fruits grew in the wild and needed only to be picked, and that fish and fowl were abundant throughout the region. The plan secured the backing of the U.S. treasury in short order, and after May 1786 assistance to London's black poor came with the understanding that they would emigrate to Sierra Leone.[14] For their part, black Londoners had many reasons to support the plan. Hundreds of them were starving and sick, many were harassed by the police as vagrants, and there were few economic opportunities open to them.

Black leaders such as Olaudah Equiano, who was the first commissary for the mission, supported the plan as an effective means toward abolition and as one that would open up new markets for British manufacturing. "I doubt not," he wrote, "if a system of commerce was established in Africa, the demand for manufactures will most rapidly augment, as the native inhabitants will sensibly adopt the British fashions, manners, customs, &c. In proportion to the civilization, so will be the consumption of British manufactures."[15] Three ships left London in April 1787 and arrived at Sierra Leone in May, just at the start of the wet season. The timing could not have been worse. The rains hindered the settlers' attempts at building shelter, so they had to live in tents. They also had trouble finding adequate provisions, and disease plagued them from the outset. In less than a year, the population dwindled from an initial 400 to 130 people. Many died, while others deserted the colony—some leaving to work at slave forts along the coast, and some risking their liberty to join slavers headed for the West Indian islands.[16]

Within two years the colony was all but wiped out. But it was revived with the assistance of Granville Sharp and the willingness of black Nova Scotians to emigrate. In 1790, Sharp began organizing the St. George's Bay Company for the purpose of carrying on "an honest and honourable trade with Africa, in order to discourage and supersede the detestable traffic in slaves."[17] Comprised primarily of merchants, this company was to revive the colony of Sierra Leone and reorganize it to make it more profitable.

Since Sharp was able to secure 100 subscribers, all that was needed was settlers to populate the colony. This time the settlers would come not from London but from the British province of Nova Scotia. In 1783, more than 16,000 black Loyalist refugees from the thirteen colonies landed in Nova Scotia. The British promised them land and freedom there, where the black colonists originally planned to settle for good, but kept few of these promises, as blacks endured poverty, wage labor, and the threat of racial violence, priming them for a change. After Parliament incorporated the Sierra Leone Company (the former St. George's Bay Company) in May 1791, approximately 1,300 black Nova Scotians decided to make their move to Sierra Leone, where they did not have as much political freedom as their earlier counterparts from London and were once again deceived about the amount of land they would receive. The colony fared so poorly that in 1807 the company petitioned the government to take it over as a Crown colony, which the government did after the passage of the Abolition of the Slave Trade Act, and it soon became a haven for freed slaves.[18]

Despite Sierra Leone's initial struggles, black leaders in Massachusetts such as Paul Cuffe still felt that emigration could serve as a powerful force for abolitionism and Christian evangelism. From the time of his 1780 foray into the political arena petitioning the Massachusetts General Court until the early nineteenth century, Cuffe devoted himself almost exclusively to his trading and business ventures. Shortly after marrying Alice Pequit in 1783, he went into business with his brother-in-law, Michael Wainer, and they traded along the eastern seaboard, including southern ports where slavery was a visible part of the market economy. In 1799 he purchased 140 acres of land in Westport, Massachusetts, and opened a school for both black and white children of the village. He then built a second ship in 1806 and started building connections with abolitionists throughout the country. That year he sailed to Wilmington, Delaware, and met with John James, a Quaker and the president of the Delaware Abolition Society.[19]

Cuffe's meeting with James made him well-known to Quaker abolitionists in Delaware and Philadelphia, and joining a Quaker meeting in Westport in 1808 similarly helped Cuffe foster connections with Quaker abolitionists throughout the Atlantic world. Among these was James Pemberton, an influential member of the Pennsylvania Abolition Society. After receiving information from abolitionists in London, Pemberton wrote a letter to Cuffe informing him "that divers persons of eminent stations and character in that city are so affected with a desire that, the prohibition of the slave trade may be improved for their benefit by promoting the civilization of The people of that country."[20] In 1808, these abolitionists had formed the African Institution of London to improve the condition of the Sierra Leone colony. With encouragement that his efforts would be supported by his newfound Quaker network, Cuffe began making plans for a voyage to Sierra Leone.[21]

Cuffe's motivation for this voyage was to help black people around the Atlantic world advance themselves politically and economically. "As I am of the African race," he noted in a letter to Delaware abolitionists John James and Alexander Wilson, "I feel myself interested for them and if I am favored with a talent I think I am willing that they should be benefitted thereby."[22] James and Wilson soon wrote to British abolitionist William Dillwyn on Cuffe's behalf and secured the support he would need to undertake his voyage. On 27 December 1810, Cuffe embarked on his trip to Sierra Leone with a crew of nine and arrived in March 1811. While in the British colony, Cuffe met with the governor and local African leaders, sharing with them his plans to stimulate commerce. In April 1811 he received a six-month trading license from the African Institution in London and a request to come to England to meet with the organization's leaders. He sailed from Africa to England in July 1811 and stayed for two months.[23]

In London, Cuffe made personal contacts with some of the most prominent abolitionists and planned to establish an organization in Sierra Leone that would foster connections between blacks in Africa and America as well as with antislavery activists in England. He lodged with William Allen of the African Institution and met leading abolitionists such as William Dillwyn, Zachary Macauly, William Wilberforce, and Thomas Clarkson. In August he met with the entire African Institution, where the members "expressed Great Satisfaction in the information I gave them and felt Also that I was Endeavouring to Assist them in maintaining the good cause."[24]

While earlier black Atlantic abolitionists such as Olaudah Equiano had advocated settlement in Africa largely as a colonialist measure, so that Europeans could profit from trade with the natives, Cuffe went further and argued for African self-determination. He helped forward this cause on his return to Sierra Leone in December 1811 when he met with local leaders and helped organize the Friendly Society of Sierra Leone, a "legitimate trading" group that would promote the production of goods for export to England and the United States and thereby undermine the Atlantic slave trade. Satisfied that his vision of encouraging American blacks to settle in Africa was a viable possibility, Cuffe set sail for the United States in February 1812.[25]

Because of the hostilities between England and America that preceded the War of 1812, Cuffe's ship was impounded on his return, but this gave him the chance to travel to the capitol and meet with governmental leaders. He used his Quaker networks to help get his ship back, appealing to Rhode Island abolitionist Moses Brown, who in turn connected him with the attorney general of Rhode Island. Armed with letters of recommendation from both men, Cuffe met with Secretary of State Albert Gallatin and President James Madison. During this meeting he discussed his emigration plans and remarked in his journal that Gallatin "observed to me any thing that the government could do to promote to Good Cause that I was Presuing Consisting with the Constitution they would cortenly be alwas Readey to render me their help or any Information that I could give or point out ways that traffick might be Discouraged They were Ever Was ready to Receive such information."[26] Cuffe's efforts were clearly paying off, as he was able to discuss illicit slave trading and spread knowledge of his plans among the top government officials in the country to secure promises future assistance.

On his way home to Boston, Cuffe stopped in Baltimore, Philadelphia, and New York City, where he built connections between black and white abolitionists and helped organize institutions to correspond and eventually trade with the Friendly Society of Sierra Leone. In Baltimore he met with Elisha Tyson, a Quaker abolitionist, and Daniel Coker, pastor of the African Methodist Episcopal Church, and they had "much agreabel Conversation on the mode to aid Africa." Coker became a forceful proponent of emigration in his own right, helping settle the colony of Sherbro, located near Sierra Leone, in 1820. Cuffe then moved on to Philadelphia, where he introduced his friends and business partners John James and Alexander Wilson to Absalom Jones and James Forten. With Jones and Forten, Cuffe also met Benjamin Rush, the president of the Pennsylvania Abolition Society, and noted that "it was proposed that there Should be a Society gathered for the purpose of aiding assisting and Communicating with the Sierra Leona Friendly Society as Well as With the African Institution in London."[27]

Two days later Cuffe was in New York City, where he arranged a meeting between twenty Quakers and twenty African American leaders and helped form a society similar to the ones in Philadelphia and Baltimore.

With the outbreak of war, Cuffe was unable to return to Sierra Leone, although he did build awareness and support for his plans through correspondence. Shortly after his return to Westport in May 1812, he wrote Prince Saunders, J. Roberts, and Perry Lockes, members of the African Society in Boston, to inform them of his plans and tell them about the organizations he helped build in Philadelphia, Baltimore, and New York City. Other correspondents included William Allen, the Friendly Society of Sierra Leone, Thomas Clarkson, Richard Allen, Jedidiah Morse, and Samuel Mills, a student at the Andover Theological Seminary who was interested in his emigration plan and would play an important role in establishing the colony of Liberia.[28]

When the war between America and England ceased in 1815, Cuffe started to more urgently pursue his plan for bringing settlers to Sierra Leone. He told Peter Williams Jr., secretary of the New York African Institution he helped organize, that "I once more call on thee to arouse the minds of your citizens to that zeal for the good of their countrymen in Africa."[29] He expressed a similar sentiment to Daniel Coker, writing, "I now call thy attention to arouse the minds of Citizens of Baltimore of the ancestors of Africans who have to do or may feel their minds Zealously inguaged for the good of their fellow creators in Africa and have a mind to visit or remove to that countery to give their names."[30] The war may have seen a temporary lull in emigrationist efforts, but the time for inaction was over, according to Cuffe.

In Cuffe's mind, tribal and ethnic divisions that may have held sway before slavery were unimportant. All black people in America were the descendants of Africans, and the condition of blacks in Sierra Leone convinced him that Africans and African Americans had shared interests that could be achieved through mutual cooperation. This is why institution building was so important to him and why he continued to press for blacks in America to move to what he saw as their native land. His ideology represents a maturing of the Ethiopianism espoused by John Marrant and Prince Hall in the 1790s and can be seen as the beginning of black nationalism in America. Even as blacks were increasingly accepting

Christianity and American political ideals of republicanism, they now began embracing an African identity in earnest.[31]

Cuffe embarked on his second journey to Sierra Leone in December 1815, but not without some difficulties. For months he heard nothing from the African Institution in London, from whom he hoped to receive financial support and a license to trade in the colony. He took forty black passengers with him on the journey, thirty-two from Boston, two each from Providence and Newport, and four from Philadelphia. When he arrived in February 1816, he was able to secure land grants for the emigrants but was unable to unload the majority of the goods he had brought to sell in order to help defray the expenses of the trip. Worse yet, he saw continued evidence of the illegal slave trade, as impounded ships were brought to the colony, and the pernicious effects of alcohol on the native population. While he was happy to assist the emigrants in getting to Africa, in many ways the trip was a disaster for him, and he was back in America by May 1816.[32]

After this trip Cuffe continued to correspond with black leaders on the eastern seaboard and whites interested in black emigration, but within a year widespread black interest in African emigration waned due to their distrust of white colonizers' motives. White leaders such as Samuel Mills, Jedidiah Morse, and Robert Finley wrote Cuffe for information about his voyage and for his thoughts on the establishment of a permanent, government-funded colony for blacks in Africa. Finley played a key role in creating the American Colonization Society in Washington in 1816 and believed that if a colony were established on the coast of Africa, laws could then be passed "permitting the emancipation of slaves on condition that they shall be colonized."[33] John T. Peters, president of the Hartford Auxiliary Colonization Society, likewise noted that his organization wanted to "encourage, and ultimately to produce an entire emancipation of slaves in America; and last, though not least—to break up and destroy that inhuman and accursed traffic, the SLAVE TRADE."[34]

Although some colonizationists, like Finley and Peters, supported abolitionism, other founding members of the American Colonization Society were prominent slaveholders more interested in strengthening the institution by colonizing free blacks. John Randolph of Roanoke, one of the society's first members, stated that "it was a notorious fact . . . that the existence of this mixed and intermediate population of free negroes was viewed by every slave holder as one of the greatest sources of insecurity, and also unprofitableness, of slave property." At this same meeting, Henry Clay wondered whether there could be "a nobler cause than that which, while it proposes to rid our country of a useless and pernicious, if not a dangerous portion of its population, contemplates the spreading of the arts of civilized life" to Africa?[35] Years earlier, Thomas Jefferson had supported colonization because he believed blacks and whites could never live peaceably in the same nation: "Deep-rooted prejudices entertained by the whites, ten thousand recollections, by the blacks, of the injuries they have sustained; new provocations; the real distinctions which nature has made; and many other circumstances, will divide us into parties, and produce convulsions which will probably never end but in the extermination of the one or the other race." He suggested that blacks be educated or prepared for a trade until age eighteen for women and twenty-one for men, at which time "they should be colonized to such place as the circumstances of the time should render most proper."[36]

These sentiments led black leaders such as James Forten and Richard Allen to reconsider their support for African emigration. Forten came to believe that colonization would strengthen slavery in the United States because, "diminished in numbers, the slave population of the southern states, which by its magnitude alarms its proprietors, will be easily secured."[37] The *National Intelligencer* reported that at the American Colonization Society's first meeting, "it was not proposed to deliberate on, or consider at all, any question of emancipation, or that was connected with the abolition of slavery. It was upon this condition alone . . . that many gentlemen from the south and west" had attended the meeting.[38] Forten noted further in a letter to Cuffe that African Americans in Philadelphia believed that colonization was a scam designed to rid the nation of free blacks. "We had a large meeting of males at the Rev. R. Allen's Church, the other evening," he wrote. "Three Thousand at least attended, and there was not one sole that was in favor of going to Africa."[39] Shortly after receiving this letter in January 1817, Paul Cuffe died at his home in Westport.

While the momentum of the African emigration movement began to lose steam, a desire for Haitian emigration excited the black populace, with Prince Saunders among its chief proponents. Saunders was born around 1775 in Lebanon, Connecticut, and was the teacher of the African School in Colchester, Connecticut, by the time he was twenty-one. In

1807 he attended Dartmouth College, and a year later Dartmouth president John Wheelock recommended him to William Ellery Channing, one of the benefactors of Boston's African School, as a good candidate for improving the condition of free blacks in the city. In November 1808, Saunders became the teacher of the African School in Boston and was soon heavily involved in the life of the community, as he joined both the African Masonic Lodge and the African Society. While in Boston, Saunders got engaged to one of Paul Cuffe's daughters, and he and Thomas Paul joined Cuffe, before his death, as the three most forceful advocates of black emigration in Massachusetts. In 1815, Saunders and Thomas Paul sailed to England, where they met the prominent English abolitionist William Wilberforce, who persuaded Saunders to become an adviser to Henri Christophe, the emperor of north Haiti. It was this experience that convinced Saunders that Haiti, and not Africa, would be the best place for black Americans to settle.[40]

Saunders sailed for Haiti and met Christophe on 16 February 1816. Christophe was immediately impressed with Saunders' education and manners and also liked the fact that he had "striking Negro features" (just then the Haitian emperor was engaged in a civil conflict with mulattos). Saunders became a courier for Christophe, taking his correspondence to England, with which Haiti was trying to secure diplomatic recognition. In the late autumn of 1816, Saunders returned to Haiti and organized several schools in just one month. By mid-1817, he was back in America, this time in Philadelphia, where he became a lay reader at Absalom Jones's St. Thomas's African Episcopal Church. It was here that he first began to write and speak about Haitian emigration, at a time when support for African emigration was dwindling among blacks and increasing among whites.[41]

In a tract written for the American Convention for Promoting the Abolition of Slavery, Saunders argued that Haitian emigration could help abolish slavery in America. He proposed emigration to the republic because he believed that "the period has arrived, when many zealous friends to abolition and emancipation are of the opinion, that it is time for them to act in relation to an asylum for such persons as shall be emancipated from slavery."[42] Speaking to whites' fears about living in a multiracial society, Saunders aimed to strengthen the economy and society of the young republic of Haiti while furthering the goals of American abolitionists. He also believed that abolitionism was evidence of true Christianity.

If those who helped the poor could expect God's favor, then how much more might those expect who "have delivered their fellow beings from the inhuman grasp of the unprincipled kidnapper, or saved them from dragging out a miserable existence"?[43]

Saunders returned to Boston in the spring of 1818 and published a second edition of his *Haytien Papers* to spread knowledge about the country. Originally published in England, the *Haytien Papers* contained more than 100 pages of laws, legal documents, and government papers about the economy, government, and culture of Haiti. Appended to this volume were his "Reflections on the Abolition of the Slave Trade," an essay aimed at spreading knowledge about abolition and building support for the continuation of the movement. He noted that the abolition of the slave trade was among the great events of the nineteenth century and attempted to foster a sense of pride among his African readers. "Let us recollect that African blood flows in our veins," he wrote, "and that we are under the necessity of exerting our utmost efforts to live in the great practice of society; our progress more or less influencing the opinions that the Europeans will form of us."[44] His philosophy evinced the influence of both black Freemasonry and the African Society in Boston, organizations he belonged to and which believed that blacks must lead moral lives in order to help their brethren still in bondage.

Along with Saunders' efforts to promote Haitian emigration, leaders of the Caribbean republic tried to lure American blacks to the island to stimulate the economy and hasten U.S. recognition of their country. During the 1810s, both Henri Christophe and Alexander Pétion, leaders of North and South Haiti, actively recruited African Americans by offering easy routes to citizenship and rewards of $40 dollars to black sailors for every emigrant they secured. Their efforts did not lead to widespread emigration in the 1810s due in part to the civil conflict that plagued the nation, but in 1822 a new leader, Jean Pierre Boyer, unified the country and opened the way for a massive influx of African American emigrants. Like Christophe and Pétion, Boyer believed that black emigration from America would stimulate the economy and improve relations between Haiti and the United States. He accordingly offered to pay emigrants' travel expenses and supply them with land and materials. Boyer's push for black emigration was also an ideological one, as he claimed that all people of African descent would find brotherhood and equality in Haiti.[45]

With the combined efforts of Haitian leaders and Prince Saunders to encourage black American emigration, the movement soon gained popularity along the eastern seaboard. As noted earlier, Thomas Paul traveled to Haiti as a missionary in 1823, and he published a letter on his return in Boston's *Columbian Sentinel,* stating that Haiti is "the best and most suitable place of residence which Providence has hitherto afferred to emancipated people of colour." And while James Forten and Richard Allen had rejected African colonization in 1817, they formed the Haytien Emigration Society of Philadelphia in 1824 to encourage emigration. Like thousands of whites during the same period, they likely saw Haiti as a frontier outlet that would allow black people to enjoy the fruits of their freedom, an "empire of liberty" analogous to Thomas Jefferson's conception of the American West. Their work led to the emigration of 6,000–13,000 blacks to Haiti during the 1820s. However, their vision did not pan out as expected. In their eyes, too few blacks decided to emigrate, and those who did soon returned because of language barriers, religious differences, and frustrations over land distribution, which took much longer than emigrants anticipated. For their part, Haitian leaders became wary of supporting further emigration, feeling it might not be the best idea to have a significant population with different political interests among them.[46]

Despite these drawbacks to Haitian emigrationism, the efforts of black leaders such as Prince Saunders and Thomas Paul of Massachusetts played a central role in connecting black abolitionists throughout the North and making them determined to fight for equal rights in America. Black emigration plans helped keep antislavery activism alive and well at a time when many white abolitionists felt their work was finished. The institutions and abolitionist network that Cuffe helped build proved vital to the movement in the 1820s. Through trial and error, black abolitionists came to realize that immediatism, and not gradual abolition coupled with colonization, was their best option, and they set out with renewed vigor to try to convince the nation of this.

7

Abolitionism and the Politics of Slavery in Early Antebellum Massachusetts

The period in which Haitian emigration flourished also saw a tremendous growth in the popularity of abolitionism in America and a commitment by many northerners to halt the spread of slavery. This commitment was sometimes based on moral principles and sometimes on political calculations but was influenced primarily by the alarming spread of slavery to the West after the War of 1812. Developments such as the Missouri Crisis in 1819 and the 1822 Denmark Vesey conspiracy helped revitalize the debate over slavery at the national level by the late 1820s, with activists in Massachusetts continuing to push their agendas of abolition and racial equality. Like they had done since the revolutionary era, African Americans in the Bay State called for both immediate emancipation and an end to racial discrimination. To achieve their goals, they continued the community building they began in the 1770s, published antislavery tracts and essays in newspapers, petitioned the government for an end to slavery, and built antislavery organizations such as the Massachusetts General Colored Association.

The 1820s and 1830s saw a number of important changes in the antislavery movement. First, the number of activists sharply increased from previous eras. While still constituting only a small percentage of the northern population, there were now thousands more activists committed to ending slavery. Second, while abolitionists such as Prince Hall had alluded to the specter of Saint Domingue as an implicit warning to whites of the consequences of slavery, activists in the 1820s such as David Walker explicitly called for southern slaves to rebel against their masters and free themselves. And, perhaps the most radical transformation in American antislavery, women openly participated in the movement to a greater degree than ever before by publishing tracts, forming antislavery societies, and speaking to audiences of men and women.[1]

Like their predecessors, antebellum black abolitionists worked tirelessly to keep the issue of slavery at the forefront of public consciousness at a time when southerners and northerners alike wanted to muffle the issue. Many whites felt that in the wake of the Missouri crisis, the Vesey conspiracy, and Nat Turner's rebellion, any discussion of slavery would tear the union apart or, worse, ignite a massive slave rebellion on the scale of the Haitian revolution.[2] Black abolitionists in Massachusetts, however, ignored these appeals and continued to agitate the issue of slavery and racial discrimination. Their efforts were successful in rousing antipathy toward colonization and pushing white abolitionists such as William Lloyd Garrison, David Lee Child, and a host of other activists from advocating gradual abolition to calling for immediate emancipation. Black abolitionists also influenced national politics in this period. Martin Van Buren pushed for a renewed two-party system in part to alleviate the sectional tensions over the issue of slavery, and the agitation of abolitionists influenced the 1832 nullification controversy in South Carolina. By drawing from and building on the tested strategies of their predecessors, African American abolitionists in Massachusetts remained key figures in the movement that would abolish slavery within a generation.

From an international perspective, the opponents of slavery and the slave trade had cause to be pleased in the late 1810s and early 1820s. Both England and the United States had abolished the international slave trade in 1808 and the Dutch did so in 1814. In 1817, Spain signed a treaty with Great Britain promising to abolish the slave trade by 1820, and most of Spain's former colonies did likewise in order to secure diplomatic recognition. By the mid-1820s, all the countries of mainland Spanish America had enacted statutes prohibiting slave imports from Africa, and slavery was abolished in Santo Domingo in 1823 when Haiti conquered that half of Hispaniola. That same year, British abolitionists formed the Society for the Mitigation and Gradual Abolition of British Colonial Slavery, which helped revive popular abolitionism in England and gave hope to activists throughout the Atlantic world that the institution was slowly eroding.[3]

While slavery was on its way to extinction in key areas throughout the Western Hemisphere, the institution expanded in the American South during the early nineteenth century. In Andrew Jackson's 1814 Treaty of Fort Jackson, the United States acquired 14 million acres of land from the Creek Indians, spurring a massive migration to the Southwest that was one of the largest in American history. During the 1810s, the population of Alabama increased twelvefold to 128,000, and that of Mississippi doubled to 75,000, with slaves comprising over 30 percent of the population in both states. Overall, the number of slaves in the nation increased 30 percent between 1810 and 1820, jumping to 1,538,038 enslaved persons. The first two decades of the nineteenth century also saw an intense cotton boom with the advent of the cotton gin and the acquisition of these new lands in the Southwest, with production increasing from 73,000 bales a year in 1800 to 730,000 bales by 1820. And this increased production more than doubled the value of slaves, with the price of a prime field hand jumping from $400-500 in 1814 to $1,000-1,100 in 1819. At the same time, the value of land in states such as Virginia, Maryland, and North Carolina dropped, making slaves the most valuable asset planters had.[4]

Given these figures, it is not surprising why southerners erupted with outrage when, in 1819, James Tallmadge proposed restricting slavery in Missouri. Tallmadge, a congressman from New York, introduced his famous amendment barring the further introduction of slavery into Missouri and its gradual abolition on 13 February 1819. When the legislative impasse was finally resolved in 1821 by the admission of Missouri as a slave state, Maine as a free one, and a prohibition of slavery north of the 36° 30' line, the politics of slavery had changed drastically in America. The rising antislavery sentiment among northerners convinced a small but important minority of southerners "that strict construction of the Constitution and a firmer commitment to state rights were the only sure safeguards for their increasingly peculiar institution."[5]

This strengthened commitment to states' rights was evident in South Carolina's response to the Vesey conspiracy of 1822. According to traditional accounts, in the spring of 1822 Denmark Vesey, a free black carpenter residing in Charleston who was aware of the Missouri debates, planned a massive slave revolt for 14 July. His coconspirators included a conjurer named Gullah Jack and other craftsmen and sailors from the region. In May, a slave informed his master of the conspiracy, and the authorities apprehended Vesey less than a month later and arrested 135 people, executing thirty-five of them. While the existence of this conspiracy has recently come under question, South Carolina authorities at the time were invested in making people believe it was real and, in response, passed one of the South's Negro Seamen Acts in December 1822, which required the jailing of black sailors in any of the state's ports. While this law was designed to limit contact between free and enslaved blacks, it violated the constitution by imprisoning citizens of other states. State leaders justified the law as a necessary security measure and resisted attempts by the federal government to supersede it.[6]

In the short term, the Missouri controversy and Vesey conspiracy muted debates over slavery at the national level and helped strengthen the colonization movement. Politicians were hesitant to agitate the issue of slavery after 1822 for fear that the discussion would tear the union apart. During the 1820s, Martin Van Buren began trying to revive the New York–Virginia coalition that had supported the Jeffersonian Republicans before James Monroe ushered in an era of one-party rule primarily to avoid the sectionalism and factions that had characterized the Missouri debates. Robert J. Turnbull of South Carolina also worked to mute discussion of slavery by the national government, arguing that slavery was the province of the states. Turnbull, an immigrant from east Florida, stated in an 1827 pamphlet that any discussion of slavery's morality by Congress posed a danger to South Carolina's very existence as a state. Along with his entreaty, the American Colonization Society became increasingly popular among whites during the 1820s. Many saw the society as a solution to the problem of slave rebellions, and auxiliary branches cropped up throughout the country, with the first Massachusetts branch opening in Boston in 1823.[7]

Blacks throughout the North defied southerners' injunctions not to agitate the issue of slavery. In New York, this defiance came in the form of *Freedom's Journal,* an antislavery newspaper that Samuel Cornish and John Russwurm began printing in March 1827. In their opening editorial on 16 March 1827, Cornish and Russwurm wrote, "It is our earnest wish to make our Journal a medium of intercourse between our brethren in the different states of this great confederacy."[8] Cornish was a minister who founded the first black Presbyterian congregation in New York City, and Russwurm was the first black graduate of Bowdoin College in 1826. Both men wanted to provide a voice for African Americans throughout the nation that could create unity and help undermine slavery, but they recognized that this burden fell on blacks themselves. "We wish to plead our own cause. Too long have others spoken for us ... The civil rights of a people being of the greatest value, it shall ever be our duty to vindicate our brethren, when oppressed, and to lay the cause before the publick."[9] The paper covered a broad range of topics, including the Haitian revolution, the effects of racial discrimination and how blacks could counter them, the colonization movement, and the place of Africa in world history. But most of all, *Freedom's Journal* served as a venue where blacks throughout the North could air their antislavery arguments, as they believed that the apparent vice and poverty experienced by northern free blacks was connected to the continuing presence of slavery in the nation and a lack of proper moral instruction. The content of the paper demonstrates the editors' awareness of abolitionism as a long political struggle dating back to the eighteenth century, and it served to connect African Americans to the larger black Atlantic.[10]

Freedom's Journal used the work and memory of eighteenth- and early-nineteenth-century abolitionists from Massachusetts to support the contemporary movement against slavery. Immediately following the opening editorial was a piece about Paul Cuffe reprinted from the *Liverpool Mercury* of 1812 that detailed his early life and activism in the eighteenth century and his efforts to encourage black settlement to Sierra Leone in the 1810s. Reprinting this biographical piece gave blacks throughout the nation an example of an active leader who rose from humble origins to prominence as both a businessman and activist. "Born under peculiar disadvantages, deprived of the benefits of early education, and his meridian spent in toil and vicissitudes," it reads in part, "he has struggled under disadvantages which have seldom occurred in the career of any individual. Yet under pressure of these difficulties he seemed to have fostered a disposition of mind which qualify him for any station in life in which he may be introduced."[11] If this was true of Cuffe, it could also be true for the readers of the paper in the 1820s.

The paper also reprinted some of Phillis Wheatley's work. In the paper's second issue, the editors wrote that "any thing relating to Phillis Wheatley, who by her writings has reflected honour upon our name and character, and demonstrated to an unbelieving world that genius dwells not alone in skins of whitish hue, will not surely be deemed uninteresting by the

readers of Freedom's Journal."[12] Following this statement was a brief narrative of Wheatley's life and extracts of her work, including her poems
"On the Death of an Infant" and "Hymn to the Morning." Showing off the
literary prowess of a young enslaved woman served a similar function as
the publication of Cuffe's memoir—encouraging blacks that they could
achieve anything and countering the same ideas of black inferiority that
Wheatley opposed in her own day. Including Wheatley in the paper also
helped keep alive the memory of one of the earliest black voices to oppose
slavery and probably introduced many contemporaries to her work. In
this way, the paper served as a link between eighteenth- and nineteenth-
century abolitionists.

Freedom's Journal also printed contemporary antislavery essays and
speeches by black abolitionists in Massachusetts, including David Walker.
Walker was born in Wilmington, North Carolina, to a free mother and
enslaved father around 1796. He spent some time in Charleston during the
early 1820s and may have been present when Denmark Vesey planned his
1822 conspiracy, which was centered in Charleston's African Methodist
Episcopal Church. By 1825, Walker was in Boston, where he joined the
African Masonic Lodge and the May Street Methodist Church, an independent black congregation formed in 1818 and headed by Samuel Snowden. In
1826, Walker helped found the Massachusetts General Colored Association,
an antislavery organization that gained a national reputation for advocating
the immediate emancipation of southern slaves, opposing the colonization
movement, and working to create unity among northern free blacks.[13]

Black unity was the key theme of Walker's speech to the Massachusetts
General Colored Association, which was reprinted in *Freedom's Journal* on
19 December 1828. At the semi-annual meeting of the organization, Walker,
by now one of the most prominent black abolitionists in Boston, said that
"the primary object of this institution, is, to unite the colored population,
so far, through the United States of America, as may be practicable and
expedient; forming societies, opening, extending, and keeping up cor-
respondences, and not withholding any thing which may have the least
tendency to meliorate *our* miserable condition."[14] Building on the work
of Massachusetts activists such as Prince Hall and Paul Cuffe to organize
African Masonic Lodges and African organizations throughout the country,
Walker called for blacks to build institutions to foster greater connections
among free blacks in order to more effectively coordinate strategies and

goals. He also argued that disunity among blacks is what kept them from "rising to the scale of reasonable and thinking beings," and it was by keeping blacks ignorant that masters were able to keep them enslaved.[15]

Walker's speech to the Massachusetts General Colored Association also contained hints of arguments he would make in his *Appeal to the Coloured Citizens of the World,* a pamphlet that drew from the Puritan tradition of the jeremiad and is one of the seminal texts in the history of abolitionism in America. He argued that blacks have an obligation to help their brethren suffering under slavery, but also that God will assist them. He wrote, "It is indispensably our duty to try every scheme that we think will have a tendency to facilitate our salvation, and leave the final result to that God, who holds the destinies of people in the hollow of his hand," and who ever has, and will, repay every nation according to its works."[16] Here he implied that America has sinned against God for holding blacks in slavery and that the nation would be judged for this crime. This argument was one in a long line of jeremiads by Massachusetts' black activists, ranging from Caesar Sarter to Prince Hall. And like these earlier activists, Walker argued that black America represented God's new covenanted nation: "I verily believe that God has something in reserve for us, which, when he shall have poured it upon us, will repay us for all our suffering and miseries."[17] Walker's God was intimately involved in earthly affairs and interested in the cause of American blacks, who must also work to help themselves to achieve freedom from slavery and racial discrimination.

In *Appeal to the Coloured Citizens of the World,* Walker built on the themes he articulated in his earlier speech by calling for black unity and self-help. He began with the premise that American blacks were "the most degraded, wretched, and abject set of beings that ever lived since the world began" and stated that his purpose was "to awaken in the breast of my afflicted, degraded, and slumbering brethren, a spirit of inquiry and investigation respecting our miseries and wretchedness in this Republican Land of Liberty."[18] He argued that slaves in America were worse off than those in any country the world has known in order to arouse his readers to greater exertions on behalf of the antislavery movement. The plight of the ancient Israelites paled in comparison, according to Walker, because slaves such as Joseph had great authority in Egypt, while black men in America could not even serve as constables or on juries. Furthermore, Egyptian slavery was milder because they at least recognized the humanity of their bondsmen by providing them with good land and allowing them to intermarry with Egyptians, something masters in the United States denied vociferously.[19]

Walker also stated that blacks' degraded condition in America owed to ignorance, and he called for black leaders to help educate their brethren. Ignorance caused both violence and disunity in the slave community and prompted blacks to have an irrational fear of white people, so that eight whites could effectively control fifty blacks. The solution to this problem was self-help and a stronger sense of community among blacks in America—slave and free. "Men of colour, who are also of sense," he wrote, "I call upon you . . . to cast your eyes upon the wretchedness of your brethren, and to do your utmost to enlighten them—go to work and enlighten your brethren!"[20] He likewise implored black leaders to "let the aim of your labours among your brethren, and particularly the youths, be the dissemination of education."[21] As black abolitionists in Massachusetts had thought since the 1780s, Walker believed that increased educational opportunity was one of the best means to fight slavery. And for those blacks in the North who believed they need not interest themselves in the affairs of slaves because they were free, he called on them to travel to the southern states without free papers and see if they got jailed or sold as a slave. Walker recognized the disparity of interests among the black communities in America, but he believed that the continued existence of slavery posed a problem that all blacks must work to alleviate.[22]

Another key theme of his *Appeal* is the pernicious influence of Christianity as practiced by whites. Walker posited that, historically, Christianity had only hurt blacks, as it was a Catholic priest, Bartolome de las Casas, who was among the first to recommend bringing African slaves to the New World. Instead of being a benevolent religion, Walker argued that based on "the way in which religion was and is conducted by the Europeans and their descendants, one might believe it was a plan fabricated by themselves and the *devils* to oppress us."[23] Instead of the true Christian religion, he believed that avarice had taken over the country, as evidenced by the fact that there was a growth among anti-Masonic organizations and temperance and sabbatarian societies throughout the North but still little attention by whites to slavery. These arguments were shared by many of his contemporaries and future black abolitionists, such as Frederick Douglass, whose 1852 "Fourth of July" address articulated some of the same arguments concerning religion that Walker shared in this text.[24]

Walker saved much of his animus for the American Colonization Society and those who believed blacks were unfit for republican government. Like the black leaders of Philadelphia did in their 1817 meeting at Bethel Church, David Walker argued that colonization is a plan "to get those of the coloured people, who are said to be free, away from among those of our brethren, whom they unjustly hold in bondage, so that they may be enabled to keep them the more secure in ignorance and wretchedness."[25] Both slave masters and free blacks such as Walker recognized the threat posed to the institution by the presence of African Americans who were not enslaved, and he asked for opposition to the plan to strengthen black solidarity. Many colonizationists claimed that their plan was one that would redeem Africa from paganism, so Walker asked whether proponents such as Henry Clay care "a pinch of snuff about Africa—whether it remains a land of Pagans and of blood, or of Christians, so long as he gets enough of her sons and daughters to dig up gold and silver for him?" If blacks were to leave the United States, Walker suggested that they consider migrating to England, whose people were "our greatest earthly friends and benefactors," or to Haiti, as his abolitionist predecessor Prince Saunders had advocated.[26]

In each of the four parts of his *Appeal,* Walker offered a scathing indictment of antiblack racism and called into question the political and religious principles of the American revolutionary tradition. He had read Thomas Jefferson's charges of black inferiority in *Notes on the State of Virginia* and responded by asking, "Has Mr. Jefferson declared to the world, that we are inferior to the whites, both in the endowments of our bodies and our minds? It is indeed surprising, that a man of such great learning, combined with such excellent natural parts, should speak so of a set of men in chains."[27] Fifty years after penning his *Notes,* Jefferson's ideas about blacks held more sway than they did in the revolutionary era, and Walker recognized this. He called for any of his brethren "who has the spirit of a man" to buy a copy of Jefferson's book and write refutations of its racial ideologies, because those ideas continued to garner respect from whites.[28]

Walker also employed some of the harsh rhetoric prevalent throughout the text in critiquing racism and intransigence toward abolitionism. He wrote, "The whites have always been an unjust, jealous, unmerciful, avaricious and blood-thirsty set of beings, always seeking after power and authority." This type of rhetoric was sure to alienate many, but that was exactly the point; he felt that blacks must display courage for the cause of the enslaved even when it would anger others. And turning the tables on the common racial presumptions of the day, Walker, speaking of white people, wondered "whether they are as good by nature as we are or not."[29] He placed himself squarely within larger currents of black racialist discourse during the nineteenth century, much of which rejected environmentalism while also positing the innate superiority of blacks, thereby mirroring the racist logic of whites.[30]

Walker often used jeremiads to support his case against slavery and racism. In many ways, he saw himself as a prophet like his contemporary Nat Turner, who would be martyred for the cause: "I write without the fear of man. I am writing for my God, and fear none but himself; they may put me to death if they choose."[31] Willing to sacrifice his life for the cause of abolition, Walker argued that Americans would sacrifice their prosperity as a nation if they continued holding slaves. "I tell you Americans! That unless you speedily alter your course, you and your Country are gone . . . For God Almighty will tear up the very face of the earth."[32] As Thomas Jefferson stated in his *Notes on the State of Virginia,* Walker believed that a just God could not allow slavery to persist forever. Referring to the Latin American revolutions, he said that the principal reason that Spaniards are now "running about the field of battle cutting each other's throats" was their involvement with slavery. And in one of his more prescient statements, he posited that "although the destruction of the oppressors God may not effect by the oppressed, yet the Lord our God will bring other destructions upon them—for not unfrequently will he cause them to rise up one against another, to be split and divided, and to oppress each other, and sometime to open hostilities with sword in hand."[33] Walker continued and strengthened the tradition of the black jeremiad that Massachusetts' black abolitionists such as Caesar Sarter and Prince Hall began in the revolutionary era by arguing that a civil war was probable if Americans did not abolish slavery.[34]

Indeed, Walker believed that violence in the form of a slave rebellion or war might very well be necessary to overthrow the institution. While black petitioners in the 1770s and Prince Hall in the 1790s had alluded to both the threat posed to whites by American slave rebels and the specter of Saint Domingue, none were as explicit as Walker in calling for slaves to rebel against their masters. His premise was simple. White people think nothing of murdering blacks to enslave them; "therefore, if there is an attempt made by us, kill or be killed. Now, I ask you, had you not rather be killed than be a slave to a tyrant, who takes the life of your mother, wife, and dear little children?" Drawing from the Haitian revolutionary tradition, Walker told slaves that "it is no more harm for you to kill a man, who is trying to kill you, than it is for you to take a drink of water when thirsty."[35] He believed that white people would not give blacks respect unless they proved their manhood, and this they could likely only do by violent resistance to slavery. While these beliefs were not very influential during the 1830s, as pacifism reigned among black and white abolitionists, in the 1840s and 1850s many black thinkers, including Henry Highland Garnet and Frederick Douglass, accepted the idea that violence would be necessary to abolish slavery.[36]

Despite the harsh rhetoric throughout his *Appeal*, Walker believed that blacks could overcome ignorance and whites could learn to live without slavery. When he read the history of Africa, "among whom learning originated," and about how Hannibal nearly conquered Rome, he believed there was hope for the future of blacks in America.[37] He based this hope partly on the belief that God would raise up another Hannibal who would assist blacks in their cause. As far as whites, he noted simply that they must "treat us like men, and there is no danger but we will all live in peace and happiness together . . . there is not a doubt in my mind, but that the whole of the past will be sunk into oblivion, and we yet, under God, will become a united and happy people." White people might think this goal unrealistic, but Walker believed that "nothing is impossible with God."[38]

There is a tension between Walker's views on the necessity of violence to overthrow slavery and his statement that whites and blacks can live together peaceably that is indicative of the evolving views of black abolitionists since the eighteenth century. The *Appeal* differs from earlier black jeremiads in that Walker seems to argue that God's judgment has already been ordained. In his view, whites can theoretically avoid the violence that will end slavery, but their behavior to date makes this scenario unlikely. His position here is markedly different from the jeremiads of Phillis Wheatley or Prince Hall, who seemed to be more hopeful at the prospects for abolition and for averting God's judgment on white America.

David Walker's pamphlet and other activities helped strengthen the antislavery movement by spreading the influence of the black press in the North and his own ideas throughout the country. As well as participating in the Massachusetts General Colored Association, he served as one of three agents in the state for *Freedom's Journal,* with the other two being Reverend Thomas Paul and John Remond, a well-known caterer and abolitionist from Salem. As an agent, Walker worked to raise funds for the paper and increase its subscription base. By the time the third edition of the *Appeal* was pub-lished in 1830, *Freedom's Journal* had folded, but former editor Samuel Cor-nish started *The Rights of All,* and Walker similarly called for blacks to help circulate the paper and contribute to its success in any way possible.[39] For his own work, Walker used networks of sailors to distribute it throughout the South. One white sailor whom authorities in Charleston arrested on 27 March 1830 for distributing the *Appeal* testified that while in Boston "a coloured man of decent appearance & very genteely dressed" came aboard his ship and said that "he wished him (Smith) to bring a packet of pamphlets to Charleston for him and to give them to any negroes he had a mind to, or that he met."[40] The black man who approached Smith was presumably Walker, and he cautioned Smith to keep his actions unknown to whites. Unfortunately for him, he was unable to do so and was sentenced to one year in prison and fined $1,000 for "distributing some pamphlets of a very seditious & inflammatory character among the Slaves & persons of color" in Charleston. Walker's strategy here presaged the later campaign waged by the American Anti-Slavery Society to inundate the South with abolitionist literature and helped to harden the battle lines between abolitionists and defenders of slavery.[41]

Soon after Walker published his work, other southern states took ac-tion to make sure it stayed out of the hands of slaves. The *Appeal* made its way to ports from Virginia to Louisiana, and white leaders confiscated it wherever they found copies. Because it showed up in Virginia in 1830, authorities at the time attributed a connection between Walker's writ-ing and Nat Turner's 1831 uprising in Southampton, but this connection is unlikely.[42] According to Sean Wilentz, when the *Appeal* was printed, "legislators in Georgia and Louisiana became so alarmed that they enacted harsh new laws restricting black literacy, including a ban on antislavery literature."[43] When the final edition of the work appeared in June 1830, the mayor of Savannah wrote to Boston mayor Harrison Gray Otis and demanded Walker be stopped. Otis replied, saying he had no power to do so. Walker's fiery denunciation of American slaveholders helped contribute to unified southern opposition to abolition and had long-term implications for the politics of slavery. By pushing southerners toward censoring and confiscating mail, which northern whites would strongly object to as a violation of their constitutional liberties, Walker helped bring in thousands of new activists to the movement.

Perhaps even more significant was his influence on white abolitionists such as William Lloyd Garrison. Garrison started his antislavery career as a colonizationist and advocate of gradual abolition, yet by 1831 he was a proponent of immediate emancipation, writing one year later, "I am constrained to declare, with the utmost sincerity, that I look upon the colonization scheme as inadequate in design, injurious in its operation, and contrary to sound principle."[44] Garrison never did adopt the belief that violence was necessary to overthrow slavery, but he did say that if his strategy of moral suasion did not convince masters to free their slaves, then the physical strength of the slaves would do so. Walker and Garrison also shared strikingly similar rhetorical styles. In his opening editorial to the *Liberator,* Garrison wrote: "I am aware that many object to the severity of my language, but is there not cause for severity? I will be as harsh as truth, and as uncompromising as justice."[45] Garrison's language here is very like the rhetoric Walker used in his own writings. And Garrison's newfound insistence on immediate abolition strongly suggests the powerful influence that activists such as David Walker had on his thinking in particular and the growth of abolitionism in general.

Black abolitionists continued to cooperate with white activists to get themselves heard and to influence whites' antislavery rhetoric and activities. Blacks comprised the majority of subscribers to Garrison's *Liberator* in its earliest years and contributed their fair share of articles and other writings to the paper. Garrison's 1832 *Thoughts on African Colonization* likewise drew heavily from the work of blacks, as it reprinted dozens of minutes from anticolonization meetings throughout northern black communities. One such meeting occurred in Boston on 12 March 1831 and included the leading African American abolitionists in the state—Reverend Samuel Snowden, Robert Roberts, James G. Barbadoes, Masonic leader John T. Hilton, Reverend Hosea Easton, and Thomas Dalton. A committee was formed to consider the establishment of another American Colonization Society branch in the state and resolved that Boston's black residents should strenuously oppose any attempts to send them to Africa and "every operation that may have a tendency to perpetuate our present political condition."[46]

White abolitionists such as David Lee Child also included blacks' voices in their publications to bolster their own cases against slavery. Child, a justice of the peace in Boston and one of the most prominent white antislavery activists in the city, appended affidavits from black abolitionists regarding the kidnapping of free blacks to his tract *The Despotism of Freedom*. Black kidnappings in Boston became more widespread during the 1820s, with slave traders selling free African Americans into southern slavery.[47] To address this issue, black abolitionists Robert Roberts and James G. Barbadoes gave Child affidavits in November 1833. In Barbadoes's account, he described the kidnapping of his son Robert H. Barbadoes in New Orleans in 1818. According to James, Robert was imprisoned for five months and denied any communication with the outside world. "He was often severely flogged to be made submissive, and deny that he was free born."[48] Robert encountered another slave who was later freed and who wrote to James Barbadoes to inform him of Robert's situation. Robert eventually gained his freedom, but James's account, along with Robert's, demonstrated that slavery was not solely a southern problem but a national one, as blacks throughout the country had to fear for their safety.

A key development in the growth of interracial activism among abolitionists in the early 1830s was cooperation in antislavery societies. Prior to this period, organizations such as the Pennsylvania Abolition Society and the Massachusetts General Colored Association consisted solely of whites or blacks, but this changed in 1832. In December 1831, Child, Garrison, and Isaac Knapp, Garrison's partner at the *Liberator,* among other activists, met at the African Baptist Church in Boston to organize the New England Anti-Slavery Society. The organization's constitution stated that "every person of full age, and sane mind, has a right to immediate freedom from personal bondage," demonstrating again the impact that black abolitionists' insistence on immediate emancipation had on their white coworkers. Along with pushing for the abolition of slavery, the society endeavored "by all means sanctioned by law, humanity, and religion . . . to improve the character and condition of free people of color."[49] Signers of the constitution included John T. Hilton, James G. Barbadoes, Hosea Easton, and Thomas Paul, making this organization the first interracial antislavery society in the nation. And just two years later, black and white abolitionists formed the Anti-Slavery Society of Salem, which similarly had as its goal immediate emancipation and included black activists such as Charles Lenox Remond.[50]

The New England Anti-Slavery Society adopted some of the strategies that black abolitionists pioneered in the eighteenth and early nineteenth centuries. Intimately tied to Thomas Paul's activism in the 1810s and 1820s was his missionary work with the Boston Baptist Association and his efforts to spread Christianity in America and Haiti. In an August 1832 meeting, the new organization reaffirmed the importance of this strategy to abolitionism, resolving that "we consider the cause of Missions and efforts to evangelize the heathen of vast importance to our country and to the world, and that the main objects of this Society are intimately connected with such efforts."[51] Just one month later the members voted to raise $50,000 to establish a school for black youths on the manual labor system and appointed James Barbadoes and John Hilton to the fundraising committee. Their presence on this committee demonstrates the commitment that this organization had to interracial cooperation, and the means they employed to bring about abolition demonstrate the influence of blacks' ideas, ones that had their genesis among some of the earliest black activists in the city.

Greater interracial cooperation among abolitionists in Massachusetts marked the emergence of a new generation of black abolitionists in the state. Like David Walker, however, this new generation was greatly influenced by the work of its predecessors. For one, activists such as James G. Barbadoes, John T. Hilton, and Samuel Snowden joined or formed organizations similar to the ones begun by earlier abolitionists. In 1818, Snowden became the pastor of Boston's second black church, Hilton became the leader of the African Masonic Lodge during the 1820s, and Barbadoes took part in the National Negro Conventions of the 1830s, where Hosea Easton, Robert Roberts, and Snowden joined him as delegates from Massachusetts. Along with Thomas Paul, Snowden had first introduced William Lloyd Garrison to local blacks in 1830, a crucial step in Garrison's decision to start his paper in Boston.[52]

Of equal importance to institutional continuity were family ties among black abolitionists. Primus Hall continued the work his father began in the 1780s by opening his home to the African School and helping found the African Baptist Church in 1805. Other children of these early black leaders made their impact felt as well. Scipio Dalton was a member of the black Masons and played a leading role in founding the African Society and the African Baptist Church, and his son, Thomas Dalton, became the first president of the Massachusetts General Colored Association. Thomas Lewis was similarly a black Mason and helped form the two organizations that Scipio Dalton did, and his son, Walker Lewis, became another founder of the association in 1826. And Thomas Paul's brother, Nathaniel Paul, became a minister in New York and an abolitionist speaker, while Thomas Paul Jr. was an apprentice to William Lloyd Garrison. Paul's daughter, Susan, became one of the most distinguished female activists in the abolition movement, joining the Massachusetts Anti-Slavery Society and the Boston Female Anti-Slavery Society. While abolitionist tactics and strategies evolved in important ways, these familial connections provided a sense of continuity between the stages of the movement and helped strengthen the work of both black and white abolitionists in the 1820s and beyond.[53]

As Susan Paul's activism suggests, the 1830s witnessed a sharp departure from the earlier abolitionist movement as more women became openly involved and active in the cause. To be sure, women had always been vital to the success of abolitionism in Massachusetts by initiating freedom suits, publishing poetry, and raising funds for processions celebrating the end of the slave trade. They were barred, however, from membership in organizations such as the African Masonic Lodge, the African Society, and the Massachusetts General Colored Association, as black leaders in Boston and throughout the state adhered to the traditional gender roles of American society. This situation began to change in the 1820s, however, as women challenged the premises of the "cult of true womanhood," an ideology that propagated four basic virtues for proper female behavior: piety, purity, domesticity, and submissiveness.[54]

By arguing that their innate piety and purity uniquely qualified them for reform work, women started becoming involved in the temperance and sabbatarian movements and soon extended their work to abolitionism. Susan Paul's Boston Female Anti-Slavery Society had similar goals as its male counterparts but was also concerned specifically with the condition of black women. In early 1834, members organized a primary school for black girls and the Samaritan Asylum, which was a home for indigent and orphaned black children. They cooperated with their counterparts in Salem, who in 1834 had formed the Salem Female Anti-Slavery Society, by accepting children from that town into their Samaritan Asylum. Both organizations helped raise funds for the movement, with the Salem society giving Garrison $100 for his trip to London to attend the British and Foreign Anti-Slavery Society convention. Overall, Massachusetts women organized more than forty female antislavery societies during the 1830s and were instrumental in the 1837 establishment of the National Convention of Anti-Slavery Women.[55]

Women were also vital in the petition campaigns waged by abolitionists in the 1830s. Shirley Yee notes how, "for black women, petitioning served as a way both to protest slavery and race discrimination and to participate in a political system that excluded them from full citizenship on the basis of race and sex."[56] Black and white women excelled at this, contributing more than 40 percent of the 34,000 signatures on congressional petitions between 1831 and 1835. Along with their signatures, women initiated many of these petition campaigns, hoping to both pressure national leaders into supporting abolition and individual masters into freeing their slaves. This work helped increase the mass appeal of abolitionism in the North and slowly undermine the institution of slavery.[57]

If the growth of female abolitionism represented a radical break from the earlier stages of the antislavery movement, many of the strategies and arguments black women advanced demonstrate the influence of their predecessors' ideas about respectability and black unity. Maria Stewart's writings, for instance, drew heavily from both the work of her intellectual mentor, David Walker, and the goals that black abolitionists in the state had worked toward since the 1780s. Stewart was a self-educated woman and a member of Thomas Paul's African Baptist Church. After the death of her husband in 1829, she underwent a conversion experience that led to her involvement in the antislavery cause. She published her first tract in 1831, *Religion and the Pure Principles of Morality,* in which she called for black unity and self-improvement.[58]

Her focus on black unity was reminiscent of Walker's admonitions in his *Appeal.* Her belief that ignorance was too widespread in Boston's black community provided another spur to her activism. Stewart believed strongly that "the day on which we unite, heart and soul, and turn our attention to knowledge and improvement, that day the hissing and reproach among the nations of the earth against us will cease."[59] In a later publication she similarly argued that "were the American free people of color to turn their attention more assiduously to moral worth and intellectual improvement, this would be the result: prejudice would gradually diminish, and the whites would be compelled to say, unloose those fetters."[60] Advocating a politics of respectability, Stewart called for free blacks to remain above reproach in order to assist their southern brethren. If blacks could not unite themselves and elevate their character, they would receive no help from whites: "Shall we, for a moment, persist in a course that will dampen the zeal of our benefactors?"[61]

Stewart saw herself as an instrument of God in the reformation of the black community and, like Walker, sometimes spoke in prophetic tones. "It was God alone who inspired my heart to publish the mediations thereof," she noted in a speech before the African-American Female Intelligence Society. "And it was done with pure motives of love to your souls, in the hope that Christians might examine themselves, and sinners become pricked in their hearts."[62] As her contemporaries and previous black abolitionists in Massachusetts had done, Stewart called for blacks to repent of their sins and live moral lives. Although the present outlook was grim for African Americans, she retained hope that they could improve themselves and foretold that "many powerful sons and daughters of Africa will shortly arise, who will put down vice and immorality among us, and declare by Him that sitteth upon the throne that they will have their rights."[63]

Along with these entreaties, Stewart critiqued the sexism prevalent in American society and castigated men for failing to improve blacks' condition. She despised the fact that black girls could be no more than servants because of the racism and sexism they faced and argued that if the colonists refused to be servants to the British, then neither should black women be satisfied with their condition. She also believed that the future of the race lay in the hands of black women: "O woman, woman! Upon you I call; for upon your exertions almost entirely depends whether the rising generation shall be any thing more than we have been or not."[64] Perhaps, for Stewart, the primary reason the future of the race lay in the hands of women was the failures of black men. In her speech at the African Masonic Lodge she boldly proclaimed that "if you are men, convince them that you possess the spirit of men," further asking, "Where can we find among ourselves the man of science, or a philosopher, or an able statesman, or a counsellor at law?"[65] Her language again reflects Walker's, especially in her critique of black manhood, but moves beyond his influence in "insisting upon the right of women to take their place in the front ranks of black moral and political leadership."[66]

Maria Stewart's work and writings are representative of the shifting courses of abolitionism in the late 1820s and 1830s. While employing some of the same strategies as her predecessors in Massachusetts, she advanced arguments that cemented her place as one of America's first black feminist writers, which was in itself a novel development in American abolitionism. Stewart also presented herself as a prophet sent to do God's work, a move shared by her friend David Walker, who employed a rhetorical style unlike any previous black antislavery writer. With their insistence on immediate emancipation, opposition to the colonization plan, and calls for black uplift, black abolitionists during this period helped broaden and advance the radical abolition movement.[67]

Afterword

The work of abolitionists such as David Walker and Maria Stewart in the late 1820s and early 1830s helped keep the issue of slavery in the forefront of national politics. In 1833, activists from around the North, including Boston's James Barbadoes, formed the American Anti-Slavery Society, and within two years there were 200 local chapters around the country. By 1838 there were 1,350 auxiliary societies, with a total membership of 250,000 people, or 2 percent of the American population. A primary strategy of this organization was to inundate the South with abolitionist tracts, of which they printed 1 million by the end of 1835. (When burglars broke into the Charleston post office in June 1835 and burned a bag of antislavery publications, President Andrew Jackson supported their actions, even calling for federal legislation allowing censorship of abolitionist materials in the South.[1])

At the same time, abolitionists began to flood Congress with petitions calling for the abolition of slavery in the capital and the entire country, along with a restriction on the spread of slavery to the West. The result was that on 25 May 1836, Congress adopted a gag rule, a motion by South Carolina representative James Henry Hammond to table all antislavery petitions before Congress. This rule was in effect until 1844 but backfired on slavery's defenders. Whereas prior to the gag rule only 8-20 percent of eligible male voters signed abolition petitions, 37 percent did so after. By restricting the constitutional liberties of whites, the supporters of slavery actually helped increase abolitionism's appeal across the North.[2]

Despite abolitionism's growing appeal, antislavery activists faced sharp challenges to their efforts throughout the nation. Much of the hatred of abolitionism related to slavery and a desire to perpetuate the institution, but this was not all. After Britain abolished colonial slavery in 1834, many abolitionists there looked to America and began collaborating with activists here, which "led some to call the movement an Anglo-American aristo-cratic plot."[3] Furthermore, the active participation of women upset those who believed the abolitionists were overturning all social conventions, leading to sharp opposition to the movement. In the mid-1830s, mob activity increased, with much of the animus directed toward free blacks and abolitionists. In 1835, Harrison Gray Otis gave an anti-abolition speech in Boston, and soon thereafter a mob attacked William Lloyd Garrison and nearly killed him. That year there were sixty-eight mobs in the North that killed eight people, and seventy-nine mobs in the South killed sixty-three people. Most of these mobs were led by local notables, as "elites, especially businessmen, were intensely and even violently hostile to the spread of abolitionism," according to Paul Goodman.[4] So while black abolitionists in Massachusetts had their share of successes during this era, they also saw a rise in white racism and had to contend with violent reactions to their work.

It was in this context that South Carolinian John C. Calhoun gave his 1837 speech to the U.S. Senate, when he told his audience that "abolition and the Union cannot co-exist."[5] His statement is indicative of the effect that abolitionists had in pushing southerners and defenders of slavery to more radical positions. In a dialectic that would last for the next thirty years, antislavery agitation hardened the position of slavery's support-ers, which in turn helped increase the popularity of abolitionism when northerners felt that the "slaveocracy" was gaining too much power and violating their civil liberties. In this era, Massachusetts black activists exerted a significant influence on the course of the movement. They helped change the nature of American abolitionism by firmly rejecting colonization and pushing whites to support immediate emancipation. They were also at the vanguard of greater female participation in the movement and advanced uncompromising arguments against slavery that influenced abolitionists until the Civil War.

While much was new about their efforts, there was also much that drew from the ideas and tactics of black activists over the past fifty years.

Petitioning continued to be an important strategy, along with interracial cooperation on antislavery publications. Institutions that the first generation of abolitionists established, including the African Masonic Lodge and the African Baptist Church, remained important centers of activity, while familial connections served to socialize this new generation of activists. And, most important, some of the arguments they employed in the antebellum period were similar to those first advanced by activists such as Caesar Sarter, Phillis Wheatley, and Prince Hall—namely, that slavery must be immediately abolished or America would face God's wrath, that blacks must treated as equal human beings, and that blacks must help their own cause by living moral lives and educating themselves.

This situation demonstrates that the northern antislavery movement was not a failure, as some scholars have suggested, and that instead of the antebellum period being a new and radical phase of the movement, it was a continuation of the radical abolitionism that blacks in Massachusetts began in the 1770s. From its inception, African Americans were at the center of this radical antislavery activity, a movement that was global in its nature and that was profoundly influenced by the ideals of Reformed theology. The jeremiad, first articulated by Caesar Sarter in the 1770s, remained a key rhetorical tool that both white and black antislavery activists employed during the Civil War and, indeed, one that continued to play a significant role in the black freedom movement of the nineteenth and twentieth centuries. Black leaders from Frederick Douglass to Ella Baker to Malcolm X have in some way drawn from the ideas, rhetorical strategies, and organizational tactics of Massachusetts' black abolitionists. By boldly asserting and working for their right to freedom and equality, these antislavery pioneers inaugurated a tradition of protest that exerted a powerful influence in their own time and that has had lasting implications for African American politics and culture in the present.

Notes

INTRODUCTION

1. Walker, *David Walker's Appeal,* preface.
2. Ibid. Throughout much of the text I use the terms "black" and "African American" interchangeably to avoid repetition. The only exception is in chapter 1, where I generally use the terms "black" and "African."
3. Sarter, "Address," 1.
4. Zilversmit, *The First Emancipation,* 55.
5. Carey, *From Peace to Freedom;* David Brion Davis, *The Problem of Slavery in Western Culture;* David Brion Davis, *The Problem of Slavery in the Age of Revolution;* David Brion Davis, *Inhuman Bondage;* Minardi, *Making Slavery History.*
6. Newman, *The Transformation of American Abolitionism.*
7. Quarles, *Black Abolitionists;* Pease and Pease, *They Who Would Be Free;* Yee, *Black Women Abolitionists;* Stauffer, *The Black Hearts of Men;* Aptheker, *Abolitionism.*
8. Bay, *The White Image in the Black Mind;* Rael, *Black Identity and Black Protest in the Antebellum North;* Maffly-Kipp, *Setting Down the Sacred Past.* For more on the creation of a black historical tradition during the nineteenth century, see Ernest, *Liberation Historiography;* and Hall, *A Faithful Account of the Race.*
9. Saillant, *Black Puritan, Black Republican.* When discussing religious thought in Massachusetts prior to the 1730s, I primarily use the term "Puritan." After this, I alternate between "Calvinism," "Reformed theology," "Edwardsianism," and "the New Divinity," where appropriate. This is not to suggest that even before 1730 there were not significant shifts in Puritan thought. For some of the most significant theological developments in New England from the seventeenth thru the nineteenth centuries, see Holifield, *Theology in America;* Reis, *Damned Women,* esp. ch. 5; Staloff, *The Making of an American Thinking Class;* Crisp and Sweeney, *After Jonathan Edwards.*
10. Bercovitch, *The American Jeremiad;* Moses, *Black Messiahs and Uncle Toms;* Howard-Pitney, *The Afro-American Jeremiad.*

11. Stout, *The New England Soul;* Bailey, *Race and Redemption in Puritan New England;.* For Willard, see Lowrie, *The Shape of the Puritan Mind.* Lovelace, *The American Pietism of Cotton Mather.* Another biographer of Mather's discusses the fact that Mather owned slaves and felt that they should be treated well but does not examine Mather's specific views on the institution; see Silverman, *Life and Times of Cotton Mather,* 263-64. Lastly, Middlekauf's *The Mathers* is completely silent on Mather's views on slavery and their influence on treatment of slaves in colonial Massachusetts.

1. PURITANS AND SLAVERY

1. Bremer, *The Puritan Experiment,* 25-46.

2. Ibid.

3. Winthrop, "A Model of Christian Charity," 15.

4. Bremer, *The Puritan Experiment,* 16-18, 23. For Puritan conversions of Native Americans, see Richter, *Facing East from Indian Country;* and Bailey, *Race and Redemption in Puritan New England.*

5. Bremer, *The Puritan Experiment,* 21. See also Cotton, *A Treatise of the Covenant of Grace,* 67-76, 87-101, 107-11.

6. Winthrop, "A Model of Christian Charity," 15. Elizabeth Reis argues "in practice, the theology of predestination was Calvinist when it came to getting into heaven, but Arminian in terms of getting into hell"; see *Damned Women,* 19.

7. Winthrop, "A Model of Christian Charity," 14.

8. Staloff, *The Making of an American Thinking Class,* 15, 26, 143.

9. "Bond-Slavery," 4.

10. *The General Laws and Liberties of the Massachusets* [sic] *Colony,* 20. For the biblical basis of some of the Puritans' views on slavery, see Exodus 21:20 (KJV), "And if a man smite his servant, or his maid, with a rod, and he die under his hand; he shall surely be punished"; and Exodus 21:16 (KJV), "And he that stealeth a man, and selleth him, or if he be found in his hand, he shall surely be put to death."

11. Towner, *A Good Master Well Served,* 103-13.

12. "Emmanuel Downing to John Winthrop" in *Winthrop Papers,* vol. 5, 38.

13. Melish, *Disowning Slavery,* 14-23.

14. Adams and Pleck, *Love of Freedom,* 4, 29.

15. *A Coppie of the Liberties of the Massachusetts Collonie in New England,* 218.

16. Saltonsall, "Petition of Richard Saltonsall, 1645," 6-7.

17. *Records of the Governor and Company of the Massachusetts Bay in New England,* 46.

18. Winthrop, *Winthrop's Journal: History of New England,* vol. 2, 252-53.

19. Willard, *A Compleat Body of Divinity,* 614.

20. Mather, *A Good Master Well Served,* 10.

21. Saffin, *A Brief and Candid Answer to a Late Printed Sheet,* 6.

22. Ibid., 8-9. For Adam's story, also see Goodell, "John Saffin and His Slave Adam," 87-112.

23. Saffin, *A Brief and Candid Answer,* 7-9.

24. *A Report of the Record Commissioners of the City of Boston, 1701-1715,* 72.

25. LaPlante, *Salem Witch Judge*, 180-81, 199-210.

26. Sewall, *The Diary of Samuel Sewall*, 432-33.

27. Ibid., 433.

28. Sewall, *The Selling of Joseph a Memorial* (Boston, 1700), in Bruns, ed., *Am I Not a Man and a Brother*, 11. For the Puritan belief that the idea of God is innate in all men, see Miller, *The New England Mind*, 270.

29. Sewall, *The Selling of Joseph*, 10-14.

30. Ibid., 11-12.

31. Ibid.

32. *A Report of the Record Commissioners of the City of Boston*, 5.

33. Ibid., 72.

34. Ibid., 232; *A Report of the Record Commissioners of the City of Boston*, 82-83. For the link between militia service and citizenship in New England, see Sweet, *Bodies Politic*, 198-99.

35. Willard, *A Compleat Body of Divinity*, 614.

36. Mather, *Diary of Cotton Mather*, vol. 2, 278.

37. Ibid., 579. Slaveholding among the New England clergy was fairly common. Between 1717 and 1783, about 118 Harvard-educated New England ministers held more than 200 slaves. See Piersen, *Black Yankees*, 196.

38. Philemon 1:10, 16 (KJV).

39. Mather, *Diary of Cotton Mather*, vol. 2, 532.

40. Ibid., vol. 1, 176.

41. Ibid.

42. Ibid., vol. 2, 663; Sensbach, *Rebecca's Revival*, 92-93. For the relationship between literacy and slave resistance, see Wood, *Black Majority*, 324; and Williams, *Self-Taught*, 7.

43. Mather, *A Good Master Well Served*, 16, 17, 9.

44. Mather, *The Negro Christianized*, 14.

45. Ibid., 21.

46. Raboteau, *Slave Religion*, 127-53; Sobel, *Trabelin' On*; Klein and Vinson, *African Slavery in Latin America and the Caribbean*, 165-66; Canizares-Esguerra, *Puritan Conquistadors*.

47. Piersen, *Black Yankees*, 14-22; Daniels, *In Freedom's Birthplace*, 457. For the distinction between slave societies and societies with slaves, see Berlin, *Many Thousands Gone*, 17-28, 95-108.

48. Kulikoff, *Tobacco and Slaves*, 23-67; Wood, *Black Majority*, 36, 308-24; Dunn, *Sugar and Slaves*, 96, 99, 117-31, 230.

49. Wood, *Black Majority*, 8-25; Morgan, *American Slavery, American Freedom*, 28-31. For the introduction of rice as a staple crop in South Carolina and its impact on Low Country society, see Berlin, *Many Thousands Gone*, 142-76.

50. See *Winthrop's Journal: History of New England*, vol. 2, 26, for his observation in 1641 of the baptism of "a Negro woman belonging to Rev. Stoughton of Dorchester, Massachusetts, being well approved by divers years of experience for sound knowledge and true godliness" (26). For the increased importation of slaves to Boston after the Royal African Company lost its monopoly in 1698, see Gould, *Barbaric Traffic*, 15. For population statistics, see U.S. Bureau of the Census, *Historical Statistics of the United States*, 13, 756.

51. Pierce, ed., "The Records of the First Church in Boston," vol. 39, 101-13; ibid., vol. 40, 370-425.

52. For requirements for church membership, see Stout, *The New England Soul,* 18.

53. Second Church Record Book, vol. 4: Baptisms and Admissions, 1689-1716, and vol. 5: Baptisms and Admissions, 1717-1741, Massachusetts Historical Society; Brattle Street Church, *The Manifesto Church,* 100-187; Old South Church Records, microfilm reel 4, Congregational Library.

54. Edwards, *A Faithful Narrative of the Surprizing Work of God,* 159; Gura, *Jonathan Edwards,* 76-77.

55. Whitefield, *George Whitefield's Journals,* 464.

56. For the full story of the conversion of the Ethiopian, see Acts 8:26-39 (KJV).

57. Brattle Street Church, *The Manifesto Church,* 100-187; Old South Church Records, microfilm reel 4, Congregational Library. For the black population of Boston in 1742, see Greene, *The Negro in Colonial New England,* 338.

58. *The Confession of Flora Negro to the New-Gathered Congregational Ch[urc]h in Chebacco,* in Seeman, "Justise Must Take Plase," 408, 410.

59. Ibid., 396.

60. Chauncy, *Seasonable Thoughts on the State of Religion in New England,* 226; *Enthusiasm Describ'd and Cautioned Against.*

61. 6 May 1742, Diary of Daniel Rogers, Manuscript Collections, New-York Historical Society.

62. 30 April 1743, Diary of Daniel Rogers, Manuscript Collections, New-York Historical Society.

63. 14 June 1747 and 2 April 1749, Diary of Daniel Rogers, Manuscript Collections, New-York Historical Society.

64. Phillis Cogswell, *Conversion Narrative,* 413.

65. Edwards, "Sinners in the Hands of an Angry God," 91.

66. Cogswell, *Conversion Narrative,* 413.

2. BLACK ABOLITIONIST WRITERS IN
THE AGE OF REVOLUTION

1. For Wheatley's role in the public sphere and the impact this had on abolitionism, see Nott, "From 'Uncultivated Barbarian' to 'Poetical Genius,'" 21-32. James Kloppenberg has argued that the blend of Christianity and republicanism, despite their disparate views on virtue, was quite common among revolutionary era intellectuals; see "The Virtues of Liberalism," 9-33. Manisha Sinha moves beyond the notion of blacks' application or appropriation of revolutionary ideas to examine their critique of the revolutionary tradition; see "To 'Cast Just Obliquy' on Oppressors, 149-60.

2. David Hume, "Of National Characters," in *Essays, Moral and Political,* 208.

3. Richard Nisbet, *Slavery Not Forbidden by Scripture,* 21.

4. Ibid., 22.

5. Ibid. David Hume wrote that "as much as submission to a petty prince, whose dominions extend not beyond a single city, is more grievous than obedience to a

great monarch; so much is domestic slavery more cruel and oppressive than any civil subjection whatsoever"; see "Of the Populousness of Ancient Nations," in *Essays, Moral and Political*, 383.

6. *The Trans-Atlantic Slave Trade Database*, http://www.slavevoyages.org/tast/database/search.faces.

7. Wheatley, *Complete Writings*, xiii.

8. Odell, *Memoir and Poems of Phillis Wheatley*, 9-11. For Wheatley's August 1771 baptism, see Old South Church Records, microfilm reel 4, Congregational Library. For her connection to some of the most prominent religious figures in revolutionary New England, see Levernier, "Phillis Wheatley and the New England Clergy," 21-38. The first full-length biography of Wheatley is Carretta, *Phillis Wheatley*.

9. Levernier, "Phillis Wheatley and the New England Clergy," 31.

10. Phillis Wheatley, "An Elegaic Poem, On the Death of that Celebrated Divine, and Eminent Servant of Jesus Christ, the late Reverend, and Pious George Whitefield," in *Complete Writings*, 114.

11. For the orthodox Puritan position on salvation, see Rosenthal, "Puritan Conscience and New England Slavery," 63-64. For the growth of Christianity before and after the American Revolution that challenged many of the ideas of orthodox Calvinists throughout America, see Bonomi, *Under the Cope of Heaven;* and Hatch, *The Democratization of American Christianity.*

12. *Massachusetts Spy: or, Thomas's Boston Journal*, 11 October 1770, 3.

13. *New Hampshire Gazette and Historical Chronicle*, 19 October 1770, 3.

14. James Albert Ukawsaw Gronniosaw, *A Narrative of the Most Remarkable Particulars in the Life of James Albert Ukawsaw Gronniosaw*, in Caretta, *Unchained Voices*, 38. For a study of Hastings life and philanthropic work, see Schlenther, *Queen of the Methodists.*

15. Henry Louis Gates Jr. discusses the "trope of the talking book" in *Figures in Black*, 21-26, and in *The Signifying Monkey*, 127-37.

16. Phillis Wheatley, "On being brought from AFRICA to AMERICA," in *Complete Writings*, 13.

17. Conforti, *Samuel Hopkins and the New Divinity Movement*, 3-6; Hopkins, *An Inquiry into the Nature of True Holiness*, 35-60; Byrd, "We Can If We Will,"66-73.

18. Wheatley, "On the Death of General Wooster," *Complete Writings*, 93.

19. "Phillis Wheatley to Samson Occom, 11 February 1774," ibid., 153.

20. In the years leading up to the American Revolution, ministers began to argue that virtue and abstaining from sin was necessary for salvation as well as for success in the struggle against Great Britain. See Heimert, *Religion and the American Mind*, 457-58; Morgan, "The Puritan Ethic and the American Revolution," 3-43; Wood, *The Creation of the American Republic*, 47-53.

21. Wood, *The Creation of the American Republic*, 49. John C. Shields discusses Wheatley's use of classicism but connects it only to her reading of classical authors and not the prevalence of classicism in secular political discourse; see "Phillis Wheatley's Use of Classicism," 97-111.

22. Wheatley, "On the Death of General Wooster," 92.

23. Wheatley, "To His Excellency General Washington," *Complete Writings*, 89; Wood, *Creation of the American Republic*, 50-52.

24. Jefferson, *Notes on the State of Virginia,* 145.

25. Ibid., 146.

26. Finkelman, *Defending Slavery,* 47.

27. "To the Publick," *Complete Writings,* 8. For the trial, see Gates, *The Trials of Phillis Wheatley,* 5–16.

28. George Washington to Phillis Wheatley, 28 February 1776, in Gates, *The Trials of Phillis Wheatley,* 37, 38.

29. Higginbotham, *George Washington,* 78.

30. Rush, *An Address to the Inhabitants of the British Settlements in America Upon Slave-Keeping,* 4.

31. Clarkson, *An Essay on the Slavery and Commerce of the Human Species,* 112.

32. During the revolutionary era both black and white abolitionists started positing environmentalist theories of racial "sameness." See Jordan, *White Over Black,* 281–94. Samuel Stanhope Smith, president of the College of New Jersey, became one of the main proponents of environmentalist racial thought during this period; see *An Essay on the Causes of the Variety of Complexion and Figure in the Human Species.*

33. Phillis Wheatley to Samuel Hopkins, 9 February 1774 and 6 May 1774, *Complete Writings,* 151-52, 157-58.

34. Samuel Hopkins, *A Dialogue Concerning the Slavery of the Africans,* in Bruns, ed., *Am I Not a Man and a Brother,* 403.

35. Sassi, "This Whole country have their hands full of Blood this day," 81.

36. Hopkins, *A Discourse Upon the Slave-Trade, and the Slavery of the Africans,* 18.

37. O'Neale, *Jupiter Hammon and the Biblical Beginnings of African American Literature,* 43.

38. Jupiter Hammon, "An Evening Thought: Salvation by Christ, with Penitential Cries," in O'Neale, *Jupiter Hammon and the Biblical Beginnings of African American Literature,* 59.

39. See ibid., 63n2.

40. Jupiter Hammon, "An Address to Miss Phillis Wheatley," ibid., 75.

41. Ibid., 76.

42. For census figures see "Number of Negro Slaves in the Province of the Massachusetts-Bay," in *Collections of the Massachusetts Historical Society,* 2nd ser., vol. 3, 95-97; and *Vital Records of Newburyport, Massachusetts,* 3; Sarter, "Address," 1.

43. Sarter, "Address," 338. Manisha Sinha notes that "the idea of revolution became the basis of an oppositional tradition of black radicalism that departed dramatically from mainstream American political thought" ("To 'Cast Just Obliquy' on Oppressors," 150).

44. Sarter, "Address," 338; John Adams, "A Dissertation on Canon and Feudal Law."

45. Davis, *The Problem of Slavery in the Age of Revolution,* 45-46.

46. Sarter, "Address," 338.

47. Ibid., 338-39.

48. Ibid., 339.

49. Ibid.

50. Ibid.

51. Ibid., 340.

52. Ibid., 339.

53. Ibid.

54. Benezet, *Some Historical Account of Guinea*, 1-23; Equiano, *The Interesting Narrative*, 193-94.

55. Sarter, "Address," 339.

56. For the jeremiad as it applies to white Puritans, see Bercovitch, *The American Jeremiad*, xi. Historian David Howard-Pitney's *The Afro-American Jeremiad*, a study of the black jeremiad, begins with an analysis of the ideology of Frederick Douglass. Wilson Jeremiah Moses does place early black abolitionists such as Richard Allen and Prince Hall within this tradition of black protest, but does not discuss Sarter's essay; see *Black Messiahs and Uncle Toms*, ch.3. For a discussion of African cosmologies, see Chireau, *Black Magic*, 27, 38; Holloway, ed., *Africanisms in American Culture*, xiv. For an eighteenth-century African perspective on this worldview, see Equiano, *The Interesting Narrative*, 41.

57. Newman, ed., *Black Preacher to White America*, xix-xxv. Haynes's sole biography is John Saillant, *Black Puritan, Black Republican*.

58. Lemuel Haynes, "A Poem, Occasioned by the Sudden Death of Mr. Asa Burt," in Newman, ed., *Black Preacher to White America*, 3.

59. Ibid., 6-7.

60. Lemuel Haynes, "The Battle of Lexington," in ibid., 12.

61. Ibid., 14.

62. Ibid., 15.

63. Saillant, *Black Puritan, Black Republican*, 92.

64. Lemuel Haynes, "Liberty Further Extended," in Newman, ed., *Black Preacher to White America*, 17.

65. Ibid., 18.

66. Ibid.

67. Ibid., 19. Acts 17:26 (KJV) reads, God "hath made of one blood all nations of men for to dwell on all the face of the earth."

68. Haynes, "Liberty Further Extended," 21.

69. Ibid., 22.

70. Ibid., 22-23.

71. Ibid., 26. For Hopkins's argument that men must not do evil that good may come about, see "Dialogue on Slavery," in Bruns, ed., *Am I Not a Man and a Brother*, 403-4.

72. Haynes, "Liberty Further Extended," 29-30.

73. According to John Saillant, while Haynes's antislavery essay was not published, "it should not be considered private. His manuscripts were preserved by white people with whom he studied, to whom he preached, and from whom came information about his life . . . It seems likely that some of these contemporaries and their successors read his essays, poems, and sermons" (*Black Puritan*, 3-7, 15, 165).

3. BLACK PETITIONING AND ORGANIZED ABOLITIONISM IN REVOLUTIONARY MASSACHUSETTS

1. Abigail Adams to John Adams, 22 September 1774, Adams Family Papers, Massachusetts Historical Society. "Lord Dunmore's Proclamation Freeing Vir-

ginia's Slaves," in Escott et al., eds., *Major Problems in the History of the American South,* 105-6. See also Frey, *Water from the Rock,* ch. 2.

2. James Otis, *Rights of the British Colonies Asserted and Proved,* in Bruns, ed., *Am I Not a Man and a Brother,* 104. For Otis's background see Middlekauf, *The Glorious Cause,* 86-91.

3. Nathaniel Appleton, *Considerations on Slavery* in Bruns, ed., *Am I Not a Man and a Brother,* 128.

4. Ibid., 134.

5. For demographic data on slaves in Massachusetts, see Greene, *The Negro in Colonial New England,* 337; and Daniels, *In Freedom's Birthplace,* 457. For the New York slave conspiracy, see Lepore, *New York Burning.* For Tacky's revolt in Jamaica, see Craton, *Testing the Chains,* 125-38; and Brown, *The Reaper's Garden,* 144-56.

6. Appleton, *Considerations on Slavery,* 131-35.

7. Bills were read three times in both the House of Representatives and the Council. If the bill passed each reading, it would then be recopied and sent to the governor for approval. See *Journals of the House of Representatives of Massachusetts, 1767,* 387.

8. For records of the two bills, see ibid., 353-58, 387-93, 408-11, 420.

9. Old South Church and Congregation Records, vol.1: 1768-1802, Massachusetts Historical Society.

10. Joshua Henshaw to Col. William Henshaw, 2 November 1768, Hugh Hall Papers, Massachusetts Historical Society. Speaking of slavery and colonial resistance in Jamaica and Barbados, John Adams remarked, "We sometimes read of Insurrections among their Negroes" (*Diary and Autobiography,* 285).

11. *A Report of the Record Commissioners of the City of Boston, 1764 through 1768,* 314.

12. Old South Church Records, microfilm reel 4, Congregational Library; Pierce, ed., "The Records of the First Church in Boston, 1630-1868," *Publications of the Colonial Society of Massachusetts,* vol.40, 370-425; Oliver and Peabody, eds., "The Records of Trinity Church," 524-59; Brattle Street Church, *The Manifesto Church,* 100-187. Cornel West argues that contemporary liberation theology has its roots in eighteenth- and nineteenth-century challenges to slavery; see his *Prophesy Deliverance,* 101.

13. John Allen, *On the Beauties of Liberty,* in Bruns, ed., *Am I Not a Man and a Brother,* 260.

14. Ibid.

15. Nathaniel Niles, *Two Discourses,* in ibid., 321.

16. "Petition of Massachusetts Blacks to the Legislature, 6 January 1773," in Aptheker, ed., *A Documentary History,* 6.

17. Ibid.

18. For Edwards's ideas on virtue and liberty, see Heimert, *Religion and the American Mind,* 457-58. For the importance of virtue in revolutionary political discourse, see Wood, *The Creation of the American Republic,* 91-124.

19. "Petition of Massachusetts Blacks to the Legislature, 6 January 1773," in Aptheker, ed., *A Documentary History,* 6.

20. Ibid.

21. Ibid. For the circulation of political information throughout the black Atlantic world, see Scott, "The Common Wind."

22. Wise, *Though the Heavens May Fall*, 129-33, 186. For discussion of the Somerset case in a local paper see the *Boston News-Letter*, 15 October 1772.

23. Lover of Constitutional Liberty, *The Appendix*, 4-5.

24. A Customer, "Essay on Slavery," *Massachusetts Spy*, 28 January 1773, 3.

25. "Petition of Massachusetts Blacks to the Legislature, 20 April 1773," in Aptheker, ed., *A Documentary History*, 7.

26. Ibid.

27. Ibid. For tracts contributing to the cause of religious freedom, see Parsons, *Freedom from Civil and Ecclesiastical Slavery;* and Backus, *An Appeal to the Public for Religious Liberty.* Thomas Kidd discusses the intimate connection between civil and religious liberty in his *God of Liberty.*

28. "Petition of Massachusetts Blacks to the Legislature, 20 April 1773," in Aptheker, ed., *A Documentary History*, 7.

29. Ibid., 8.

30. Ibid.

31. John Allen, *On the Beauties of Liberty*, in Bruns, ed., *Am I Not a Man and a Brother*, 261.

32. "Petition of Massachusetts Blacks to the Legislature, 20 April 1773," in Aptheker, ed., *A Documentary History*, 8.

33. *Journals of the House of Representatives of Massachusetts, 1773-1774*, 85.

34. Ibid., 104, 221-37. On Hutchinson dissolving the General Court, see "Samuel Dexter to Jeremy Belknap, 26 February 1795," in *Belknap Papers*, 388. See also Egerton, *Death or Liberty*, 56.

35. "Petition of Massachusetts Blacks to Thomas Gage, 25 May 1774," in Aptheker, ed., *A Documentary History*, 8-9.

36. Ibid., 8-9.

37. Ibid., 9.

38. Ibid.

39. Ibid., 9.

40. Juster, *Disorderly Women*, 3-7. For an example outside of New England of religious accommodation to gender ideology, see Lindman, "Acting the Manly Christian," 393-416.

41. "Petition of Massachusetts Blacks to Thomas Gage, 25 May 1774," in Aptheker, ed., *A Documentary History*, 9.

42. "Binding out poor children was a common expedient on both sides of the Atlantic for keeping down the costs of poor relief and inculcating the offspring of the laboring poor with the requisite habits of industry and morality" (Nash, *Forging Freedom*, 77).

43. Melish, *Disowning Slavery*, 68-73.

44. See Quarles, *Black Abolitionists*, 8-14; Yee, *Black Women Abolitionists*, 2; Newman, *The Transformation of American Abolitionism*, 2-6.

45. *Massachusetts Spy*, 21 June 1775, 2. Committees of Correspondence were organizations initially set up to coordinate boycotts and responses to Parliamentary measures, but after the Coercive Acts of 1774 some of them became, in effect, extralegal governmental bodies at the local level. See Brown, *Revolutionary Politics in Massachusetts*.

46. *Massachusetts Spy*, 21 June 1775, 2.

47. For Hall's professions see Wesley, *Prince Hall,* 83; and Horton, "Generations of Protest, 243-45.

48. "Petition of Massachusetts Blacks to the Legislature, 13 January 1777," in Aptheker, ed., *A Documentary History,* 10.

49. Ibid.

50. Quarles, *The Negro in the American Revolution,* 111-33; Frey, *Water from the Rock.*

51. "Petition of Massachusetts Blacks to the Legislature, 13 January 1777," in Aptheker, ed., *A Documentary History,* 10.

52. Ibid.

53. *Journals of the House of Representatives of Massachusetts, 1776-1777,* 274; *Journals of the House of Representatives of Massachusetts, 1777,* 25.

54. "Petition of Massachusetts Blacks to the Legislature, 13 January 1777," and "The Petition of the Negroes in the Towns of Stratford and Fairfield, May 1779," both in Aptheker, ed. *A Documentary History,* 10.

55. "The Petition of the Negroes in the Towns of Stratford and Fairfield, May 1779," in ibid., 11.

56. "Petition of New Hampshire Slaves, 12 November 1779," in Bruns, ed., *Am I Not a Man and a Brother,* 452.

57. Ibid.

58. For Whipple's presence in Massachusetts during the war, see Kaplan, *The Black Presence in the Era of the American Revolution,* 46.

59. White, *Connecticut's Black Soldiers,* 19-27.

60. Thomas, *Rise to be a People,* 4-11.

61. Harris, *Paul Cuffe,* 16-19.

62. "Petition of Paul Cuffe and Other Blacks, February 10, 1780," in Bruns, ed., *Am I Not a Man and a Brother,* 454.

63. Ibid.

64. Ibid., 455.

65. Thomas, *Rise to Be a People,* 10-11.

4. ABOLITION OF SLAVERY AND THE SLAVE TRADE

1. *Constitution of the Commonwealth of Massachusetts,* http://www.mass.gov/legis/const.htm.

2. John Adams to Jeremy Belknap, 21 March 1795, Jeremy Belknap Papers, Massachusetts Historical Society.

3. Samuel Dexter to Jeremy Belknap, 23 February 1795, Jeremy Belknap Papers, Massachusetts Historical Society.

4. Belknap, "Queries Respecting the Slavery and Emancipation of Negroes in Massachusetts, Proposed by the Hon. Judge Tucker of Virginia, and Answered by the Rev. Dr. Belknap," 201-3.

5. For abolition in the North, see Egerton, *Death or Liberty,* 95-121; Jonathan Edwards Jr., *The Injustice and Impolicy of the Slave Trade,* 34.

6. Wroth and Zobel, eds., *Legal Papers of John Adams,* 54; *Slew V. Whipple, 1766,* in Bruns, ed., *Am I Not a Man and a Brother,* 105-6. For the statistics regarding freedom suits, see Minardi, *Making Slavery History,* 17.

7. *Essex Court of Common Pleas, Docket Book 1765-1770,* Rare Books and Manuscripts Collection, Philips Library; Greene, *Negro in Colonial New England,* 122.

8. For *Margaret v. Muzzy* see Wroth and Zobel, eds., *Legal Papers of John Adams,* 58-59; for *Caesar v. Taylor* see ibid., 59-60.

9. John Adams to Jeremy Belknap, 21 March 1795, Jeremy Belknap Papers, Massachusetts Historical Society.

10. Welch, "Mumbet and Judge Sedgwick," 13-14; Rose, *Mother of Freedom,* 4, 32-39.

11. Ibid., 64.

12. Ibid., 36-39, 64-65.

13. Bouvier, *Bouvier's Law Dictionary and Concise Encyclopedia,* 2890.

14. "Petition of Massachusetts Blacks to the Legislature, 25 May 1774," in Aptheker, ed., *A Documentary History,* 8-9.

15. Welch, "Mumbet and Judge Sedgwick," 14.

16. "Brom and Bett vs. J. Ashley, Esq.," in Rosenthal, "Free Soil in Berkshire County 1781," 785. Ashley immediately appealed the decision but dropped his appeal in October 1781 and paid his fine. It is not clear why Ashley dropped his appeal, but Arthur Zilversmit argues that he did so because the Massachusetts Superior Court had ruled slavery unconstitutional just one month before, in the case *Caldwell v. Jennison* decided in September 1781 ("Quok Walker, Mumbet, and the Abolition of Slavery in Massachusetts," 617-22).

17. Sedgwick, *The Practicability of the Abolition of Slavery,* 16; Rose, *Mother of Freedom,* 75-106.

18. Spector, "The Quock Walker Cases,"12-13.

19. Zilversmit, "Quok Walker, Mumbet, and the Abolition of Slavery in Massachusetts," 614-17, 622-24; and Cushing, "The Cushing Court and the Abolition of Slavery in Massachusetts," 118-21.

20. Cushing, "The Cushing Court and the Abolition of Slavery in Massachusetts," 118-21.

21. William Cushing, "Commonwealth v. Jennison, Chief Justice Cushing to the Jury, 1783," in Bruns, ed., *Am I Not a Man and a Brother,* 475. According to Zilversmit, the resolution of the 1781 cases decided the legality of slavery in Massachusetts because John Ashley dropped his appeal against Mumbet and Brom one month after hearing the results of the Jennison case, presumably reasoning that since slavery had been declared unconstitutional in the Worcester court, he would lose his case. While this may be a plausible interpretation, there is no evidence demonstrating that Ashley was aware of the Worcester cases or dropped his appeal for any other reason than being tired of fighting to retain slaves who might just run away when the opportunity arose. Zilversmit, "Quok Walker, Mumbet, and the Abolition of Slavery in Massachusetts," 622-24. See also O'Brien, "Did the Jennison Case Outlaw Slavery in Massachusetts?" 219-41; and Blanck, "Seventeen Eighty Three: The Turning Point in the Law of Slavery and Freedom in Massachusetts," 24-51.

22. Spector, "The Quock Walker Cases," 16-18. For more on black agency and judicial activism in Massachusetts, see Blanck, "Seventeen Eighty-Three," 45-49; and Egerton, *Death or Liberty,* 108-9.

23. Drescher, *Abolition*, 151; Hochschild, *Bury the Chains*, 43-48; Christopher Leslie Brown, *Moral Capital*.

24. Providence Abolition Society Minute Book, 1789-1827, Papers of the American Slave Trade, part 1, reel 19, Rhode Island Historical Society; Coughtry, *The Notorious Triangle*, 205-6.

25. "Debate at the Constitutional Convention, August 21-22, 1787," in Roger Bruns, ed., *Am I Not a Man and a Brother*, 522.

26. Ibid., 522-24.

27. Jeremy Belknap to Ebenezer Hazard, 9 March 1788, in *Belknap Papers*, 25.

28. "Petition of Massachusetts Blacks to the Legislature, 27 February 1788," in Aptheker, ed., *A Documentary History*, 20.

29. Ibid.

30. Ibid., 20-21.

31. Ibid., 21.

32. Jeremy Belknap to Ebenezer Hazard, 2 August 1788, in *Belknap Papers*, 55; *New York Packet*, 26 February 1788, 2.

33. Ebenezer Hazard to Jeremy Belknap, 5 April 1788, in *Belknap Papers*, 28-29.

34. *Massachusetts Spy*, 24 April 1788, 1-2.

35. *The Perpetual Laws of the Commonwealth of Massachusetts*, 235.

36. Jeremy Belknap to Ebenezer Hazard, 2 August 1788, in *Belknap Papers*, 55.

37. Providence Abolition Society Minute Book, 1789-1827, pp. 2-3, Papers of the American Slave Trade, part 1, reel 19, Rhode Island Historical Society.

38. Providence Abolition Society Minute Book, 1789-1827, pp. 15-18, Papers of the American Slave Trade, part 1, reel 19, Rhode Island Historical Society.

39. Moses Brown Collection, Papers of the American Slave Trade, part 1, reel 12. Rhode Island Historical Society.

5. MASSACHUSETTS BLACKS AND THE GROWTH OF THE NORTHERN ANTISLAVERY MOVEMENT

1. *Acts and Laws of the Commonwealth of Massachusetts*, 626.

2. *A Report of the Record Commissioners of the City of Boston, 1776 through 1786*, 158.

3. Ibid., 199.

4. *A Report of the Record Commissioners of the City of Boston, 1787 through 1798*, 82.

5. Ibid., 103, 159.

6. Ibid., 189.

7. Sesay, "Freemasons of Color," 15. Peter P. Hinks also discusses the early Black Masons in "John Marrant and the Meaning of Early Black Freemasonry," 105-16.

8. "A Journal of the Rev. John Marrant," in Brooks and Saillant, eds., *Face Zion Forward*, 98; "A Narrative of the Lord's Wonderful Dealings with John Marrant, a Black," in ibid., 49-73.

9. Acts 3:22-23 (KJV).

10. "A Narrative of the Lord's Wonderful Dealings with John Marrant, a Black," in *Face Zion Forward*, 49-73; *A Journal of the Rev. John Marrrant*, in ibid., 98, 148-49.

11. John Marrant, "A Sermon Preached on the 24th Day of June 1789, Being the Festival of St. John the Baptist," in ibid., 78.

12. Ibid., 80.

13. Ibid., 81.

14. Ibid., 86, 89.

15. For African American thinkers who did posit innate differences between the races, see Bay, *The White Image in the Black Mind.*

16. Brooks, *American Lazarus,* 89.

17. Prince Hall, "A Charge Delivered to the Brethren of the African Lodge on the 25th of June, 1792," in Brooks and Saillant, eds., *Face Zion Forward,* 192.

18. Ibid. For Hall's 1786 request to raise black troops, see Harry E. Davis, "Documents Relating to Negro Masonry in America," 431.

19. Prince Hall, "A Charge Delivered to the Brethren of the African Lodge on the 25th of June, 1792," in Brooks and Saillant, eds., *Face Zion Forward,* 196.

20. "Petition of Prince Hall to the General Court of Massachusetts, 17 October 1787," in Aptheker, ed., *A Documentary History,* 19.

21. Prince Hall, "A Charge Delivered to the African Lodge June 24, 1797," in Brooks and Saillant, eds., *Face Zion Forward,* 201-3.

22. Ibid., 203.

23. Ibid., 200.

24. Psalm 137: 1, 4 (KJV).

25. Prince Hall, "A Charge Delivered to the African Lodge June 24, 1797," in Brooks and Saillant, eds., *Face Zion Forward,* 204.

26. *Virginia Chronicle,* 19 October 1793.

27. *Boston Gazette,* 11 November 1793.

28. Prince Hall, "A Charge Delivered to the African Lodge June 24, 1797," in Brooks and Saillant, eds., *Face Zion Forward,* 205-6; Dubois and Garrigus, *Slave Revolution in the Caribbean,* 24-29. For the impact of the Haitian Revolution on the early American republic, see Ashli White, *Encountering Revolution:;* and Dubois, *Avengers of the New World,* 303-5.

29. Sesay, "Freemasons of Color," 173.

30. Brooks, *The American Lazarus,* 118-19, and "The Early American Public Sphere and the Emergence of a Black Print Counterpublic," 78-82.

31. Wesley, *Prince Hall,* 126.

32. Peter Mantore to Prince Hall, 2 March 1797, in Davis, "Documents Relating to Negro Masonry in America," 425.

33. Ibid., 425-26. For the establishment of the first two black churches in Philadelphia, see Newman, *Freedom's Prophet,* 53-77.

34. Prince Hall to Peter Mantore, 22 March 1797, in Davis, "Documents Relating to Negro Masonry in America," 426.

35. Levesque, *Black Boston,* 266-68; Dowling, "Rev. Thomas Paul and the Colored Baptist Churches," 295.

36. Convention of Delegates from the Abolition Societies Established in Different Parts of the United States, *To the Free Africans and other free People of color in the United States.*

37. *A Volume of the Records Relating to the Early History of Boston, 1799 to, and Including, 1810,* 14.

38. Minutes of the Boston School Committee, 1815-1836, pp. 22, 401-2, Rare Books and Manuscripts Collection, Boston Public Library.

39. Minutes of the Boston School Committee, 1815-1836, p. 155, Rare Books and Manuscripts Collection, Boston Public Library; Records of the Free African Schools, Vol. 1: Regulations, Bylaws, Reports, 1817-1832, Manuscript Collections, New-York Historical Society.

40. "A Brief Sketch of the Revival of Religion in Boston," *Massachusetts Baptist Missionary Magazine,* September 1804, 92.

41. Dowling, "Rev. Thomas Paul and the Colored Baptist Churches," 297. *Minutes of the Boston Baptist Association,* 1812, 8; 1816, 6; 1818, 11; 1819, 11.

42. Dowling, "Rev. Thomas Paul and the Colored Baptist Churches," 295-96; *Minutes of the Boston Baptist Association,* 1819, 6; Howe, *What Hath God Wrought,* 164-202, 302-3; Sellers, *The Market Revolution,* 202-36.

43. "Laws of the African Society, Instituted at Boston, Anno Domini 1796," in Porter, *Early Negro Writing,* 11.

44. *The Constitution of the New York African Society for Mutual Relief,* Rare Books and Manuscript Collections, Schomburg Center for Black History and Culture. According to Jane G. Landers, *cofradias* were corporate organizations that promoted social cohesion, reinforced extended family networks, and recognized leadership generated from within the black community" (*Atlantic Creoles in the Age of Revolutions,* 145).

45. "Laws of the African Society, Instituted at Boston, Anno Domini 1796," in Porter, *Early Negro Writing,* 11.

46. For the Free African Society of Philadelphia, see Nash, *Forging Freedom,* 109-18.

47. A Member of the African Society in Boston, *The Sons of Africans: An Essay on Freedom, with Observations on the Origin of Slavery* (Boston: Printed for the members of the Society, 1808), in Porter, *Early Negro Writing,* 13.

48. Ibid., 16.

49. Absalom Jones, "A Thanksgiving Sermon: Preached January 1, 1808, in St. Thomas's, or the African Episcopal Church," in Warner, *American Sermons,* 539; Glaude, *Exodus,* 6.

50. Morse, *A Discourse Delivered at the African Meeting-House,* 18; Dean, *A Discourse Delivered Before the African Society;* Glaude, *Exodus,* 91-99. For a larger discussion of black commemorative activity and festive life, see Piersen, *Black Yankees,* 117-28; and Shane White, "It Was a Proud Day,"13-50.

51. *Invitation, Addressed to the Marshals of the "Africum Shocietee."*

52. Ibid.

6. BLACK EMIGRATION AND ABOLITION IN THE EARLY REPUBLIC

1. Paul Cuffe to William Allen, June 1812, in Wiggins, ed., *Captain Paul Cuffe's Logs and Letters,* 226.

2. For the debates about commerce and slavery in the Atlantic world, see Gould, *Barbaric Traffic.* There have been a number of excellent studies detailing

both Paul Cuffe's emigration schemes and the movement more broadly; however, most portray it primarily as either a response to racism or the beginning of black nationalism and not as a strategy in the abolitionist movement. See Miller, *The Search for a Black Nationality*; Harris, *Paul Cuffe*; and Thomas, *Rise to Be a People*. For black emigrationism in the 1820s, see Bacon, *Freedom's Journal*, 177–204; and James, *The Struggles of John Brown Russwurm*, 44–57.

3. James Forten was initially enthusiastic about black emigration to Africa before the creation of the American Colonization Society in 1817. He would later take up the cause of Haitian emigration, largely as a response to the challenges of white racism. For a discussion of these challenges and his changing views on emigration, see Winch, *A Gentleman of Color*, 177–220.

4. "Petition of Massachusetts Blacks to the Legislature, 20 April 1773," in Aptheker, ed., *A Documentary History*, 8.

5. Samuel Hopkins and Ezra Stiles, "To the Public," in Bruns, ed., *Am I Not a Man and a Brother*, 292.

6. Ibid., 292–93.

7. Samuel Hopkins, *A Dialogue Concerning the Slavery of the Africans*, in Bruns, ed., *Am I Not a Man and a Brother*, 403.

8. Phillis Wheatley to John Thornton, 30 October 1774, in Wheatley, *Complete Writings*, 159.

9. The Free African Union Society to William Thornton, 24 January 1787, in Robinson, ed. *The Proceedings of the Free African Union Society and the African Benevolent Society*, 16.

10. William Thornton to the Free African Union Society, 6 March 1787, in ibid., 17; Staudenraus, *The African Colonization Movement*, 7.

11. "Petition of Prince Hall and Others, 4 January 1787," House Unpassed Legislation, No. 2358 (1787), Massachusetts Archives.

12. "Petition of Prince Hall and Others, 4 January 1787," House Unpassed Legislation, No. 2358 (1787), Massachusetts Archives.

13. Samuel Stevens to the Free African Union Society, 1 June 1787, in Robinson, ed., *The Proceedings of the Free African Union Society and the African Benevolent Society*, 18.

14. Byrd, *Captives and Voyagers*, 125–27.

15. Equiano, *The Interesting Narrative of the Life of Olaudah Equiano*, 193.

16. Byrd, *Captives and Voyagers*, 208–10; Pybus, *Epic Journeys of Freedom*, 114–19, 139–44.

17. Granville Sharp to the Settlers at Sierra Leone, 27 September 1790, in Hoare, *Memoirs of Granville Sharp*, 358.

18. Byrd, *Captives and Voyagers*, 167–85; Seymour Drescher, "Emperors of the World: British Abolitionism and Imperialism," in Derek R. Peterson, ed., *Abolitionism and Imperialism in Britain, Africa, and the Atlantic*, 135–37.

19. *Captain Paul Cuffe's Logs and Letters*, 45–57.

20. James Pemberton to Paul Cuffe, 8 June 1808, ibid., 77.

21. Ibid., 45–57.

22. Paul Cuffe to John James and Alexander Wilson, 10 June 1809, ibid., 86.

23. Ibid., 81–87, 105–33.

24. Paul Cuffe to John Cuffe, 12 August 1811, ibid., 145.

25. Ibid., 149–75; Equiano, *The Interesting Narrative of the Life of Olaudah Equiano,* 193–95.

26. *Captain Paul Cuffe's Logs and Letters,* 213.

27. Ibid., 214, 215. For Coker's mission to Sherbro, see *Journal of Daniel Coker.*

28. *Captain Paul Cuffe's Logs and Letters,* 224–85.

29. Paul Cuffe to Peter Williams Jr., 13 March 1815, ibid., 321.

30. Paul Cuffe to Daniel Coker, 13 March 1815, ibid., 322.

31. For more on Paul Cuffe and black nationalism, see Miller, *The Search for a Black Nationality,* 53. Also see Sidbury, *Becoming African in America.*

32. *Captain Paul Cuffe's Logs and Letters,* 399–411.

33. Finley, *Thoughts on the Colonization of Free Blacks,* 5.

34. "Address by John T. Peters," in *Constitution of the Hartford Auxiliary Colonization Society,* 8.

35. American Colonization Society, *A View of Exertions Lately Made for the Purpose of Colonizing the Free People of Colour,* 9, 5.

36. Waldstreicher, ed., *Notes on the State of Virginia by Thomas Jefferson,* 175.

37. James Forten, "To the Humane and Benevolent Inhabitants of the City and County of Philadelphia, 1818," in Porter, *Early Negro Writing,* 267.

38. *A View of Exertions Lately Made for the Purpose of Colonizing the Free People of Colour,* 5.

39. James Forten to Paul Cuffe, 25 January 1817, *Captain Paul Cuffe's Logs and Letters,* 502.

40. Arthur O. White, "Prince Saunders," 526–28.

41. White, "Prince Saunders," 528–30. Saunders's exploits in Haiti were not without their difficulties. William Bentley, pastor of the East Church in Salem, heard reports that Henri Christophe was unhappy with Saunders' expenses while in England, and others were eclipsing Saunders' talents as a schoolteacher. Bentley also discussed Haitian emigration and support for the African Baptist Church of Boston with Saunders on multiple occasions. See *The Diary of William Bentley,* 516–17.

42. Saunders, *A Memoir,* 13.

43. Ibid., 7–8.

44. Prince Saunders, *Haytien Papers,* 155.

45. Leslie M. Alexander, "'The Black Republic': The Influence of the Haitian Revolution on Northern Black Political Consciousness, 1816–1862," in Jackson and Bacon, eds., *African Americans and the Haitian Revolution,* 59–60.

46. Thomas Paul, "Letter to the Editor of the Columbian Centinel, 3 July 1824," in Porter, ed., *Early Negro Writing,* 279; Miller, *The Search for a Black Nationality,* 78; Newman, *Freedom's Prophet,* 247–58; Sara C. Fanning, "The Roots of Early Black Nationalism: Northern African Americans' Invocations of Haiti in the Early Nineteenth Century," in Jackson and Bacon, eds., *African Americans and the Haitian Revolution,* 39. For Jefferson's "empire of liberty," see Wood, *Empire of Liberty,* 357–99. For the problems American blacks encountered in Haiti, see Alexander, "The Black Republic," 62–63.

7. ABOLITIONISM AND THE POLITICS OF SLAVERY
IN EARLY ANTEBELLUM MASSACHUSETTS

1. Newman, *The Transformation of American Abolitionism*, 120-46.

2. For the influence of Haiti on the politics of slavery in the antebellum period, see Clavin, *Toussaint Louverture and the American Civil War.*

3. Drescher, *Abolition*, 187-92, 246-48.

4. For the value of land dropping and the increased amount of slaves between 1810 and 1820, see Forbes, *The Missouri Compromise and Its Aftermath*, 34, 38. For all other figures see Howe, *What Hath God Wrought*, 125-28.

5. Mason, *Slavery and Politics in the Early American Republic*, 158.

6. Howe, *What Hath God Wrought*, 160-63; Forbes, *The Missouri Controversy and Its Aftermath*, 155-62. For the argument that the conspiracy was not a real one, see Michael P. Johnson, "Denmark Vesey and His Co-Conspirators," 915-76. James O'Neil Spady has in turn questioned Johnson's argument, showing, for example, that the first two witnesses for the state came forward of their own accord; see "Power and Confession," 287-304.

7. Forbes, *The Missouri Controversy and Its Aftermath*, 135-36, 148, 223-24; "Brutus," *The Crisis;* Newman, *The Transformation of American Abolitionism*, 110.

8. Samuel Cornish and John Russwurm, "To Our Patrons," *Freedom's Journal*, 16 March 1827, 1.

9. Ibid.

10. Bacon, *Freedom's Journal*, 44-45.

11. "Memoirs of Capt. Paul Cuffee," *Freedom's Journal*, 18 April 1827, 1.

12. *Freedom's Journal*, 23 March 1827, 6.

13. Newman, *The Transformation of American Abolitionism*, 100; Walker, *David Walker's Appeal to the Coloured Citizens of the World*, viii-xi.

14. David Walker, "Address, Delivered before the General Colored Association of Boston" *Freedom's Journal*, 19 December 1828, 2.

15. Ibid.

16. Ibid.

17. Ibid.

18. Walker, *David Walker's Appeal*, 1-2.

19. Ibid., 7-11.

20. Ibid., 28.

21. Ibid., 30.

22. Ibid., 22-28.

23. Ibid., 35.

24. See Douglass, "What to the Slave Is the Fourth of July," 164-70.

25. Walker, *David Walker's Appeal*, 47.

26. Ibid., 50, 56.

27. Ibid., 10.

28. Ibid. Thomas G. Poole argues that Walker's *Appeal* "disavowed the evolving mythocultural interpretation of the United States, specifically attacking the nation's understanding of liberty and practice of Christianity" ("What Country Have I?" 536). Manisha Sinha likewise argues that Walker was the culmination

of a long line of black thinkers critiquing the revolutionary tradition in "To 'Cast Just Obliquy' on Oppressors," 158.

29. Walker, *David Walker's Appeal*, 16, 17.

30. Bay, *The White Image in the Black Mind*, 45.

31. Walker, *David Walker's Appeal*, 54. For Nat Turner's belief that he was a prophet, see Aptheker, ed., *Nat Turner's Slave Rebellion*, 136-38.

32. Walker, *David Walker's Appeal*, 39.

33. Ibid., 3.

34. In *The Afro-American Jeremiad* Howard-Pitney traces the jeremiad in black discourse from the nineteenth century to Martin Luther King Jr. but begins his analysis with Frederick Douglass.

35. Walker, *David Walker's Appeal*, 25-26.

36. For the shift in black thought away from pacifism, see Quarles, *Black Abolitionists*, 225-30.

37. Walker, *David Walker's Appeal*, 19-20.

38. Ibid., 70.

39. Ibid., 67.

40. "Testimony and Confession of Edward Smith," in Walker, *David Walker's Appeal*, 85. For the contribution of free black sailors to abolitionism and their work as information conduits, see Bolster, *Black Jacks*, 190-214.

41. Walker, *David Walker's Appeal*, 85. For the American Anti-Slavery Society's campaign to flood the South with abolitionist tracts, see Howe, *What Hath God Wrought*, 426-28.

42. Sean Wilentz points out that by his own testimony, Turner began receiving divine instruction a decade before both Walker's *Appeal* and Garrison's *Liberator* appeared (*The Rise of American Democracy*, 340).

43. Walker, *David Walker's Appeal*, vii.

44. Garrison, *Thoughts on African Colonization*, 2.

45. *Liberator*, 1 January 1831, 1. For more on Walker's influence on Garrison, see Donald M. Jacobs, "David Walker and William Lloyd Garrison: Racial Cooperation and the Shaping of Boston Abolition" in Jacobs, ed., *Courage and Conscience*, 1-2.

46. "A Voice from Boston," in Garrison, *Thoughts on African Colonization*, 21.

47. James Brewer Stewart, "Boston, Abolition, and the Atlantic World, 1820-1861," in Jacobs, ed., *Courage and Conscience*, 109.

48. "Affidavit of James G. Barbadoes," in Child, *The Despotism of Freedom*, 71.

49. Records of the New England Anti-Slavery Society, Rare Books and Manuscripts Collection, Boston Public Library.

50. "Constitution of the New England Anti-Slavery Society," Records of the New England Anti-Slavery Society, Rare Books and Manuscripts Collection, Boston Public Library; Anti-Slavery Society of Salem and Vicinity Records, Philips Library.

51. Records of the New England Anti-Slavery Society, Rare Books and Manuscripts Collection, Boston Public Library.

52. "Minutes and Proceedings of the First Annual Convention of the People of Colour," in *Minutes of the Proceedings of the National Negro Conventions, 1830-1864*, 7; Roy E. Finkenbine, "Boston's Black Churches: Institutional Centers of the Antislavery Movement" in *Courage and Conscience*, 176.

53. Horton, "Generations of Protest," 242-56; Mitchell, "The Paul Family," 75.

54. Yee, *Black Women Abolitionists*, 40. Black women established a small number of organizations in New England between 1800 and 1830, including the Ladies African Charitable Society in Portsmouth (1796) and the Colored Female Religious and Moral Society in Salem (1819). See Adams and Pleck, *Love of Freedom*, 189-90.

55. Salem Female Anti-Slavery Society Record Book, 1834-1846, p. 11, and folder 2: Correspondence, August 1834-April 1839, Philips Library; Debra Gold Hansen, "The Boston Female Anti-Slavery Society and the Limits of Gender Politics," in Yellin and Van Horne, eds., *The Abolitionist Sisterhood*, 47; Newman, *The Transformation of American Abolitionism*, 139.

56. Yee, *Black Women Abolitionists*, 134.

57. Newman, *The Transformation of American Abolitionism*, 140, 146.

58. Richardson, *Maria Stewart*, 3-8.

59. Maria Stewart, "Religion and the Pure Principles of Morality," ibid., 37.

60. Maria Stewart, "Lecture Delivered at Franklin Hall," ibid., 46.

61. Maria Stewart, "Cause for Encouragement," *Liberator*, 14 July 1832, 110.

62. Maria Stewart, "Address Delivered before the African American Female Intelligence Society," in Richardson, *Maria Stewart*, 52.

63. Maria Stewart, "An Address Delivered at the African Masonic Hall," ibid., 63.

64. Maria Stewart, "Address Delivered before the African American Female Intelligence Society," ibid., 55.

65. Maria Stewart, "An Address Delivered at the African Masonic Hall," ibid., 57.

66. Richardson, *Maria Stewart*, 19.

67. Patricia Hill Collins argues that "Maria Stewart was one of the first U.S. Black feminists to champion the utility of Black women's relationships with one another in providing a community for Black women's activism and self-determination" (*Black Feminist Thought*, 2).

AFTERWORD

1. Howe, *What Hath God Wrought*, 426-27.

2. Drescher, *Abolition*, 307-9.

3. Wilentz, *The Rise of American Democracy*, 409.

4. Goodman, *Of One Blood*, xiv; Howe, *What Hath God Wrought*, 435; Drescher, *Abolition*, 265; James Brewer Stewart, "Boston, Abolition, and the Atlantic World" in Jacobs, ed., *Courage and Conscience*, 116.

5. John C. Calhoun, "Speech in the U.S. Senate" in Paul Finkelman, *Defending Slavery*, 57.

Bibliography

PRIMARY SOURCES

Archives Consulted

Boston Public Library, Boston
Congregational Library, Boston
Massachusetts Archives, Boston
Massachusetts Historical Society, Boston
New-York Historical Society, New York City
Philips Library, Salem, MA
Rhode Island Historical Society, Providence
Schomburg Center for Research in Black Culture, New York City

Minutes and Proceedings, Recurring

Journals of the House of Representatives of Massachusetts, 1767. Boston: Massachusetts Historical Society, 1974.

Journals of the House of Representatives of Massachusetts, 1773-1774. Boston: Massachusetts Historical Society, 1981.

Journals of the House of Representatives of Massachusetts, 1776-1777. Boston: Massachusetts Historical Society, 1986.

Journals of the House of Representatives of Massachusetts, 1777. Boston: Massachusetts Historical Society, 1987.

Minutes of the Boston Baptist Association. Boston: Lincoln & Edmands, 1812, 1816, 1818-19.

Minutes of the Proceedings of the National Negro Conventions, 1830-1864. Ed. Howard Holman Bell. New York: Arno Press, 1969.

Published Sources

Acts and Laws of the Commonwealth of Massachusetts. Boston: Wright & Potter, 1893.

Adams, John. *Diary and Autobiography of John Adams, Volume I: Diary, 1755-1770.* Ed. L. H. Butterfield et al. Cambridge, MA: Harvard University Press, 1961.

———. "A Dissertation on Canon and Feudal Law." In *The Portable John Adams.* Ed. John Patrick Diggins. New York: Penguin Books, 2004.

Allen, Richard. *Life Experience and Gospel Labors of the Rt. Rev. Richard Allen.* Nashville, TN: Legacy, 1990.

American Colonization Society. *A View of Exertions Lately Made for the Purpose of Colonizing the Free People of Colour, in the United States, in Africa, or Elsewhere.* Washington, DC: Jonathan Elliot, 1817.

Aptheker, Herbert, ed. *A Documentary History of the Negro People in the United States,* Volume 1: *From the Colonial Times Through the Civil War.* New York: Carol, 1990.

———, ed. *Nat Turner's Slave Rebellion.* New York: Grove Press, 1966.

Backus, Isaac. *An Appeal to the Public for Religious Liberty, Against the Oppression of the Present Day.* Boston: John Boyle, 1773.

Belknap, Jeremy. "Queries Respecting the Slavery and Emancipation of Negroes in Massachusetts, Proposed by the Hon. Judge Tucker of Virginia, and Answered by the Rev. Dr. Belknap." *Massachusetts Historical Society Collections.* 1st ser., vol. 4. Boston: Massachusetts Historical Society, 1795.

Belknap Papers. Collections of the Massachusetts Historical Society, 5th ser., vol. 3. Boston: Massachusetts Historical Society, 1877.

Benezet, Anthony. *Some Historical Account of Guinea.* Philadelphia, 1771.

"Bond-Slavery." In *The Laws and Liberties of Massachusetts.* 1648. Ed. M. Farrand. Cambridge, MA: Harvard University Press, 1929.

Brattle Street Church. *The Manifesto Church: Records of the Church in Brattle Square Boston, with Lists of Communicants, Baptisms, Marriages, and Funerals: 1699-1872.* Boston: Benevolent Fraternity of Churches, 1902.

Brooks, Joanna, and John Saillant, eds. *"Face Zion Forward": First Writers of the Black Atlantic, 1785-1798.* Boston: Northeastern University Press, 2002.

Bruns, Roger, ed. *Am I Not a Man and a Brother: The Antislavery Crusade of Revolutionary America, 1688-1788.* New York: Chelsea House, 1977.

Brutus [Robert J. Turnbull]. *The Crisis; or, Essays on the Usurpations of the Federal Government.* Charleston, SC: A. E. Miller, 1827.

Carretta, Vincent, ed. *Unchained Voices: An Anthology of Black Authors in the English-Speaking World of the 18th Century.* Lexington: University Press of Kentucky, 1996.

Chauncy, Charles. *Enthusiasm Described and Caution'd Against. A Sermon Preach'd at the Old Brick Meeting-House in Boston, the Lord's Day after Commencement, 1742. With a Letter to the Reverend Mr. James Davenport.* Boston: J. Draper, 1742.

———. *Seasonable Thoughts on the State of Religion in New England.* Boston: Samuel Eliot, 1743.

Child, David Lee. *The Despotism of Freedom; or, The Tyranny and Cruelty of American Republican Slave-Masters.* Boston: Boston Young Men's Anti-Slavery Association, 1833.

Clarkson, Thomas. *An Essay on the Slavery and Commerce of the Human Species.* 1785. Miami, OH: Mnemosyne, 1969.

Constitution of the Commonwealth of Massachusetts. http://www.mass.gov/legis/const.htm.

Constitution of the Hartford Auxiliary Colonization Society: A List of Officers Chosen at the Organization of the Society, Together with an Address to the Public. Hartford, CT: Lincoln & Stone, 1819.

Convention of Delegates from the Abolition Societies Established in Different Parts of the United States. *To the Free Africans and Other Free People of Color in the United States.* Philadelphia: Zachariah Poulson, 1796.

A Coppie of the Liberties of the Massachusetts Collonie in New England. Collections of the Massachusetts Historical Society. 3rd ser., vol. 8. Boston: Charles C. Little & James Brown, 1843.

Cotton, John. *A Treatise of the Covenant of Grace, as it is Dispensed to the Elect Seed, Effectually Unto Salvation.* London: Peter Parker, 1671.

Davis, Harry E. "Documents Relating to Negro Masonry in America." *Journal of Negro History* vol. 21, no. 4 (1936): 411-32.

Dean, Paul. *A Discourse Delivered Before the African Society, at their Meeting-House, in Boston, Mass. On the Abolition of the Slave Trade.* Boston: Nathaniel Coverly, 1819.

The Diary of William Bentley, D. D., Volume 4: January 1811-December, 1819. Gloucester, MA: Peter Smith, 1962.

Donnan, Elizabeth. *Documents Illustrative of the History of the Slave Trade to America, Volume III: New England and the Middle Colonies.* Washington, DC: Carnegie Institute of Washington, 1930-35.

Douglass, Frederick. "What to the Slave Is the Fourth of July?" In *Narrative of the Life of Frederick Douglass, an American Slave: Written by Himself, with Related Documents.* Ed. David W. Blight. Boston: Bedford/St. Martin's, 2003.

Downing, Emmanuel. "Emmanuel Downing to John Winthrop." In *Winthrop Papers,* Volume 5: *1645-1649.* Boston: Massachusetts Historical Society, 1947.

Edwards, Jonathan. *A Faithful Narrative of the Surprizing Work of God.* In *The Works of Jonathan Edwards.* Vol. 4. Ed. C. C. Goen. New Haven, CT: Yale University Press, 1972.

——. "Sinners in the Hands of an Angry God." In *A Jonathan Edwards Reader.* Ed. John E. Smith et al. New Haven, CT: Yale University Press, 1995.

Edwards, Jonathan, Jr. *The Injustice and Impolicy of the Slave Trade, and of the Slavery of the Africans.* New Haven, CT, 1791.

Equiano, Olaudah. *The Interesting Narrative of the Life of Olaudah Equiano, Written by Himself.* Ed. Robert J. Allison. Boston: Bedford/St. Martin's, 1995.

Escott, Paul D. et al., eds. *Major Problems in the History of the American South,* Volume 1: *The Old South.* Boston: Houghton Mifflin, 1999.

Finkelman, Paul. *Defending Slavery: Proslavery Thought in the Old South, A Brief History with Documents.* Boston: Bedford/St. Martin's, 2003.

Finley, Robert. *Thoughts on the Colonization of Free Blacks.* Washington, DC, 1816.

Garrison, William Lloyd. *Thoughts on African Colonization.* 1832. New York: Arno Press, 1969.

The General Laws and Liberties of the Massachusets [sic] *Colony: Revised and Reprinted, by Order of the General Court Holden at Boston.* Cambridge, MA: Samuel Green, 1672.

Hoare, Prince. *Memoirs of Granville Sharp, Esq.* London: Henry Colburn, 1820.

Hopkins, Samuel. *A Discourse Upon the Slave-Trade, and the Slavery of the Africans* Providence, RI: J. Carter, 1793.

———. *An Inquiry into the Nature of True Holiness.* Newport, RI: Solomon South-wick, 1773.

Hume, David. *Essays, Moral and Political.* Ed. Eugene F. Miller. Indianapolis: Liberty Fund, 1987.

Invitation, Addressed to the Marshals of the "Africum Shocietee," at the Commemoration of the "Abolition of the Slave Trade," July 14th, 1816. Salem, MA, 1816.

Jefferson, Thomas. "Notes on the State of Virginia." 1782. In *Thomas Jefferson: Basic Writings.* Old Saybrook, CT: Konecky & Konecky, 2005.

Journal of Daniel Coker, a Descendant of Africa, from the Time of Leaving New York, in the Ship Elizabeth, Capt. Sebor, on a Voyage for Sherbro, in Africa, in Company with Three Agents, and About Ninety Persons of Colour. Baltimore: Edward J. Coale, 1820.

Lover of Constitutional Liberty. *The Appendix: or, Some Observations on the Expediency of the Petition of the Africans . . .* Boston: E. Russell, 1773.

Mather, Cotton. *Diary of Cotton Mather,* Volume 1: *1681-1709.* New York: Frederick Ungar, 1957.

———. *Diary of Cotton Mather,* Volume 2: *1709-1724.* New York: Frederick Ungar, 1957.

———. *A Good Master Well Served.* Boston: B. Green & J. Allen, 1696.

———. *The Negro Christianized: An Essay to Excite and Assist that Good Work, the Instruction of Negro-Servants in Christianity.* Boston: B. Green, 1706.

Morse, Jedidiah. *A Discourse Delivered at the African Meeting-House, in Boston, July 14, 1808, in Grateful Celebration of the Abolition of the African Slave Trade.* Boston: Lincoln & Edmonds, 1808.

Newman, Richard S., ed. *Black Preacher to White America: The Collected Writings of Lemuel Haynes, 1774-1833.* Brooklyn, NY: Carlson, 1990.

Nisbet, Richard. *Slavery Not Forbidden by Scripture.* Philadelphia, 1773.

Number of Negro Slaves in the Province of Massachusetts-Bay. Collections of the Massachusetts Historical Society, 2nd ser., vol. 3. Boston: John Eliot, 1815.

Odell, Margaretta Matilda. *Memoir and Poems of Phillis Wheatley, a Native African and a Slave.* Boston: George W. Light, 1834.

Oliver, Andrew and James Bishop Peabody, eds. *The Records of Trinity Church, Boston: 1728-1830.* Publications of the Colonial Society of Massachusetts. Vol. 46. Boston: The Society, 1982.

Parsons, Jonathan. *Freedom from Civil and Ecclesiastical Tyranny.* Newburyport, MA, 1774.

The Perpetual Laws of the Commonwealth of Massachusetts, from the Commencement of the Constitution, in October, 1780, to the Last Wednesday in May, 1789. Boston: Adams & Nourse, 1789.

Personal Slavery Established. Philadelphia, 1773.

Pierce, Richard D., ed. *The Records of the First Church in Boston, 1630-1868.* Publications of the Colonial Society of Massachusetts. Vols. 39 and 40. Boston: The Society, 1961.

Porter, Dorothy, ed. *Early Negro Writing, 1760-1837.* Boston: Beacon Press, 1971.

The Proceedings of the Free African Union Society and the African Benevolent Society, Newport, Rhode Island 1780-1824. Ed. William H. Robinson. Providence: Urban League of Rhode Island, 1976.

Records of the Governor and Company of the Massachusetts Bay in New England: Printed by Order of the Legislature. Vol. 3. Ed. Nathaniel B. Shurtleff. Boston: W. White, 1853-54.

A Report of the Record Commissioners of the City of Boston, Containing the Records of Boston Selectmen: 1701-1715. Boston: Rockwell & Churchill, 1884.

A Report of the Record Commissioners of the City of Boston, Containing the Records of Boston Selectmen: 1716-1736. Boston: Rockwell & Churchill, 1885.

A Report of the Record Commissioners of the City of Boston, Containing the Selectmen's Minutes from 1776 through 1786. Boston: Rockwell & Churchill, 1896.

A Report of the Record Commissioners of the City of Boston, Containing the Selectmen's Minutes from 1787 through 1798. Boston: Rockwell & Churchill, 1896.

Richardson, Marilyn. *Maria Stewart: America's First Black Woman Political Writer.* Bloomington: Indiana University Press, 1987.

Rush, Benjamin. *An Address to the Inhabitants of the British Settlements in America Upon Slave-Keeping.* New York: Hodge & Shober, 1773.

Saffin, John. *A Brief and Candid Answer to a Late Printed Sheet, Entitled, the Selling of Joseph.* Boston, 1701.

Sarter, Caesar. "Address, To Those who are Advocates for holding the Africans in Slavery," *Essex Journal and Merrimack Packet* (Newburyport, MA), 17 August 1774, 1.

Sassi, Jonathan D. "'This Whole country have their hands full of Blood this day': Transcription and Introduction of an Antislavery Sermon Manuscript Attributed to the Reverend Samuel Hopkins." *Proceedings of the American Antiquarian Society* 112 (2004): 29-92.

Saunders, Prince. *Haytien Papers.* Boston: Caleb Bingham, 1818.

———. *A Memoir Presented to the American Convention for Prompting the Abolition of Slavery and Improving the Conditions of the African Race.* Philadelphia: Dennis Heartz, 1818.

Sedgwick, Theodore. *The Practicability of the Abolition of Slavery: A Lecture Delivered at the Lyceum in Stockbridge, Massachusetts, February, 1831.* New York: Jay Seymour, 1831.

Seeman, Erik R. "'Justise Must Take Place': Three African Americans Speak of Religion in Eighteenth Century New England." *William and Mary Quarterly* 56, no. 2 (1999): 393-414.

Sewall, Samuel. *The Diary of Samuel Sewall, Volume 1: 1674-1708.* New York: Farrar, Straus & Giroux, 1973.

Smith, Samuel Stanhope. *An Essay on the Causes of the Variety of Complexion and Figure in the Human Species, to Which are Added Strictures on Lord Kaims's Discourse, on the Original Diversity of Mankind.* Philadelphia: Robert Aiyken, 1787.

Stoddard, Solomon. *The Danger of a Speedy Degeneracy.* Boston: B. Green, 1705.

U.S. Bureau of the Census. *Historical Statistics of the United States.* Washington, DC: Department of Commerce, 1961.

Vital Records of Newburyport, Massachusetts: To the End of the Year 1849, Volume 1: *Births.* Salem, MA: Essex Institute, 1911.

A Volume of the Records Relating to the Early History of Boston, Containing Minutes of the Selectmen's Meetings, 1799 to, and Including, 1810. Boston: Municipal Printing Office, 1904.

Waldstreicher, David, ed. *Notes on the State of Virginia by Thomas Jefferson, with Related Documents.* Boston: Bedford/St. Martin's, 2002.

Walker, David. *David Walker's Appeal in Four Articles: Together with a Preamble to the World.* Ed. Sean Wilentz. New York: Hill & Wang, 1995.

Warner, Michael, ed. *American Sermons: The Pilgrims to Martin Luther King Jr.* New York: Literary Classics of the United States, 1999.

Wheatley, Phillis. *Complete Writings.* Ed. Vincent Carretta. New York: Penguin Books, 2001.

Whitefield, George. *George Whitefield's Journals (1738-41).* Carlisle, PA: Banner of Truth Trust, 1998.

Wiggins, Rosalind Cobb, ed. *Captain Paul Cuffe's Logs and Letters, 1808-1817: A Black Quaker's "Voice from Within the Veil."* Washington, DC: Howard University Press, 2006.

Willard, Samuel. *A Compleat Body of Divinity in Two Hundred and Fifty Expository Lectures on the Assembly's Shorter Catechism wherein The Doctrines of the Christian Religion are Unfolded, their Truth Confirm'd, their Excellence Display'd, their Usefulness Improv'd; Contrary Errors & Vices Refuted & Expos'd, Objections Answer'd, Controversies Settled, Cases of Conscience Resolv'd; and a Great Light thereby Reflected on the Present Age.* Boston: B. Green & S. Kneeland, 1726.

Winthrop, John. "A Model of Christian Charity." *The American Intellectual Tradition,* Volume 1: *1630-1865.* 6th ed. Ed. David A. Hollinger and Charles Capper. New York: Oxford University Press, 2011.

———. *Winthrop's Journal: History of New England,* Volume 2: *1630-1649.* New York: Elibron Classics, 2005.

Wroth, L. Kinvin, and Hiller B. Zobel, eds. *Legal Papers of John Adams.* Vol. 2. Cambridge, MA: Harvard University Press, 1965.

Newspapers and Periodicals

Boston Gazette
Boston News-Letter
Essex Journal and Merrimack Packet (Newburyport, MA)
Freedom's Journal (New York, NY)
Liberator (Boston)
Massachusetts Baptist Missionary Magazine
Massachusetts Spy (Worcester, MA)
Massachusetts Spy, or Thomas's Boston Journal
New Hampshire Gazette and Historical Chronicle (Portsmouth, NH)
New York Packet (New York, NY)
Virginia Chronicle (Norfolk)

SECONDARY SOURCES

Adams, Catherine, and Elizabeth H. Pleck. *Love of Freedom: Black Women in Colonial and Revolutionary New England.* New York: Oxford University Press, 2010.

Aptheker, Herbert. *Abolitionism: A Revolutionary Movement.* Boston: Twayne, 1989.

Armitage, David, and Michael J. Braddick, eds. *The British Atlantic World, 1500-1800*. New York: Palgrave Macmillan, 2002.

Bacon, Jacqueline. *Freedom's Journal: The First African-American Newspaper*. Lanham, MD: Lexington Books, 2007.

Bailey, Richard. *Race and Redemption in Puritan New England*. New York: Oxford University Press, 2011.

Bay, Mia. *The White Image in the Black Mind: African-American Ideas about White People, 1830-1925*. New York: Oxford University Press, 2000.

Bercovitch, Sacvan. *The American Jeremiad*. Madison: University of Wisconsin Press, 1978.

Berlin, Ira. *Many Thousands Gone: The First Two Centuries of Slavery in North America*. Cambridge, MA: Harvard University Press, 1998.

Blanck, Emily. "Seventeen Eighty-Three: The Turning Point in the Law of Slavery and Freedom in Massachusetts." *New England Quarterly* 75, no. 1 (2002): 24-51.

Bolster, W. Jeffrey. *Black Jacks: African American Seamen in the Age of Sail*. Cambridge, MA: Harvard University Press, 1997.

Bonomi, Patricia U. *Under the Cope of Heaven: Religion, Society, and Politics in Colonial America*. New York: Oxford University Press, 1986.

Breen, T. H. *The Lockean Moment: The Language of Rights on the Eve of the American Revolution*. New York: Oxford University Press, 2001.

Bremer, Francis J. *The Puritan Experiment: New England Society from Bradford to Edwards*. Hanover, NH: University Press of New England, 1995.

——. *Puritanism: A Very Short Introduction*. New York: Oxford University Press, 2009.

Brooks, Joanna. *American Lazarus: Religion and the Rise of African-American and Native American Literatures*. New York: Oxford University Press, 2003.

——. "The Early American Public Sphere and the Emergence of a Black Print Counterpublic." *William and Mary Quarterly* 3rd series, vol. 62, no. 1 (2005): 67-92.

Brown, Christopher Leslie. *Moral Capital: Foundations of British Abolitionism*. Chapel Hill: University of North Carolina Press, 2006.

Brown, Richard D. *Revolutionary Politics in Massachusetts: The Boston Committee of Correspondence and the Towns, 1772-1774*. Cambridge, MA: Harvard University Press, 1970.

Brown, Vincent. *The Reaper's Garden: Death and Power in the World of Atlantic Slavery*. Cambridge, MA: Harvard University Press, 2008.

Byrd, Alexander. *Captives and Voyagers: Black Migrants Across the Eighteenth-Century Atlantic World*. Baton Rouge: Louisiana State University Press, 2008.

Byrd, James. "We Can If We Will: Regeneration and Benevolence." In *After Jonathan Edwards: The Courses of the New England Theology*. Ed. Oliver D. Crisp and Douglas A. Sweeney. New York: Oxford University Press, 2012.

Canizares-Esguerra, Jorge. *Puritan Conqistadors: Iberianizing the Atlantic, 1550-1700*. Palo Alto, CA: Stanford University Press, 2006.

Carey, Brycchan. *From Peace to Freedom: Quaker Rhetoric and the Birth of American Antislavery, 1657-1761*. New Haven, CT: Yale University Press, 2012.

Carretta, Vincent. *Phillis Wheatley: Biography of a Genius in Bondage*. Athens: University of Georgia Press, 2011.

Chireau, Yvonne. *Black Magic: Religion and the African American Conjuring Tradition.* Berkeley: University of California Press, 2003.

Clavin, Matthew J. *Toussaint Louverture and the American Civil War: The Promise and Peril of a Second Haitian Revolution.* Philadelphia: University of Pennsylvania Press, 2010.

Collins, Patricia Hill. *Black Feminist Thought: Knowledge, Consciousness, and the Politics of Empowerment.* New York: Routledge, 2000.

Conforti, Joseph A. *Samuel Hopkins and the New Divinity Movement: Calvinism, the Congregational Ministry, and Reform in New England Between the Great Awakenings.* Grand Rapids, MI: Christian University Press, 1981.

Coughtry, Jay. *The Notorious Triangle: Rhode Island and the African Slave Trade, 1700-1807.* Philadelphia: Temple University Press, 1981.

Craton, Michael. *Testing the Chains: Resistance to Slavery in the British West Indies.* Ithaca, NY: Cornell University Press, 1982.

Crisp, Oliver D., and Douglas A. Sweeney, eds. *After Jonathan Edwards: The Courses of the New England Theology.* New York: Oxford University Press, 2012.

Cushing, John D. "The Cushing Court and the Abolition of Slavery in Massachusetts: More Notes on the 'Quock Walker Case.'" *American Journal of Legal History* 5, no. 2 (1961): 118-44.

Daniels, John. *In Freedom's Birthplace: A Study of the Boston Negroes.* Boston: Houghton Mifflin, 1914.

Davis, David Brion. *Inhuman Bondage: The Rise and Fall of Slavery in the New World.* New York: Oxford University Press, 2006.

———. *The Problem of Slavery in the Age of Revolution, 1770-1823.* Ithaca, NY: Cornell University Press, 1975.

———. *The Problem of Slavery in Western Culture.* New York: Oxford University Press, 1967.

Dollar, George William. "The Life and Works of the Reverend Samuel Willard (1640-1707)." *Church History* 31, no. 2 (1962): 232-33.

Dowling, John. "Rev. Thomas Paul and the Colored Baptist Churches." *Baptist Memorial and Monthly Record* 8, no. 4 (1849): 295-97.

Drescher, Seymour. *Abolition: A History of Slavery and Antislavery.* Cambridge, UK: Cambridge University Press, 2009.

Dubois, Laurent. *Avengers of the New World: The Story of the Haitian Revolution.* Cambridge, MA: Harvard University Press, 2004.

Dubois, Laurent, and John D. Garrigus. *Slave Revolution in the Caribbean, 1789-1804: A Brief History with Documents.* Boston: Bedford/St. Martin's, 2006.

Dunn, Richard S. *Sugar and Slaves: The Rise of the Planter Class in the English West Indies, 1624-1713.* Chapel Hill: University of North Carolina Press, 1972.

Egerton, Douglas R. *Death or Liberty: African Americans and Revolutionary America.* New York: Oxford University Press, 2009.

Ernest, John. *Liberation Historiography: African American Writers and the Challenge of History, 1794-1861.* Chapel Hill: University of North Carolina Press, 2004.

Forbes, Robert Pierce. *The Missouri Compromise and Its Aftermath: Slavery and the Meaning of America.* Chapel Hill: University of North Carolina Press, 2007.

Frey, Sylvia. *Water from the Rock: Black Resistance in a Revolutionary Age.* Princeton, NJ: Princeton University Press, 1991.

Frey, Sylvia, and Betty Wood. *Come Shouting to Zion: African American Protestantism in the American South and British Caribbean to 1830.* Chapel Hill: University of North Carolina Press, 1998.

Gates, Henry Louis, Jr. *Figures in Black: Words, Signs, and the "Racial" Self.* New York: Oxford University Press, 1987.

———. *The Signifying Monkey: A Theory of African-American Literary Criticism.* New York: Oxford University Press, 1988.

———. *The Trials of Phillis Wheatley: America's First Black Poet and Her Encounters with the Founding Fathers.* New York: Basic Civitas Books, 2003.

Glaude, Eddie S., Jr. *Exodus!: Religion, Race, and Nation in Early Nineteenth-Century Black America.* Chicago: University of Chicago Press, 2000.

Goodell, Abner C., Jr. "John Saffin and His Slave Adam." In *Publications of the Colonial Society of Massachusetts, Volume 1: Transactions 1892-94.* Boston: The Society, 1895.

Goodman, Paul. *Of One Blood: Abolitionism and the Origins of Racial Equality.* Berkeley: University of California Press, 1998.

Gould, Philip. *Barbaric Traffic: Commerce and Antislavery in the 18th Century Atlantic World.* Cambridge, MA: Harvard University Press, 2003.

Greene, Lorenzo Johnston. *The Negro in Colonial New England.* 1942. New York: Atheneum, 1971.

Gura, Philip F. *Jonathan Edwards: America's Evangelical.* New York: Hill & Wang, 2005.

Hall, Stephen G. *A Faithful Account of the Race: African American Historical Writing in Nineteenth-Century America.* Chapel Hill: University of North Carolina Press, 2009.

Hancock, Scott. "The Law Will Make You Smart: Legal Consciousness, Rights Rhetoric, and African American Identity Formation in Massachusetts, 1641-1855." Ph.D. dissertation. University of New Hampshire, 1999.

Harris, Sheldon H. *Paul Cuffe: Black America and the African Return.* New York: Simon & Schuster, 1972.

Hatch. Nathan O. *The Democratization of American Christianity.* New Haven, CT: Yale University Press, 1989.

———. *The Sacred Cause of Liberty: Republican Thought and the Millennium in Revolutionary New England.* New Haven, CT: Yale University Press, 1977.

Heimert, Alan. *Religion and the American Mind: From the Great Awakening to the American Revolution.* Cambridge, MA: Harvard University Press, 1966.

Higginbotham, Don. *George Washington: Uniting a Nation.* Lanham, MD: Rowman & Littlefield, 2002.

Hill, Hamilton Andrews. *History of the Old South Church, Boston: 1669-1884.* Boston: Houghton, Mifflin, 1890.

Hinks, Peter P. "John Marrant and the Meaning of Early Black Freemasonry." *William and Mary Quarterly* 3rd series, vol. 64, no. 1 (2007): 105-16.

———. *To Awaken My Afflicted Brethren: David Walker and the Problem of Antebellum Slave Resistance.* University Park: Pennsylvania State University Press, 1997.

Hochschild, Adam. *Bury the Chains: Prophets and Rebels in the Fight to Free an Empire's Slaves.* Boston: Houghton Mifflin, 2005.

Holifield, E. Brooks. *Theology in America: Christian Thought from the Age of the Puritans to the Civil War.* New Haven, CT: Yale University Press, 2003.

Holloway, Joseph E., ed. *Africanisms in American Culture.* Bloomington: Indiana University Press, 1990.

Horton, James Oliver. "Generations of Protest: Black Families and Social Reform in Ante-Bellum Boston." *New England Quarterly* 49, no. 2 (1976): 242-56.

Howard-Pitney, David. *The Afro-American Jeremiad: Appeals for Justice in America.* Philadelphia: Temple University Press, 1990.

Howe, Daniel Walker. *What Hath God Wrought: The Transformation of America, 1815-1848.* New York: Oxford University Press, 2007.

Jackson, Maurice, and Jacqueline Bacon, eds. *African Americans and the Haitian Revolution: Selected Essays and Historical Documents.* New York: Routledge, 2010.

Jacobs, Donald M., ed. *Courage and Conscience: Black and White Abolitionists in Boston.* Bloomington: Indiana University Press, 1993.

James, Winston. *The Struggles of John Brown Russwurm: The Life and Writings of a Pan-Africanist Pioneer, 1799-1851.* New York: New York University Press, 2010.

Johnson, Michael P. "Denmark Vesey and His Co-Conspirators." *William and Mary Quarterly* 3rd series, vol. 58, no. 4 (2001): 915-76.

Jordan, Winthrop. *White over Black: American Attitudes Toward the Negro, 1550-1812.* Chapel Hill: University of North Carolina Press, 1966.

Juster, Susan. *Disorderly Women: Sexual Politics and Evangelicalism in Revolutionary New England.* Ithaca, NY: Cornell University Press, 1994.

Kaplan, Sidney. *The Black Presence in the Era of the American Revolution, 1770-1800.* Washington, DC: Smithsonian Institution Press, 1973.

Kidd, Thomas S. *God of Liberty: A Religious History of the American Revolution.* New York: Basic Books, 2010.

Klein, Herbert S., and Ben Vinson, III. *African Slavery in Latin America and the Caribbean.* 2nd ed. New York: Oxford University Press, 2007.

Kloppenberg, James T. "The Virtues of Liberalism: Christianity, Republicanism, and Ethics in Early American Political Discourse." *Journal of American History* 74, no. 1 (1987): 9-33.

Kulikoff, Allan. *Tobacco and Slaves: The Development of Southern Culture in the Chesapeake, 1680-1800.* Chapel Hill: University of North Carolina Press, 1986.

Landers, Jane G. *Atlantic Creoles in the Age of Revolutions.* Cambridge, MA: Harvard University Press, 2010.

LaPlante, Eve. *Salem Witch Judge: The Life and Repentance of Samuel Sewall.* New York: HarperCollins, 2007.

Lepore, Jill. *New York Burning: Liberty, Slavery, and Conspiracy in Eighteenth-Century Manhattan.* New York: Alfred A. Knopf, 2005.

Levernier, James A. "Phillis Wheatley and the New England Clergy." *Early American Literature* 26, no. 1 (1991): 21-38.

Levesque, George A. *Black Boston: African American Life and Culture in Urban America, 1750-1860.* New York: Garland, 1994.

Lindman, Janet Moore. "Acting the Manly Christian: White Evangelical Masculinity in Revolutionary Virginia." *William and Mary Quarterly* 3rd series, vol. 57, no. 2 (2000): 393-416.

Lovelace, Richard F. *The American Pietism of Cotton Mather: Origins of American Evangelicalism.* Grand Rapids, MI: Christian University Press, 1979.

Lowrie, Ernest Benson. *The Shape of the Puritan Mind: The Thought of Samuel Willard.* New Haven, CT: Yale University Press, 1974.

Maffly-Kipp, Laurie. *Setting Down the Sacred Past: African-American Race Histories.* Cambridge, MA: Harvard University Press, 2010.

Mason, Matthew. *Slavery and Politics in the Early American Republic.* Chapel Hill: University of North Carolina Press, 2006.

McCoy, Drew R. *The Last of the Fathers: James Madison and the Republican Legacy.* Cambridge, UK: Cambridge University Press, 1989.

Melish, Joanne Pope. *Disowning Slavery: Gradual Emancipation and "Race" in New England, 1780-1860.* Ithaca, NY: Cornell University Press, 1998.

Middlekauf, Robert. *The Glorious Cause: The American Revolution, 1763-1789.* 1982. New York: Oxford University Press, 2005.

——. *The Mathers: Three Generations of Puritan Intellectuals, 1596-1728.* New York: Oxford University Press, 1971.

Miller, Floyd J. *The Search for a Black Nationality: Black Colonization and Emigration, 1787-1863.* Urbana: University of Illinois Press, 1975.

Miller, Perry. *The New England Mind: The Seventeenth Century.* Boston: Beacon Press, 1939.

Minardi, Margot. *Making Slavery History: Abolitionism and the Politics of Memory in Massachusetts.* New York: Oxford University Press, 2010.

Mitchell, J. Marcus. "The Paul Family." *Old-Time New England* 63, no. 231 (1973): 75-77.

Moore, George H. *Notes on the History of Slavery in Massachusetts.* New York: D. Appleton, 1866.

Morgan, Edmund S. *American Slavery, American Freedom: The Ordeal of Colonial Virginia.* New York: W. W. Norton, 1975.

——. "The Puritan Ethic and the American Revolution." *William and Mary Quarterly* 3rd series, vol. 24, no. 1 (1967): 3-43.

Moses, Wilson Jeremiah. *Black Messiahs and Uncle Toms: Social and Literary Manipulations of a Religious Myth.* University Park: Pennsylvania State University Press, 1993.

Nash, Gary B. *Forging Freedom: The Formation of Philadelphia's Black Community, 1720-1840.* Cambridge, MA: Harvard University Press, 1988.

——. *The Unknown American Revolution: The Unruly Birth of Democracy and the Struggle to Create America.* New York: Viking Press, 2005.

Newman, Richard S. *Freedom's Prophet: Bishop Richard Allen, the AME Church, and the Black Founding Fathers.* New York: New York University Press, 2008.

——. *The Transformation of American Abolitionism: Fighting Slavery in the Early Republic.* Chapel Hill: University of North Carolina Press, 2002.

Nott, Walt. "From 'Uncultivated Barbarian' to 'Poetical Genius': The Public Presence of Phillis Wheatley." *MELUS* 18, no. 3 (1993): 21-32.

O'Brien, William. "Did the Jennison Case Outlaw Slavery in Massachusetts?" *William and Mary Quarterly* 3rd series, vol. 17, no. 2 (1960): 219-41.

Odell, Margaretta Matilda. *Memoir and Poems of Phillis Wheatley, a Native African and a Slave.* Boston: George W. Light, 1834.

O'Neale, Sondra A. "Challenge to Wheatley's Critics: 'There Was No Other Game in Town.'" *Journal of Negro Education* 54, no. 4 (1985): 500-511.

——. *Jupiter Hammon and the Biblical Beginnings of African-American Literature.* Metuchen, NJ: Scarecrow Press, 1993.

Patterson, Orlando. *Slavery and Social Death: A Comparative Study.* Cambridge, MA: Harvard University Press, 1982.

Pease, Jane H., and William H. Pease. *They Who Would Be Free: Blacks' Search for Freedom, 1830-1861.* Urbana: University of Illinois Press, 1974.

Peterson, Derek R., ed., *Abolitionism and Imperialism in Britain, Africa, and the Atlantic.* Athens: Ohio University Press, 2010.

Piersen, William D. *Black Yankees: The Development of an Afro-American Subculture in Eighteenth-Century New England.* Amherst: University of Massachusetts Press, 1988.

Poole, Thomas G. "'What Country Have I?' Nineteenth-Century African-American Theological Critiques of the Nation's Birth and Destiny." *Journal of Religion* 72, no. 4 (1992): 533-48.

Pybus, Cassandra. *Epic Journeys of Freedom: Runaway Slaves of the American Revolution and their Global Quest for Liberty.* Boston: Beacon Press, 2006.

Quarles, Benjamin. *Black Abolitionists.* New York: Oxford University Press, 1969.

——. *The Negro in the American Revolution.* Chapel Hill: University of North Carolina Press, 1961.

Raboteau, Alfred J. *Slave Religion: The "Invisible Institution" in the Antebellum South.* New York: Oxford University Press, 1978.

Rael, Patrick. *Black Identity and Black Protest in the Antebellum North.* Chapel Hill: University of North Carolina Press, 2002.

Reis, Elizabeth. *Damned Women: Sinners and Witches in Puritan New England.* Ithaca, NY: Cornell University Press, 1997.

Richards, Leonard L. *Shays's Rebellion: The American Revolution's Final Battle.* Philadelphia: University of Pennsylvania Press, 2003.

Richter, Daniel K. *Facing East from Indian Country: A Native History of Early America.* Cambridge, MA: Harvard University Press, 2003.

Rose, Ben Z. *Mother of Freedom: Mum Bett and the Roots of Abolition.* Waverly, MA: Treeline Press, 2009.

Rosenthal, Bernard. "Puritan Conscience and New England Slavery." *New England Quarterly* 46, no. 1 (1973): 62-81.

Rosenthal, James M. "Free Soil in Berkshire County 1781." *New England Quarterly* 10, no. 4 (1937): 781-85.

Saillant, John. *Black Puritan, Black Republican: The Life and Thought of Lemuel Haynes, 1753-1833.* New York: Oxford University Press, 2003.

Schlenther, Boyd Stanley. *Queen of the Methodists: The Countess of Huntingdon and the Eighteenth-Century Crisis of Faith and Society.* Bath, UK: Durham Academic Press, 1997.

Scott, Julius Sherrard III. "The Common Wind: Currents of Afro-American Communication in the Era of the Haitian Revolution." Ph.D. dissertation. Duke University, 1986.

Sellers, Charles. *The Market Revolution: Jacksonian America, 1815-1846.* New York: Oxford University Press, 1991.

Sensbach. Jon F. *Rebecca's Revival: Creating Black Christianity in the Atlantic World.* Cambridge, MA: Harvard University Press, 2005.

Sesay, Chernoh Momodu, Jr. "Freemasons of Color: Prince Hall, Revolutionary Black Boston, and the Origins of Black Freemasonry, 1770-1807." Ph.D. dissertation. Northwestern University, 2006.

Shields, John C. "Phillis Wheatley's Use of Classicism." *American Literature* 52, no. 1 (1990): 97-111.

Sidbury, James. *Becoming African in America: Race and Nation in the Early Black Atlantic.* New York: Oxford University Press, 2007.

Silverman, Kenneth. *Life and Times of Cotton Mather.* New York: Harper & Row, 1984.

Sinha, Manisha. "To 'Cast Just Obliquy' on Oppressors: Black Radicalism in the Age of Revolution." *William and Mary Quarterly* 3rd series, vol. 64, no. 1 (2007): 149-60.

Smallwood, Stephanie E. *Saltwater Slavery: A Middle Passage from Africa to American Diaspora.* Cambridge, MA: Harvard University Press, 2007.

Sobel, Mechal. *Trabelin' On: The Slave Journey to an Afro-Baptist Faith.* Westport, CT: Greenwood Press, 1979.

Spady, James O'Neil. "Power and Confession: On the Credibility of the Earliest Reports of the Denmark Vesey Slave Conspiracy." *William and Mary Quarterly* 68, no. 2 (2011): 287-304.

Spector, Robert M. "The Quock Walker Cases (1781-83)—Slavery, Its Abolition, and Negro Citizenship in Early Massachusetts." *Journal of Negro History* 53, no. 1 (1986): 12-32.

Staloff, Darren. *The Making of an American Thinking Class: Intellectuals and Intelligentsia in Puritan Massachusetts.* New York: Oxford University Press, 1998.

Staudenraus, P. J. *The African Colonization Movement, 1816-1865.* New York: Columbia University Press, 1961.

Stauffer, John. *The Black Hearts of Men: Radical Abolitionists and the Transformation of Race.* Cambridge, MA: Harvard University Press, 2001.

Stout, Harry S. *The New England Soul: Preaching and Religious Culture in Colonial New England.* New York: Oxford University Press, 1986.

Sweet, John Wood. *Bodies Politic: Negotiating Race in the American North, 1730-1830.* Baltimore: Johns Hopkins University Press, 2003.

Thomas, Lamont D. *Rise to Be a People: A Biography of Paul Cuffe.* Urbana: University of Illinois Press, 1986.

Towner, Lawrence William. *A Good Master Well Served: Masters and Servants in Colonial Massachusetts, 1620-1750.* New York: Garland, 1998.

The Trans-Atlantic Slave Trade Database. http://www.slavevoyages.org.

Van Cleve, George William. *A Slaveholder's Union: Slavery, Politics, and the Constitution in the Early American Republic.* Chicago: University of Chicago Press, 2010.

Welch, Richard E., Jr. "Mumbet and Judge Sedgwick: A Footnote to the Early History of Massachusetts Justice." *Boston Bar Journal* 8, no. 1 (1964): 12-19.

Wesley, Charles H. *Prince Hall: Life and Legacy.* Washington, DC: United Supreme Council, 1977.

West, Cornel. *Prophesy Deliverance! An Afro-American Revolutionary Christianity.* Anniversary Edition. 1982. Louisville, KY: Westminster John Knox Press, 2002.

White, Arthur O. "Prince Saunders: An Instance of Social Mobility among Antebellum New England Blacks." *Journal of Negro History* 60, no. 4 (1975): 526-35.

White, Ashli. *Encountering Revolution: Haiti and the Making of the Early Republic.* Baltimore: Johns Hopkins University Press, 2010.

White, David O. *Connecticut's Black Soldiers, 1775-1783.* Chester, CT: Pequot Press, 1973.

White, Shane. "'It Was a Proud Day': African Americans, Festivals, and Parades in the North, 1741-1834." *Journal of American History* 81, no. 1 (1994): 13-50.

Wilentz, Sean. *The Rise of American Democracy: Jefferson to Lincoln.* New York: W. W. Norton, 2005.

Williams, Heather Andrea. *Self-Taught: African American Education in Slavery and Freedom.* Chapel Hill: University of North Carolina Press, 2005.

Winch, Julie. *A Gentleman of Color: The Life of James Forten.* New York: Oxford University Press, 2002.

Wise, Steven M. *Though the Heavens May Fall: The Landmark Trial That Led to the End of Human Slavery.* Cambridge, MA: Da Capo Press, 2005.

Wood, Gordon S. *The Creation of the American Republic.* Chapel Hill: University of North Carolina Press, 1969.

———. *Empire of Liberty: A History of the Early Republic, 1789-1815.* New York: Oxford University Press, 2009.

Wood, Peter. *Black Majority: Negroes in Colonial South Carolina from 1670 Through the Stono Rebellion.* New York: Alfred A. Knopf, 1974.

Yee, Shirley J. *Black Women Abolitionists: A Study in Activism, 1828-1860.* Knoxville: University of Tennessee Press, 1992.

Yellin, Jean Fagan, and John C. Van Horne, eds. *The Abolitionist Sisterhood: Women's Political Culture in Antebellum America.* Ithaca, NY: Cornell University Press, 1994.

Zilversmit, Arthur. *The First Emancipation: The Abolition of Slavery in the North.* Chicago: University of Chicago Press, 1967.

———. "Quok Walker, Mumbet, and the Abolition of Slavery in Massachusetts." *William and Mary Quarterly* 3rd series, vol. 25, no. 4 (1968): 614-24.

Index